60¢

Main Fleet to Singapore

MAIN FLEET TO
Singapore

Captain Russell Grenfell, R.N.

*

New York
THE MACMILLAN COMPANY
1952

Contents

★

Illustrations

★

PLATES

9

MAPS

Introduction

*

In writing this book, I am fortunate to have had the help of a number of persons who took leading parts in or were closely connected, directly or indirectly, with the operations or happenings with which the book deals. To all of these I wish to express my very best thanks for all the trouble they took in supplying me with information that I could not otherwise have obtained and in contending with my many queries. Such merits as this book may have will be due in large part to their generosity and patience. I wish, in particular, to record my indebtedness to Lady Phillips, Admiral of the Fleet Lord Chatfield, P.C., G.C.B., O.M., K.C.M.G., C.V.O., Admiral Sir Geoffrey Layton, G.B.E., K.C.B., K.C.M.G., D.S.O., Admiral Sir Ragnar Colvin, K.B.E., C.B., Admiral Sir Arthur Palliser, K.C.B., D.S.C., Admiral Sir William Tennant, K.C.B., C.B.E., M.V.O., Air Chief Marshal Sir Robert Brooke-Popham, G.C.V.O., K.C.B., C.M.G., A.F.C., Lieut.-General Sir William Dobbie, G.C.M.G., K.C.B., D.S.O., Lieut.-General Sir Lionel Bond, K.B.E., C.B., Lieut.-General A. E. Percival, C.B., D.S.O., O.B.E., M.C., and Air Vice-Marshal Sir Paul Maltby, K.B.E., C.B., D.S.O., A.F.C. I must, however, emphasize that none of them is in any way responsible for any of the opinions I have expressed, many of which some of them will not have read. Nor would it be proper to suggest that they necessarily agree with my presentation of the facts.

I am also very grateful to Mr. Henry Newnham for the trouble he was so kind as to take in reading the proofs.

For the naval operations in the central Pacific and the Coral Sea I have relied mainly on Captain Samuel Morison's excellent 'History of United States Naval Operations in World War II' and the 'Battle Report' series compiled by Captain Walter Karig,

U.S.N.R., and others. Captain Morison's books, of which six volumes have so far been published, are the nearest counterpart in the United States to our official histories over here.

I much regret that I cannot make similar acknowledgment to our own official historians, but it is from lack of opportunity. If rumour be true, we have an extremely high-powered, streamlined, and efficient team at work on the official histories of the late war. But at the time of writing, more than five years after the end of the war, they have produced no naval histories. In this same period, it has been possible for the Americans to publish six volumes of semi-official naval history, and for Mr. Churchill, with all the cares of Leader of the Opposition to support, to publish four of his own.

Since, however, the Governmental version of what happened in the late war still remains hidden behind the Safety Curtain, Mr. Churchill's revealing volumes are all the more valuable as works of reference; and, as the reader will find, I have not failed to make use of them. One of the most noteworthy features of these volumes is the extreme candour which informs them. There can have been few, if any, great wartime statesmen who, writing contemporaneously, have been so frank about the war of their time. Mr. Churchill has been frank not only about the mistakes of other people but, to his very great credit, frank about his own; and for this example of objectivity and self-disclosure, history will always owe him a debt of gratitude.

For the sake of brevity, I have referred in my footnotes to Mr. Churchill's books *The Second World War* as Churchill, Vol. . . . ; and to Captain Morison's books, mentioned above, as Morison, Vol. . . .

The photographs for plates 1 and 2 were supplied by the British Overseas Airways Corporation; those for plates 9 and 10 by the Press Association; for plate 14 by Pamela Booth; and all the rest by the Imperial War Museum.

CHAPTER ONE

The Rise of Westernized Japan up to the end of the Russo-Japanese War

★

The Far Eastern territories belonging to Britain in the year 1939 had all been gained for her through superior sea power. The particular method of acquisition had varied. Some had been bought, some leased, and some obtained by Treaty. Others had been conquered by soldiers of the British Army. But lease, purchase, cession or conquest had in each case been made possible by the supremacy of the British Navy among the fleets of the world. But for this, the soldiers could not have been transported eastward; or, had they got there, could have been turned out by superior forces sent by any foreign nation possessing command of the sea. Paramount sea power was the basic condition of British colonization in the Far East; or indeed anywhere else. By the middle of the nineteenth century, it had brought Queen Victoria the sovereignty over Australia, New Zealand, Hong Kong, the Straits Settlements, and parts of Borneo, while a British rajah ruled in Sarawak.

At this mid-century period, and indeed for long after, Britain was universally acknowledged as the leading sea Power of the world. Her numerous naval victories during the French Revolutionary and Napoleonic wars, and especially the dazzling successes of Lord Nelson, had given the British Navy a prestige that no other Power had as yet thought of challenging. Indeed, its dominant position was so firmly established as virtually to be taken for granted by everyone. And, for that reason, the safety of Britain's overseas possessions east of Suez can have troubled

13

the mind of no British statesman. Who could attack them? The British fleet could be reasonably certain of frustrating any attempt by a European Power; and outside Europe the only country with any pretence to a modern navy was the United States of America. But its fleet was then small compared to those of the European nations. The absolute security felt by British business men in places like Hong Kong can be gauged by the arrogance with which some of the heads of the great mercantile houses expected captains of the King's ships to pay them the first call of ceremony.

Yet the seeds of change were nevertheless being sown. In the eighteen-fifties, in the heyday of British naval supremacy, came two occurrences which were destined to have a profound effect on the Far Eastern situation. One was the Crimean War, by which Britain and France barred Russia's way to the Mediterranean from the Black Sea by confirming the closure of the Dardanelles to her warships. The Russian part of the Baltic being iced-up in winter, Russia had been anxious to secure access to warm water through the narrow waterways from the Black Sea controlled by Turkey.

Frustrated in this endeavour to reach the Mediterranean to the southward, Russia turned her gaze to the east. Far away, at the other end of the Asian continental mass, was the Pacific Ocean, bordered by the long coastline of China which reached right down into tropic waters. And China was governed by the Manchu dynasty, already well-advanced in the process of decay which had characterized all previous Chinese Imperial houses. Within two years of the end of the Crimean War, China had been induced to cede a large part of the Amur basin to Russia, and a period of Russian expansion in Central and Eastern Asia had begun. Some years later, the great trans-Siberian railway was commenced. Year by year it wound farther and farther east towards the Pacific coast. One branch was due to end at Vladivostock, a port on the Sea of Japan that Russia had managed to obtain from China in 1871. But as Vladivostock harbour is frozen over in the winter, plans were also laid to take another line south through Manchuria to the ice-free ports of Talienwan[1] and Port Arthur in the Gulf of Pechili. These two ports still belonged to China, but Russia looked forward to arranging for their lease or cession.

But, after a time, Russia began to realize that unexpected obstacles were looming up in the Far East to the fulfilment of her programme in that area; having said which, we can now conveniently go back to consider the second occurrence of the eighteen-fifties which was to have far-reaching effects in Eastern waters.

While the Crimean War was in progress, the opening-up of Japan was in its initial stages. In the seventeenth century the Japanese had done a remarkable thing. They had decided that contact with the outside world was undesirable and that, in consequence, they would in future live in seclusion, forgoing all communication with other nations, sufficient unto themselves. No foreigners should intrude their unwelcome presences in the Japanese islands, and no Japanese should wander to other lands. The Japanese would tolerate neither traders nor visitors, into Japan or away from it.[2] To enforce the latter part of that principle, it was ruled that no ocean-going ships were to be built by Japanese.

In this condition the Japanese people remained for two and a half centuries, shut off from the world, living their own lives in their own way, trading with no one but harming no one.

There is a widespread belief in the modern twentieth-century world, finding support in very high places, that trade and peace are interdependent. Thus, the Prime Minister of England, Mr. Neville Chamberlain, declared in November 1939 that:

'There can be no lasting peace unless there is a full and constant flow of trade between the nations concerned.'

These sentiments were echoed five years later by President Roosevelt, who said on 11th October 1944 that:

'Opportunities for the citizens of every country to trade with

---

[1] Known as Dairen to the Japanese and Dalny to the Russians.

[2] The only exception was in favour of the Dutch, who were allowed to conduct a strictly limited trade and to maintain a few commercial representatives in Japan.

the citizens of other countries . . . are essential to world peace.'

Mr. Roosevelt's successor did not hesitate to endorse that opinion. On 4th July 1947 President Truman made the statement that:

'Two years ago the United States and fifty other nations joined in signing that great declaration of independence known as the Charter of the United Nations. We did so because we had learned at staggering cost that the nations of the world cannot live in peace and prosperity if at the same time they try to live in isolation.'

These are three witnesses, each a world figure of outstanding authority and all saying exactly the same thing. Yet the historian is bound to note that their testimony is wholly at variance with the practical example provided by Japan. The Japanese lived in isolation for 250 years, and for those 250 years remained at peace with the outside world, a vastly longer holiday from external warfare than any of the principal trading nations can record over the same period. It is difficult not to think that, in spite of the one Prime Minister and two Presidents quoted, Japan remained at peace precisely because she was in isolation, especially since she had been involved in foreign wars before her policy of isolation began and was to be repeatedly so involved shortly after it was terminated.

The ending of the Japanese isolation was initiated by the arrival in Japan of an American squadron of warships under Commodore Perry in 1853. It came laden with commercial samples and brought a proposal that Japan should open her ports to foreign trade.

The Japanese were, however, not prepared to discard their way of life at the first summons. Several years of indecision and internal controversy ensued, during which more foreign pressure was exerted on them to abandon their economic exclusiveness. The British, French, and Russians in turn ranged themselves alongside the Americans; and faced with this mounting insistence the Japanese authorities eventually gave way. In 1858, two years after the end of the Crimean War, the necessary treaty was signed and Japan was thenceforth to be included in the international trading system. The statesmen in Whitehall who had joined so eagerly in the measures to this end would not have foreseen the day when Japanese bicycles would be selling in England at half the domestic cost of manufacture.

Having made their decision, albeit under coercion, the Japanese wasted no time in vain resentments or, as the Chinese did a few years later, in plotting the ejection of the 'foreign devils' who had forced their way into the home circle. Instead, they set about discovering what the new mechanized world was like. They were in an extraordinary position. For over two centuries they had virtually stood still while the Western nations, in material matters at least, had been making rapid progress. When Commodore Perry had first appeared in 1853, Japanese warriors were still using bows and arrows and wearing body armour.

Nothing could have exceeded the resolution and activity with which the Japanese began the work of catching up the rest of the world. Selected men were sent abroad to many countries to study engineering, shipbuilding, railways, commerce, administration, and all other subjects in which the Western peoples had any lessons to teach; and instructors were engaged to come to Japan to train the Japanese in the ways of modern warfare. Naturally, the Japanese rulers turned for this to those nations with the highest reputations—Britain for the navy and France for the army. But after the French defeat in The Franco-Prussian War, the French instructors were sent home and replaced by Germans.

Astonishing progress was made in all directions. The task of changing the country from a state of medieval feudalism to one of highly organized nineteenth-century industrialization was a colossal one. Yet the almost magical speed and efficiency with which the Japanese effected the metamorphosis can be gauged from the fact that in a little over forty years they were fighting a successful war against a major Western Power.

In the early days, when they were just emerging from the seclusion of many generations and taking their first look around the outside world, the problems of national security and strategic areas would naturally be among the first to engage their attention. The nearest land to Japan was Korea, across the Straits of Tsushima to the northward. This country was then a weak and inefficient kingdom from which the Japanese would have nothing to fear. But it would be a different matter if a stronger outside Power got control of the Korean peninsula. That would be most dangerous from the Japanese point of view, and it became Japanese policy to keep Korea independent. To Japan it represented almost exactly what the Low Countries have traditionally meant to England.

The first people to manifest designs against this independence were the Chinese, who in the 1880s began a process of infiltration and encroachment. Though the Japanese attitude remained conciliatory, Chinese intransigence brought matters to a head in 1894, and an act of aggression by Chinese warships against a Japanese squadron took place. The results were unfortunate for China. Both ashore and afloat, the Japanese completely outclassed their enemies, the Chinese fleet was almost wholly destroyed, and Japanese armies not only drove the Chinese out of Korea but attacked and captured the south Manchurian port of Talienwan and the strongly fortified naval harbour of Port Arthur in the Liao-tung peninsula, as well as Wei-hai-wei on the Shantung coast. All three were secured to Japan by the treaty of peace, together with a strip of the south Manchurian coast and the island of Formosa.

At this point the two separate threads of national development that we have been examining begin to come into collision. The Japanese successes against China, leading to the hoisting of the flag of the rising sun at Talienwan and Port Arthur, were by no means to Russia's taste. The building of the Trans-Siberian railway was now well advanced and it would not be long before a branch of the line should, if all went well, be reaching down towards those same two ice-free ports which the Russians had had in mind for their own use, and which had indeed provided one of the reasons for the railway itself. It was therefore vastly irritating, to say the least, to have these upstart Japanese walking in first. Somehow they must be got rid of.

The method to be employed needed, however, some care in its selection. Russia could hardly order the Japanese away all by herself. To do so would inevitably arouse outside suspicion of her own motives and might well bring the British, none too friendly, into active opposition. A promising solution was a combination of Powers to bring the necessary pressure to bear; and this is what Russia managed to organize, France and Germany agreeing to join her in depriving the Japanese of their conquests. What brought these two accomplices to Russia's aid? France being allied to Russia, her adhesion to the plot is understandable on that ground. But why Germany? Because she had wind of what was afoot and wanted to share in the eventual spoils.

At all events, no sooner was the China-Japanese peace treaty ratified than the three conspirators 'advised' Japan to relinquish her gains of Chinese territory, including the two ports mentioned. The three Powers stated that their objects were to restore the integrity of China, to remove a threat to the Chinese capital, and to promote the peace of the Far East. Faced with so powerful a combination, Japan could do nothing but withdraw. Port Arthur and other south Manchurian acquisitions were handed back to China, and only Wei-hai-wei and Formosa remained to Japan out of her war gains.

The Japanese people were naturally outraged at this development. But worse was to follow. The Russians were only biding their time before they appropriated the prizes that Japan had been forced to give up. To do so at once would have been too blatant. A decent interval must elapse.

Whether it was by chance or collusion that Germany moved first cannot be known. But three years later, in 1898, she made the murder of two of her missionaries the excuse for seizing the harbour and hinterland of Tsingtao on the Chinese coast just below the Shantung promontory, which she rapidly fortified and converted into a naval base. As if by pre-agreement, Russian ships steamed into Port Arthur and Talienwan and Russian troops occupied the Liao-tung peninsula. At the same time the French demanded and received the use of the harbour of

Kwang-chow-wan in the south. The British, not to be outdone, secured a lease of additional territory adjoining Hong Kong harbour and arranged with the Japanese for the transfer to Britain of Wei-hai-wei in north Shantung, of which a lease was obtained from China 'for as long as the Russians remained in Port Arthur'.

The feelings of the Japanese can be imagined. They had recently been intimidated into abandoning the most important of

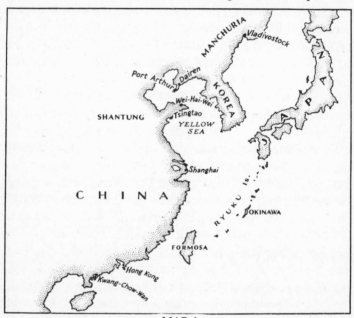

MAP 1

their legitimate conquests by a trio of Powers uttering high-sounding phrases about the integrity of China and the peace of the Far East. It could now be seen for how much the integrity of China and the peace of the Far East had really counted with this trio. The Japanese had been not only despoiled but tricked. It was but forty years since they had emerged from seclusion and begun to take stock of the world at large. It was a world abounding in sentiments of liberality and moral rectitude, in anti-slavery movements and humanitarian activity. Yet after their experience in 1898, the Japanese could not have been blamed if they reached the conclusion that, in matters of international politics, aggression and duplicity were by no means obsolete but, on the contrary, remained effective instruments in use by the best people.

As it was, the establishment of Russia in the Liao-tung peninsula and the intentions she soon displayed of further expansion in the area aroused Japan's worst fears. Here was the very situation she most dreaded, the possibility of a first-class Power securing a position of dominance on the nearby mainland. The Japanese began to increase their armed forces and particularly their fleet. In 1894, when they had fought the Chinese, they had had nothing bigger than protected cruisers. By 1901, they were the possessors of six up-to-date battleships, all built in England. Across the Gulf of Korea there was now a Russian battle fleet in Port Arthur, sent out from the Baltic soon after the seizure of the port.

Britain liked the appearance of a strong Russian naval force in the Far East no more than did Japan, and just as little as she had ever wanted to see one in the Mediterranean. A squadron of British battleships was sent to the China station. But if Russian battleships were a menace to British possessions and interests in the Far East, so also were Japanese. At the turn of the century, however, no one quite knew what value to place on Japan for war purposes. On previous form, the white races were generally to be classed as superior in warlike skill to Orientals, and although the Japanese were known to be martially inclined they were militarily an unknown quantity, and most Europeans were disposed to put their money on the Russians in the event of a Russo-Japanese clash. Britain undoubtedly regarded the Russians as the greater danger of the two; and so the British Government decided to give its diplomatic support to Japan. In 1902, there was concluded an Anglo-Japanese Alliance, the main purpose of which was to ensure that if Russia and Japan came to blows it should be a straight fight between the two.[1] Neither

[1] As a matter of fact, the Japanese had been negotiating for two alliances simultaneously; an Anglo-Japanese Alliance against Russia, and a Russo-Japanese Alliance, presumably against England. The Anglo-Japanese Alliance won.

the French nor the Germans would be likely to join Russia in a Far Eastern war with the certainty of having the British fleet against them.

The Boxer rising of 1900 had given Russia the opportunity to occupy Manchuria; and though she gave a promise to evacuate after the rising had been suppressed, it was soon clear that she did not really mean to budge. By the year 1903, relations between Russia and Japan had become seriously strained. Having gained effective control of Manchuria, the Russians were making ominous moves in the direction of Korea and were increasing their political pressure on the Korean Government. On this vital issue, the Japanese were determined not to yield. They had watched the Russians coming closer and closer to their country for a number of years, and they knew that if Korea went the way of Manchuria, Japan would not only be under constant menace from Russian forces close at hand but would find herself soon excluded from trading relations with all north China. Japanese diplomatic remonstrances in St. Petersburg became more frequent and grew sharper in tone.

There had undoubtedly been a tendency, perhaps a natural tendency, among many Russians to regard the Japanese, an Oriental people until recently stagnating in feudal backwardness, as rivals whom there was no need to take too seriously. But as the situation between the two countries grew increasingly critical there were certain of the Czar's advisers who began to wonder whether the Japanese could, after all, be thrust aside out of the Russian path of expansion. Among these was the Minister of War, General Kuropatkin, who had come to entertain serious doubts about Russia's comparative strength; and he made the drastic proposal that Russia should abandon her ambitions in Manchuria and Korea and concentrate instead on development in the Vladivostock area further north. Generals are so often held up to public obloquy as the world's principal warmongers that it is instructive to find, in this case, a General's voice foremost among those raised for conciliation and peace. It will not be the last time that this phenomenon is recorded in this volume.

Kuropatkin was, however, overborne at the instance of the

powerful commercial interests which had sunk much capital in Far Eastern development and did not intend to be deprived, through fear of a war which they assumed their country was bound to win, of the profits about to accrue. The Russian Government remained obdurate against Japanese protests and warnings.

By early February of 1904, the Japanese had made up their minds to fight, as the only alternative to being devoured by the Russian octopus whose tentacles were now very near to the Japanese islands. Japanese war plans inevitably hinged on the command of the sea. Without it, Japan could not send her armies over to the mainland; while if the Russians gained it they could in due course invade and might conquer Japan. Command of the sea was vital to the Japanese. Yet their Naval Staff had a most daunting problem to face. Naval strength was then to be measured in terms of battleships. Of these the Japanese had six, whereas the Russian Port Arthur fleet contained seven. But the real Japanese weakness lay in the fact that while the Japanese battle fleet, already just inferior in Far Eastern waters, had no reserves, the Russians possessed in the Baltic a battleship force about equal in strength to their Port Arthur fleet. The Japanese Navy would therefore be taking on a Russian one double its size. They were bold men in Tokyo who decided to accept the risk.

In these circumstances, the early destruction or at least crippling of the Port Arthur fleet was all-important. Under the compelling necessity of gaining every possible advantage in the desperately unequal fight, the Japanese Admiralty decided on a surprise attack. Governments brought face to face with the grim possibility of national subjugation are inclined to pay small heed to the niceties of international law. Negotiations with Russia were broken off on February 5th, and the Japanese ambassador demanded his passports. On the night of February 8th, without a declaration of war, Japanese destroyers made torpedo attacks on the Russian battleships anchored outside Port Arthur and severely damaged three of them, thus giving the Japanese a temporary superiority of six to four, sufficient for their immediate purposes.

Much criticism was levelled at the Japanese in certain countries for this attack made before formal declaration of war. British comment took a different line. *The Times* military correspondent said that 'the Japanese Navy has opened the war by an act of daring which is destined to take a place of honour in naval annals'; while the leading article declared that it was 'quite impossible for Russia to endeavour to make capital out of the disconcerting promptness with which Japan has delivered her attack. The cases in which a formal declaration of war precedes the outbreak of hostilities have been comparatively rare in modern history. Russia, at all events, has honoured the tradition more in the breach than the observance.'

The Japanese destroyers were greatly helped by an extraordinary lack of precautions in the Russian fleet. Though the whole world knew that the situation between the two countries was critical,[1] that fleet was anchored outside the harbour with the usual lights burning, with torpedo nets not out and with guns not manned. It was a gift to the Japanese which may well have cost the Russians the war; for from that initial blow the Port Arthur fleet, which proved to the general surprise to be as inefficient as it was negligent, never fully recovered.

Though the Japanese now had local command of the sea, it was imperative for them to make an early end of the Port Arthur fleet before the strong Baltic fleet could come out to reinforce it. The investment of Port Arthur by an army under General Nogi was begun as quickly as possible. Efforts to induce the Russian fleet to accept decisive action being unavailing, it became clear it would have to be sunk in harbour. But Port Arthur harbour is guarded by a ring of hills which had been heavily fortified and which the Russian garrison defended with bitter determination. Precious months passed; and in October, with Port Arthur still holding out, it was learnt that the Russian Baltic fleet had started on its way east. The Japanese efforts to capture Port Arthur re-

[1] *The Times* of 21st January 1904 reported 'numerous applications from New Zealanders to serve in the Japanese army and navy in the event of war'; while *The Times* of February 5th printed a cable from its St. Petersburg correspondent that 'it is now almost impossible to believe that war can be averted'.

doubled. Heavy loss of life was incurred but still without effect. At last, in December 1904, with the Baltic fleet at Madagascar, Nogi's army captured a height called 203 Metre Hill, the top of which gave a view of the harbour. Heavy howitzers were brought up and the Port Arthur fleet was sunk at its anchors.

It had been a race against time. The Japanese fleet had perforce been watching the sea exit from Port Arthur till the last, and after ten months of active service, including a fleet action, was in sore need of repair and rest before the next round of the contest. Fortunately for it, the Russian Baltic fleet was in rather worse state of inefficiency than the Port Arthur squadron and was making only a very slow passage eastward. It was not till May that it was approaching the Straits of Tsushima on its way to Vladivostock. There it was met by the Japanese fleet under Admiral Togo, who achieved one of the completest naval victories on record, practically the whole Russian fleet being sunk or captured.

The Japanese fleet had performed the outstanding feat of capturing or destroying the greater part of a hostile navy of double its strength. But it had done something more than that. For the first time in history, an Eastern race, on the sea at least, had met one of the white races in combat and had administered a smashing defeat to it. The news went flashing through oriental lands. British officers of the Indian Army heard of it as the talk of the bazaars.

CHAPTER TWO

Power Rivalries in the Far East from 1905 to the end of World War I

*

The end of the Russo-Japanese war, which came a few months after Tsushima, left Japan with Port Arthur and Talienwan (or Dairen) and eliminated Russian influence from Korea and most of Manchuria.[1] It also gave Japan a new position in the world. She was now universally recognized as a World Power to be taken seriously.

She was, too, a stronger naval power than before the war; for though two battleships had been lost in the war, the Russian battleships sunk in Port Arthur were raised and added to the Japanese fleet, and one of the Baltic battleships had been captured afloat at Tsushima.

From the point of view of the protection of British Far Eastern interests, Japan was now the nation that mattered most. For the time being, however, she and Britain were joined by alliance, and Japanese sentiment towards the British, in consequence of the latter's moral support against Russia, was extremely cordial. All the same, there were now the political ingredients for an increasing antagonism between the two countries; though developments in other parts of the world were operating to keep this inevitable tendency in the background. In Europe, the German challenge to Britain's naval supremacy was being energetically pressed, and British attention was being more and more centred on what was happening in Kiel and Wilhelmshaven, to the ex-

[1] Russia having been ejected from Port Arthur, Britain should have returned Wei-hai-wei to China. But a revised lease was obtained from her and the British stayed on.

clusion of possible dangers in other parts of the world. Sir John Fisher, First Sea Lord of the Admiralty, was convinced of a coming German war and his policy was to concentrate British naval strength in home waters. The China station was left with only a few cruisers, and Japan became, through the tautening of the Western rivalry, the major naval Power of the Far East.

What use would Japan make of her newly won position there and in the world? In human affairs, ambition usually stands next behind fear in the psychological queue, and steps quickly up into the vacant space when fear moves away. Having hurled back the Russian attempt to expand into North China, would Japan proceed to take Russia's place in the exploitation of the same area? We shall have a chance of judging before long.

Meanwhile, a period of recovery was her primary need. The war with Russia had been exhausting and expensive. Moreover, within a year or two of the end of the war, a new naval fashion had come in with the building by Britain of all-big-gun 'Dreadnought' battleships, which rendered all pre-existing types practically obsolete. Japan, if she was to keep her place, would have to conform; and this would mean renewed heavy expenditure. At that time, too, the number of nations with sizeable fleets was fairly large. Besides Britain, still the major sea power, the Germans, Americans, and French were all superior to the Japanese in naval strength, and the Austrians and Italians not much inferior. It would therefore be necessary for the Japanese to walk warily if their ultimate aims were likely to antagonize foreign opinion.

Nevertheless, by 1910 they felt that the world situation made it safe for them to announce the annexation of Korea. Britain, under increasing threat from the growing German High Seas Fleet, acquiesced. The Anglo-Japanese Alliance was renewed two years later for a further period of ten years.

Up to now, American sentiment had also been friendly to Japan. It had been the American fleet that had first broken in on Japanese seclusion. The United States had openly sympathized with Japan over the dispute with Russia, and the American President had taken the initiative in arranging the Peace Conference between the two warring countries which had led to the Treaty of Portsmouth of 1905. Just before the outbreak of the Russo-Japanese War, *The Times* correspondent in Japan had reported that:

'Various speeches recently delivered by Japanese publicists have shown that the nation believes itself to be fighting to secure Anglo-Saxon ideals for Asia instead of a military despotism. . . . Several Tokyo journals rejoice that America is now in the same camp with Japan, since the latter desires nothing beyond a practical assertion of the principles recognized constructively by the new commercial Treaty between China and the United States—namely, the Open Door and the recognition of China's sovereignty over Manchuria.'[1]

The mention of the Open Door is worth particular notice. This principle had also found a place in the Anglo-Japanese Treaty of Alliance, one of the declared objects of which was equal opportunity for all nations in China.

A year after the annexation of Korea, Japan's real intentions towards China began to show themselves. Not that her full policy was immediately apparent to the whole world. It is the custom of few nations to proclaim their final object from the housetops in advance. Outsiders have usually to piece together their conclusions on this score from a succession of episodes pointing in one direction or another; and it was some time before Japan's purpose became too clear to be mistaken.

After the death of the redoubtable Empress Dowager of China in 1908, informed circles in Shanghai and Hong Kong became aware that Japan was taking an increasingly active, though hidden, part in Chinese politics. At this time, the Manchu dynasty was generally regarded as being on its last legs. For two thousand years, China had been ruled by a series of conquering dynasties, each of which had gradually decayed with time and corruption until power had fallen from its nerveless grasp. The Manchu dynasty was nearing the end of the usual span and was, as most observers agreed, about due for early collapse.

The revolution that broke out in China in 1911 was the signal

[1] *The Times* of 18th January 1904.

that the Manchu Emperors had had their day. It began in the south of China and there is not much doubt that it was encouraged and speeded by Japanese intrigue. It is probable that the Japanese hoped the revolution would split China into two parts, north and south, which might give them the chance to dominate one half or perhaps both.

Unfortunately for the Japanese, the revolution spread all over China and resulted not only in the overthrow of the boy-Emperor but in the establishment of a Chinese republic under Yuan-Shih-Kai, China's ablest statesman. This was evidently by no means to the Japanese liking. To detach a part of China from the crumbling Empire was one thing. But for the whole of China to be converted into a unified democracy, as looked like happening, quite another. With the old effete Imperial system swept away, it was possible that so capable a man as Yuan-Shih-Kai might effect a reorganization of his country on Western lines, as had been done in Japan forty years before, which might interfere considerably with the realization of certain Japanese ambitions. Yuan-Shih-Kai was informed that Japan would on no account recognize a Chinese republic, and the Japanese announced their intention of commencing military operations to restore the Manchus.

At this point, however, Britain intervened and insisted that Japan should leave China alone to work out her own salvation. This action by Britain caused the first rift in the Anglo-Japanese accord and gave rise to openly expressed hostility in Japan to the Anglo-Japanese Alliance.

The Japanese lost no time in setting to work to repair this initial setback. The second Chinese revolution, which broke out in 1913, was largely their doing. For months, Japanese arms and money had been poured into the south of China and active intrigues were carried on with the southern leaders; and in the actual rebellion many Japanese officers fought on the side of the south. All, once again, to no purpose. The revolution was a complete failure, and the famous Sun-Yat-Sen, the southern leader, fled to Japan in a Japanese ship.

But world events were shaping themselves in Japan's favour.

In 1914, war broke out in Europe. With all the European Powers at each others' throats, the way was open for Japan to pursue any Far Eastern aims of her own without fear of active interference except by the United States, who was thought unlikely to take action by herself. In the words of Count Okuma, the Japanese Prime Minister, 'it was Japan's opportunity of 1,000 years'.

But, first of all, the Japanese Government had to consider whether they would make any move in support of the Anglo-Japanese Alliance. There was actually a strong body of opinion in Japan, and especially in the Army, opposed to participation. The Elder Statesmen, however, realized that entry into the war would enable Japan to eject the Germans from Tsingtao and thereby gain a foothold for herself in one of the richest provinces of China. Thus, self-interest was in harmony with loyalty to the British ally.

The Germans, for their part, had known in advance that they could not hope to hold Tsingtao in a war against a superior sea Power; and, shortly after the outbreak, had opened negotiations with China for the handing back of the Tsingtao territory. China, on the point of acceptance, was assured by Britain that she and Japan intended to eject Germany from Tsingtao by force of arms but that China need have no misgivings about the result. This assurance was based on a declaration by Japan that she had no selfish designs on Chinese territory, to the integrity of which she was in principle devoted. The Japanese had evidently well learnt the lesson given them by the three Western Powers in 1895 that 'the integrity of China' was the master-phrase in Far Eastern affairs.

Relying on the British assurance, China refused the German offer, and Japan declared war. Plans for this contingency had evidently been long prepared, for within a week or two a well-organized amphibious force was on its way to besiege Tsingtao, two British men-of-war and two British battalions joining the expedition shortly after its arrival at the disembarking beach. Tsingtao was strongly fortified but, being without hope of relief, surrendered on November 7th. In spite of what the Chinese had been told, it remained in Japanese hands for the next eight years.

Two months after the fall of Tsingtao, Japan presented to China what came to be known as the Twenty-one Demands. These gave so clear an indication of Japanese expansionist ambition in China that they are worth some notice. They were in five groups:

Group 1 dealt with the situation arising from the eviction of the Germans from Tsingtao. China was to agree to endorse any settlement that Japan might make with Germany, and was to grant Japan concessions for railway building in the Shangtung province. No concessions on the coast of Shangtung were to be made to a third Power.

Group 2. The leases of Port Arthur and of two Manchurian railways were to be extended to ninety-nine years. Other concessions were to be made in South Manchuria and Eastern Inner Mongolia which, including the Japanese right to provide military, political and financial advisers for the two provinces, would have had the effect of making them virtually Japanese protectorates.

Group 3 dealt with some important iron- and coal-mines in the Yangtse valley. These were to be a joint concern of Japan and China, and outside interests were to be excluded.

Group 4 stipulated that China was not to lease or cede to a third Power any harbour, bay or island along the entire coast of China.

Group 5 was the most drastic of all, and included the demand for the employment by China of influential Japanese as advisers in political, financial and military affairs, while the police departments of important areas were to be joint Japanese and Chinese concerns.

By these demands, the Japanese policy towards China was starkly revealed. The Twenty-one Demands were obviously designed to give Japan almost complete domination over China, politically and commercially. A study of the map shows that in obtaining control of eastern Inner Mongolia, southern Manchuria and Shangtung province and in acquiring a belt of influence on the Yangtse, the Japanese would virtually have surrounded the then seat of the Chinese Government at Peking. As if this were not enough, Group 5 demands would give Japan the control of the Chinese police, army, navy and finance.

In presenting these demands, Japan informed China that if absolute secrecy were not maintained, the conditions would be made more severe. When, however, in spite of this threat, the details began to leak out, the whole set of demands was denied. Eventually, when denial was no longer possible, Japan dropped Group 5 and communicated to Britain, as her Ally, the list of the remaining four groups. Despite the obviously predatory nature of even these reduced demands, Japan coolly described them as 'outstanding questions which she was taking up with China in order to preserve the peace of the Far East and to establish more friendly relations with that country'. The peace of the Far East was another dialectical legacy from the year 1895.

On learning what was afoot, both Britain and the United States presented strong notes of protest. But Japan, for reasons that we shall be able to estimate in a moment, paid little heed. In May 1915, she delivered an ultimatum to the Chinese Government and forced it to submit to the demands of Groups 1 to 4 and to one demand of Group 5.

The main result of the diplomatic pressure that Britain attempted to apply on this occasion was a severe fall in British popularity among the Japanese. The Anglo-Japanese Alliance had already, as we have seen, come under criticism in Japan before 1914. German influence in the country, on the other hand, was strong. German officers had trained the Japanese Army, and since the Army was both more numerous and necessarily closer to the people than the British-trained Navy, there was relatively more sympathy among the Japanese for German than for British ideas. The similarity between the German and Japanese autocratic systems of government also provided a natural link between the two nations.

The pro-German sentiments among the Japanese, reacting on the opposition of the British Foreign Office to the Twenty-one Demands, gave rise to a violent anti-British Press campaign in Japan which lasted throughout 1915 and 1916. Contempt and ridicule were poured on the British war effort, including the conduct of the small British forces which had co-operated with the Japanese in the siege of Tsingtao. Nor can this abuse have been distasteful to the Japanese Government, since it was itself acting in a manner calculated to injure the British cause and estrange the British Government. For instance, during the greater part of the war, Japan gave asylum to Indian seditionists whose extradition was urgently desired by Whitehall but refused by Tokyo. It was not the conduct of a friendly nation, still less of an ally.

The explanation of this equivocal attitude on the part of the Japanese is almost certainly to be found in their confident belief that Germany would win the war. For this there were, indeed, obvious superficial grounds. The German Army was deep inside France, while the Russian Army was in a sorry plight and shortly to disintegrate. In 1917, British military experts in the Far East reported that Japan not only expected but hoped that Germany would be victorious; and there is little doubt that the Japanese Government attempted and probably achieved an understanding with the Germans. There is reason to think that the final and sudden victory of the Allies came to Japan as a distinctly unpleasant shock. In fact, on the day of the German surrender, the Japanese were so taken aback that it needed a reminder from the allied ambassadors in Tokyo to make them put out any flags.

In time of war, expediency tends regrettably to push principle roughly aside. In 1917, when the German unrestricted U-boat offensive had created an urgent demand for more convoy escorts, the British Government, in exchange for the despatch of Japanese destroyers to the Mediterranean for convoy duty, pledged itself to support Japan's claim for the post-war retention of Tsingtao. It was a betrayal of the assurances given to China in 1914 which had induced her to forgo the proffered return of the territory by the Germans to Chinese sovereignty. The Anglo-Japanese pledges then given had both been dishonoured, first by the Japanese and now by the British.

Nor were the British alone among the anti-German nations

in making moral concessions to necessity at the expense of the Chinese. In 1917, the United States came into the war against Germany, and in consequence became anxious to remove any outstanding differences with Japan, the chief among which derived from the American note to Japan objecting to the Twenty-one Demands. There was an exchange of notes between Viscount Ishii and Mr. Lansing, in the course of which the United States recognized that 'territorial propinquity creates special relations between nations and consequently Japan has special interests in China'. This statement was received with astonishment and dismay by the Chinese, who hastened to proclaim that they would refuse to be bound by agreements relating to themselves arranged between foreign Powers.

It is to be noted that in the Lansing-Ishii agreement, which virtually gave American approval to the Twenty-one Demands, Japan again complacently reaffirmed her adherence to the principle of the integrity of China. It cannot unhappily be called a rare phenomenon in international affairs for solemn declarations to be out of strict accord with the facts or actions to which they relate. But that they should shout defiance at each other, as they did here, was diplomatically inartistic.

There is no particular objection, on the other hand, to be taken to the principle that 'territorial propinquity creates special relations between nations'. It is, indeed, a matter of common sense, and history offers a multiplicity of examples of its working. The traditional English interest in the Low Countries is one: the Monroe Doctrine another.

There were several reasons why the Japanese should have a special interest in the state of affairs on the Chinese mainland. One that we have already noticed was that its closeness to their country would make the establishment of a powerful foreign State on Chinese territory a serious threat to Japanese security. But another and almost equally potent reason related to the question of the raw materials of industry.

In these, Japan is poorly provided. Her home islands contain quite inadequate supplies of iron, coal, oil and several other minerals important for a modern industrialized country, and especially one which aspired to make its own way in a mechanizing world. Where was Japan to look for the extra quantities she needed? The obvious place was China, whence most of her requirements except oil and rubber and tin could be met. In particular, China had plenty of coal and iron, the main ingredients of industrial prosperity and martial strength. There were, of course, supplies in other parts of the world. But if Japan relied on them, she might find herself industrially starved in war, either through the action of the supplying countries or through her sea life-lines being severed by a superior naval enemy. The short sea routes to China, being covered by the Japanese islands and the Japanese-owned Ryukus and Formosa, would naturally be much more secure.

The attractions of China as the main source of Japan's essential raw materials were further enhanced by that huge country's perennial weakness, political corruption, and obstinate backwardness. Unlike Britain, who faces a continent customarily harbouring a number of exceedingly powerful and well-organized nations, Japan had to deal with a great, flabby giant of much potential wealth but little inclination for self-development and poor military aptitude. There was therefore a fair prospect for the Japanese to gain that measure of control, if necessary by force, over Chinese resources which would ensure to them those essential supplies both in peace and war which would be their best guarantee of independence, commercial prosperity, and strategic security. The Japanese could not, it is true, get absolutely all they needed from China. But they could get a great deal.

The morality of such a policy towards China, especially when sought by such rough means as the Twenty-one Demands of 1915, may be debatable. It is, however, the way of all nations not to be over-scrupulous where what they regard as their vital interests are involved. The United States happens to be singularly fortunate in the matter of raw materials and therefore has no need to be particularly sensitive about external sources of supply. But Americans would hardly claim that, over the key strategical matter of the Panama Canal, their own methods of getting what they wanted were entirely kid-gloved.

CHAPTER THREE

The Far East from 1918-36

*

The outcome of the war of 1914–18 considerably increased Japan's international standing. The German fleet had been almost eliminated; the Austrian fleet altogether. France was utterly exhausted and Russia in the throes of revolution. At the Peace Conference of 1919, Japan became one of the 'Big Five'. She was now a first-class Power, and was possessed of a fleet that was of major importance in world politics. Only one other nation had gained instead of lost as a result of the war. The United States had replaced Britain as the most powerful country on the globe.

But though Japan had done well for herself in power and influence, her international relationships had undergone considerable change. Before the war, both America and Britain could be counted as her friends. They were so no longer, though Britain was still her nominal ally for a few more years.

Japan's conduct during the war had given both these countries much to think about. They knew she had harboured strong sympathies for the German enemy, with whom they suspected she had been flirting. Moreover, they were by now well aware of her real intentions towards China and of what these would mean to themselves. They had been hostile to Russia's expansion into Manchuria because they had had reason to think she intended to squeeze all foreign commerce out of the areas she occupied. They had conversely favoured Japan largely because she had paid lip service to the 'open door' in China. By the end of the war, however, they could tell that any Japanese assurances of this kind were fraudulent. Wherever the Japanese had established themselves they had practised unfair discrimination in favour of Japanese goods, some of their methods of doing so being:

(a) Delays at Japanese banks and discount houses;
(b) Delaying foreign goods at the ports, while Japanese goods were handled promptly;
(c) Special rebates and lower freight charges on Japanese goods both on the railways and at sea.

It was clear that Japan meant to follow the same general line as the Russians before them. Japanese-occupied China was to be reserved for the commercial benefit of the Japanese. The 'open door' was to be fully open for them but no one else.

In these circumstances, what was to be done about the Anglo-Japanese Alliance? The Americans had by now come to regard it with great disfavour. British feelings on the subject were somewhat mixed. The Foreign Office realized the disadvantages of renewing an alliance with a nation which had given so many proofs of disloyalty towards it. On the other hand, it was felt that by remaining allied to Japan, Britain could exercise a measure of restraint upon her which would be impossible if the connection were broken. This was, however, an ignoble argument. An alliance inevitably implies support of the ally and his policy; and to enter into an alliance for the opposite purpose of obstructing him is essentially dishonest.

There was a further strong reason against renewal. An alliance, if only by implication, must be directed against somebody. With the general thinning-out of navies as a result of the war, there were now few Powers capable of getting at Japan at all. Russia could do so by land, but in 1922 was in a state of internal turmoil; while in any case large-scale continental warfare in eastern Asia against the new-born hope of the Socialist world was unlikely to appeal either to the British Government or people. No one else was now a menace to the Japanese except the United States; and it was unthinkable that Britain should side with Japan against America, even had the Anglo-Japanese Alliance not expressly excluded that contingency.

When the time came, the Alliance was properly allowed to

lapse. But its non-renewal was softened and to some extent disguised by the merging of the Alliance in a Four-Power Treaty between the United States, Britain, Japan and France. This multiple Treaty had little or no practical value, but it enabled the Japanese face to be partially saved.

This step was taken at the Washington Conference of 1921–2, called by the Americans to effect a treaty of naval limitation and so avoid a post-war competition in naval armaments. For this purpose, the United States took the bold step of producing, without previous consultation, proposed ratios of naval strength to be accepted by the principal naval Powers. These ratios, applying primarily to the larger classes, were as follows:

U.S.A.	5
Britain	5
Japan	3
France	1·75
Italy	1·75

When these figures were brought out of the hat, both the Japanese and French were bitterly affronted. The French had a long and honourable naval history, and had for two centuries been the runners-up to Britain as the chief naval Power of the world. They did not take kindly to a ratio about half that of the Japanese.

The latter, however, were no better pleased. They had been steadily working their way up in the world, and their ambitions had been mounting with their achievements. To be 'frozen' for a long period at 60 per cent of the American and British strength was a horrid insult, and might also be distinctly damaging to the position of the dominant military party in Japan. This party had naturally made the most of the successes of the previous eighteen years and particularly of the Russo-Japanese war, the result of which had not been presented to the Japanese public in its true colours. At sea, the Japanese had certainly done wonders. But on land the fight had been less one-sided. Big battles in Manchuria had led to a virtual stalemate. While the Russian armies were far from final defeat, Japan's resources were nearing their end and an early peace was essential to her; which the intervention of the American President had fortunately brought about.

But this aspect of the war had been kept from the Japanese people, who had therefore acquired a false idea of what had been effected, and so suffered an attack of swelled head. This was even admitted by some of the Japanese leaders. Thus General Toji, speaking in 1912, said:

'The Japanese were poisoned with vainglory after the war with Russia and have, in consequence, become luxurious and conceited. Neither the military authorities nor the statesmen have told the nation the truth about the war and its real ending. Instead, they have made irresponsible, exaggerated speeches and encouraged the people in pride and vanity.'

To accept a position of admitted inferiority at sea was therefore most embarrassing politically for the Japanese Government, as it was personally distasteful to its members.

For some time, it was touch and go whether the Japanese representatives at Washington would sign. The members of the British delegation, to whom they were still linked by alliance, endeavoured to smooth them down and made to them the happy suggestion that they might accept provided there was agreement by the other signatories not further to develop any naval bases in the Western Pacific. By this means, suggested the British naval officers, Japan would be protected against attack by the larger fleets of Britain and America which, without bases, would not be able to get at Japan. This formula saved the day and the Japanese signed. Their reluctance had been entirely psychological; materially they gained more out of the Treaty than anyone else, as we shall see.

The nation that might have been expected to kick the hardest against the American big ship ratios raised no objections. By long tradition, Britain was the foremost sea Power in the world, with a fleet of commanding superiority. At the turn of the century the ruling political principle in regard to the Navy was the Two-Power Standard, which meant that the Navy of Britain was to be equal to the next two strongest navies combined. When

Mr. Churchill became First Lord of the Admiralty in 1911, he made the concession to the growing sea power of Germany of openly reducing the planned British lead to 60 per cent over the nearest rival.

The British tradition of a superior fleet was still, in 1921, very strong indeed and was not merely a matter of sentiment. The British fleet *was* the largest in the world. In 1914, it had had a core of 32 Dreadnought capital ships to the United States' 11. In 1919, Britain had 40 to the United States' 18. But the U.S.A. had a very large building programme in hand, whereas Britain had only the *Hood* under construction and was beginning to break up large numbers of her wartime fleet. Nevertheless, at the time of the Washington Conference the state of the British, American and Japanese Dreadnought battlefleets was as follows:

	Completed	Building or projected
Britain	30	4
U.S.A.	20	15
Japan	11	4

The British lead over the American fleet was large, and even when the current building programmes were completed the United States would have no more than a rough parity, while the British battlefleet would be more than twice as strong as that of Japan. The Japanese could not have built their battlefleet up to 60 per cent of the British had not the Washington ratios sliced the British strength drastically down to meet theirs.

After nearly thirty years, there are few people now who realize that the main sacrifice in the Washington Naval Treaty fell on the British. They saved money, certainly, but that is all they did save. The Americans saved more money in stopping the construction of a number of new ships, and they leapt at a stroke into coequality with the strongest naval power without having to go to the expense of building their way up to that position. The Japanese saved money, too, and they gained considerably in naval strength proportionately to the United States and Britain.

Britain it was who lost on the deal. By accepting the main American ratios, she surrendered her long-standing sea supremacy among the nations of the world, she abandoned her ancient freedom to protect in the way she thought best her vital maritime communications, and she agreed to forgo her previous commanding lead over the Japanese. The British Government was, however, in a difficult position. To challenge the American President's arbitrarily chosen ratios would probably mean wrecking the Conference, and it was thought most inadvisable for Britain, as the American public's hereditary whipping-boy, to risk doing that. Besides, Britain owed the United States a lot of money; and the American authorities were making it clear that it was none the less owed because it had been spent, among other things, in keeping the American Continent safe from the German fleet which in 1914 was second only to the British.

There were contemporary British critics of the Washington naval proposals who disliked them on principle. These critics argued that if Britain wished to avoid a naval building race with the Americans she should tell them to go ahead with building what they liked and good luck to them. No one in Britain contemplated a war with the United States, and if the latter felt inclined to possess the largest fleet in the world, Britain had no cause for apprehension. But for Britain to tie her hands in the all-important matter of sea power, not only in relation to America but other countries too, was a fundamental mistake. There was much to be said for this view. The Anglo-American parity was no more than superficial, since in the event of another world crisis the Americans would be bound to leap ahead with a building programme that Britain would be unable to match. But for the sake of a false semblance of naval equality with America, the British Government gave away any chance of equality in the Far East, where it mattered a great deal.

One peculiar feature of the occasion was the earldom bestowed on Mr. Balfour. Whatever his previous services to the country, whatever his eminence and distinction as an individual, whatever his tact and skill in the Washington negotiations, it was odd that the opportunity taken for doing him high honour was his signature to a treaty abolishing the centuries-old supremacy of Britain on the seas.

The Far East from 1918–36

The standstill agreement about naval bases expressly excluded the proposed British base at Singapore. This project had been decided on shortly after the war and was the offspring of the changed world conditions the war had brought about. Naval—or any other—war plans have to visualize some country as the potential enemy; and the almost complete elimination of Germany as a naval Power in Europe, combined with the unpleasant political conduct of the Japanese during the war, served to make the British Admiralty's thoughts turn eastward.[1] The next challenge seemed likely to come from Japan.

If so, the need for a good fleet base in the Far East was evident. Hong Kong would not do. Its harbour was too small and shallow for a big fleet of modern ships, and it was unduly vulnerable to land attack. The protective leased territory on the mainland side of the harbour was only fifteen miles deep. Should the Japanese be able to land an army anywhere near, they might well be able to march round and capture the base from the land side, as they had done at Port Arthur.

For the main Far Eastern base, the Admiralty had therefore chosen Singapore. It had plenty of deep water, a sheltered anchorage, and several hundred miles of the British Malayan Peninsula behind it. It was on the corner between the Indian Ocean and the China Seas and would serve both to cover the former and to act as a base of advance into the latter. But it was also a long way from Japan and could logically be described, therefore, as mainly defensive in character. It was so accepted at the Washington Conference.

The opportunity was taken of the meeting of the Powers at Washington to bring Anglo-American pressure to bear on Japan to abandon her aggressive designs on China and relinquish the concessions she had screwed out of the Chinese during the war while the rest of the world was otherwise engaged. Her representatives were made to realize that any special advantages remaining to Japan out of the Twenty-one Demands must be liquidated and that Tsingtao must be returned to China.

This port was by now probably the most promised place in

[1] Their military co-operation was unexceptionable.

42

the Far East. The Germans had offered it to China in 1914, and a week or two later the British, with Japanese backing, had also promised it to her. In 1917, with the Japanese still in possession, the British had promised it to them at the Peace Conference, a promise that the Conference of 1919, with American approval, duly confirmed. But at Washington two years later, this confirmation was repudiated by its British and American signatories and Tsingtao reverted to Chinese control.

By the end of the Washington Conference, Japan had suffered a severe diplomatic reverse. Her plans on the Chinese mainland had been brought to a halt, her gains of the war years had been prised away from her, and she found herself diplomatically isolated, condemned to a stipulated inferiority in naval armaments to Britain and the United States, which two countries not only were to have substantially larger fleets than hers but, to make matters much worse, were now united in firm dislike of and opposition to Japan's whole Far Eastern policy.

It is hardly surprising that in the course of the following years, the feeling in Japan towards the United States and Britain grew increasingly sour.[1] These two Powers were standing between Japan and what she believed to be her destiny, and she did not like them for it. Moreover, salt was rubbed into psychological wounds when the Americans passed a law forbidding Japanese immigration into the United States, while the 'White Australia' policy gave similar offence. If Japan remained quiescent for the next eight or nine years, it should have been fairly obvious to London and Washington that it was only because she was biding her time. The Western nations now had sufficient evidence for guessing what her long-term policy in the Far East was, and they could reasonably suppose it would be resumed in its previous form should changing circumstances provide the opportunity.

The animosity of the Japanese towards America was not unilateral. In the years following the Washington Conference, Japan came to occupy for many Americans the position of national enemy No. 1. The American armed forces thought primarily in

---

[1] Though the chief hostility was to the United States.

terms of a Japanese war. To American civilians a Japanese invasion was a very real bogey. Even those living far in the interior of their huge country expected to wake up any morning to find Japanese soldiers scrambling over the garden wall. On the basis of ordinary probability, these American fears were quite groundless. The American fleet being 66 per cent stronger than the Japanese, the American population much larger, the country's material resources and industrial productivity much greater, a Japanese invasion across the 4,000 odd miles of the Pacific Ocean was practically inconceivable.

Not that the average pre-war Briton showed much superior wisdom where sea power was concerned. There were many eminent men who wrote agitated letters to the Press round about 1939 to say that a German capture of the Channel Ports would be fatal to this country, since it would give the Nazis submarine bases on the Atlantic. Therefore an army of continental size must be used to keep these vital bases out of German hands. What these letter-writers failed to understand was that if enemy ships themselves can be successfully disposed of, the bases from which they emerge cease to matter. In the event, the Germans did capture the Channel ports, their occupation by the enemy did not prove fatal to Britain, and the U-boat offensive was eventually defeated at sea, and would have been defeated sooner had not the previous false ideas on the subject clouded the issue.

It would seem that even Mr. Churchill shared in this pessimistic view of Britain's chances of survival in the event of a German victory on land; for he had written before the war that 'if France broke, everything would break, and the Nazi domination of Europe and potentially of a large part of the world would seem to be inevitable'. Holding such views, Mr. Churchill's offer of common citizenship with France in June 1940 has the appearance of a despairing attempt to avert the irretrievable disaster that he clearly believed the fall of France must entail. His amazing proposal to the French is, indeed, hardly explicable on any other basis.

The Washington Treaty left the British naval staff with a much more complicated problem to solve than it did their American counterparts. If, now that the Anglo-Japanese Alliance was no more, the Japanese fleet constituted a direct menace to British interests in the Far East, then undoubtedly a British fleet of comparable size to the Japanese was required in Far Eastern waters. This meant an Eastern fleet of at least ten capital ships, the number to which Japan had been limited by the recent treaty.

Admiral of the Fleet Lord Jellicoe had gone out to Australia and New Zealand just before the Washington Conference to advise these countries on defence policies. To him, the drastically changed balance of naval force in the world called plainly for a considerable redistribution of British naval strength. He recommended that there should be an Anglo-Dominion Pacific fleet of fifteen battleships based on Australia. Though to the war-weary British world of 1920 such a project seemed grandiose and impossibly expensive, there is no doubt that in principle Jellicoe was right. The chief post-war naval danger was in the Pacific, and it was in the Pacific therefore that the fleet required to meet that danger should have been stationed. The necessity for a fleet to be trained on its probable battle-ground had been recognized by Admiral Fisher in his concentration of British naval strength in the North Sea before 1914, when Germany was the main rival.

When Jellicoe reported, there were quite enough capital ships in the British Navy for thirteen to have been sent permanently to the Pacific.[1] But the subsequent Washington Treaty limitations ruled any such transfer entirely out. After Washington, there were not even enough ships for the British Admiralty to detach to the East the ten required to match the Japanese fleet. The ratios of 5 : 5 : 3 for the British, American and Japanese fleets might give the Americans enough naval strength, seeing that the ever-friendly British fleet covered the United States from attack from the East. But they certainly did not suffice for the British, who had to protect themselves both in European and Far Eastern waters. The post-war fleets of France, Italy, Baltic Russia, Spain and so on might not be individually imposing; but all together they added up to quite a few ships. Even the severely restricted German Navy of Versailles proportions

---

[1] The other two were to be provided by Australia and New Zealand.

counted for something. The traditions of British statesmanship and the security instincts of the British people demanded the maintenance of a fleet in European waters that gave an obvious margin of safety.

There were also some awkward administrative drawbacks to the use of Singapore as a permanent base. The tip of the Malayan peninsula is almost on the Equator, making life in a warship very uncomfortable. The naval base area was twenty miles by road from Singapore city, had no pre-existing social amenities, and can indeed be described without much exaggeration as being situated in jungle surroundings.

These geographical limitations were not lightly to be brushed aside. Men joining the British Navy might want to see the world. But they also wanted to get an occasional glimpse of their wives and families. Since these latter, for climatic reasons, could not suitably be brought out to a place like Singapore for prolonged periods, it became politically impracticable to station nearly two-thirds of the Navy on Singapore, far from their homes, in a hot and trying climate, in conditions of isolation and discomfort.

Some of the worst of these objections could have been avoided if Lord Jellicoe's advice had been taken to base the Pacific fleet on Sydney. There the officers and men could have brought (or found) their wives and set up their homes. There, too, were docking and repair facilities on a fair scale already available, the expansion of which to deal with the biggest classes of ship would have been a much quicker job than the creation of a new major repair base out of nothing at Singapore.

Singapore, it is true, would unquestionably have to be used as an operating base in time of war, and Sydney was no less than 4,000 miles away from it. But Sydney was also 4,000 miles from Japan, as compared with 10,000 miles from England to Japan by the shortest route and 15,000 miles if the Mediterranean were closed—as it was in 1941. Moreover, *Sydney faced the Pacific Ocean*; and a fleet with its home base on the Pacific would have been thinking in terms of Pacific warfare. Sydney was therefore a better home port for a Pacific fleet than Chatham, Portsmouth or Devonport. Some repair facilities were certainly needed at

Singapore: say, enough for emergency repairs, plus a floating dock. But Sydney was the best place for the main repair and recreational port.[1]

Why, then, were the claims of Sydney ignored? One cannot tell with any certainty. But there is some ground for supposing that the Sea Lords in Whitehall may have felt jealous of the possibility that a large fleet based on Australia might gradually slip out of their control. It is not without significance that only a year or two before, in May 1918, the Admiralty had made a proposal to the Imperial Conference of that year which would virtually have had the effect of abolishing separate Dominion navies. This proposal was for 'a single navy under a central naval authority', which authority would, of course, have been in London. British admirals with such an idea in their minds would hardly feel a natural enthusiasm for the basing of a substantial fraction of the Navy on Australia, more or less for good.

There were therefore weighty arguments, from the Admiralty's point of view, against the stationing in the Far East of a British battlefleet capable of looking the Japanese Navy in the face. And so the Admiralty settled the matter by sending no battle fleet at all. The post-war China squadron consisted of a few cruisers, just as before the war when Japan was an ally. The bulk of the fleet remained in the Mediterranean and Home Waters.

The British Government and the naval staff at the Admiralty reassured themselves by arguing that in the event of trouble in the Far East, the fleet could always go out there. Elaborate plans were made for its transference, and the 'passage of the fleet to Singapore' became one of the standard exercises at the Staff College. For such exercises, it was always conveniently assumed that there would be no simultaneous complications in Europe to prevent the whole fleet moving half-way across the world.

The problem of reinforcing the Far East was made no easier by the wave of anti-war fervour that spread over Britain after

---

[1] There were a number of public critics of the choice of Singapore rather than Sydney, among them Colonel Repington, military correspondent of *The Times*.

the 1914–18 war. The British people had suffered severely in the war. Loss of life had been very heavy, and loss of treasure beyond all expectation. Having entered the war the richest country in the world, Britain emerged from it with heavy war debts. Post-war exhaustion and poverty brought a strong reaction against war itself and all to do with it. Pacifism throve, and the men who had done the fighting became objects of public disdain; while the League of Nations Union, supported by a mixed multitude of vague idealists, university professors, anti-war careerists, and opinionated intellectuals, mostly quite ignorant of strategy, drew all the applause.

Politicians of all parties, their ears to the ground, paid lip-service to the prevailing emotion. Collective security became their watchword, whether or no they believed in it, as many did not. Its foremost advocates were the Labour politicians who, with little or no experience of the responsibilities of government and convinced that warfare was an upper-class machination, worked on the happy assumption that foreigners could somehow or other be relied upon to pay for the defence of the British Empire. The Labour Party therefore consistently opposed all defence expenditure, even continuing their opposition up to the very outbreak of war in 1939. It did not seem to strike its members as odd that they should have been clamouring for war against Germany for the previous year or more but nevertheless fighting hard against the means of waging it.

To these persistent anti-warriors, the Singapore base was a special bugbear. It would cost the imposing sum of £20 million and they railed at this huge loss to the social services. When they came into brief power in 1924, they stopped work on the base; and after their successors had restarted it, they made it a constant object of criticism. As might be expected when a defence project becomes a political shuttlecock, work on the base languished. With a determined effort, it could have been finished in five years. But, after ten years, the building of the main graving dock had only just been started.

It happened that a Labour Government was again in power in 1930 when the London Naval Conference of that year took place. The Washington Treaty had a duration of ten years; after which, while the ratios might remain in force, it had been agreed that battleship replacement would begin. The British Admiralty had been looking forward eagerly for this to happen. A ten-year naval holiday was a serious thing from an administrative point of view. The plant for heavy armament making is very costly to provide and expensive to maintain, while the personnel for working it is very highly specialized. A steady programme of work is therefore needed to keep the arms factories and their operatives on a remunerative basis, or even on armament work at all. Armament firms without orders lose their expert men to other industries, and must themselves either go out of business or convert their machinery to other use.

This was the broad position in naval armament matters in Britain in 1930, when the Naval Conference assembled. Starved of work, the firms were in a bad way, and the Admiralty was counting on a resumption of building to bring about an industrial revival.

But the Labour Ministers were sworn foes of armaments in any form and were resolved to use the Conference, not to bring a little life back into the gunmakers' pallid cheeks, but to bleed them still further. They agreed to a further standstill of six years in battleship construction, and they came to the almost worse compact to bring cruisers and destroyers under the ratio system, involving a considerable amount of scrapping of these classes, too. From this disastrous decision dates the acute shortage of convoy escorts at the beginning of the 1939 war and the resultant loss of millions of tons of shipping and thousands of merchant seamen's lives that might have been saved.

It is true that both the American and Japanese navies were bound by the same prolonged restrictions as the British. But the last were the chief sufferers, since they had much the greater commitments in the way of seaborne communications that needed protection. They therefore had the most to lose from a further period of naval limitation. The capital ship strengths had now come down to 15 : 15 : 9 for the British, American and Japanese fleets.

The political craving for disarmament in Britain was not, of course, lost on the Japanese. They must have felt that if they kept quiet, events would sooner or later play into their hands. Nine years after the Washington Conference, their opportunity came. The economic crisis which began to develop in 1929 paved the way. By 1931 it had the world fast in its grip, and led to a certain episode which the Japanese evidently took as their signal for action. Ill-considered pay cuts were applied to the men of the British Navy, and the Home Fleet at Invergordon broke out in open mutiny. This occurred in the middle of September. Four days later, a bomb wrecked a train in Manchuria, in consequence of which the Japanese marched in and occupied Mukden, the capital, where they installed a nominee emperor as the head of a new Manchurian State (which they christened Manchukuo) under their supervision and control. Japanese expansion in China had recommenced.

There was a great hullabaloo in the world. All the British pacifists, as is their way, called loudly for war against Japan. The League of Nations passed minatory resolutions and sent a Commission under Lord Lytton to Manchuria to investigate and report. In due course, the Commission declared that Japan had been very wicked. No one, however, did anything; and the Japanese stayed where they were. This slap in the eye for the League of Nations administered by Japan did not deter the League enthusiasts from proceeding with their Disarmament Conference billed for 1932, regardless of the lesson that even with armaments as they were the League organization had been unable to prevent the Japanese breaking the new international rules.

Having successfully disregarded the League in 1931, the Japanese did so again in the early part of the following year. The Manchurian *coup* had been an army triumph. There was then much jealousy between the Japanese Army and Navy, and in February 1932 the Japanese Admiral at Shanghai thought he would gain some prestige for his Service by landing a naval force to deal with some anti-Japanese actions by the local Chinese. His landing party ran unexpectedly into the Cantonese 19th

Route Army and received rough handling. The affair developed, troops were sent from Japan, and for about six weeks there was heavy fighting in parts of the Chinese city, with much destruction of property.

Again, the League talked a lot but did nothing. Though the threat to British interests in China was obvious, the great Admiralty plan to move the fleet east in case of danger was not put into force. Quite apart from the disorganizing effects of the Invergordon mutiny, there was as yet no safe base in the Far East for the main fleet's use. Owing to previous political opposition, the Singapore base was far from ready. Its defences were incomplete and its repair facilities only half-installed.

Nor were these the only difficulties that arose when the question of coercing Japan was examined as a matter of immediate urgency. Singapore, completed or not as a base, is 1,500 miles from Shanghai and 2,000 miles from Manchuria. The communications from Japan to both these areas ran through the Yellow Sea, the approaches to which were guarded by the Japanese bases of the Pescadores, to the south of Formosa, and Okinawa to the north of it. The problem of police action by a British fleet based on Singapore was therefore none too straightforward, even were that fleet in superior force to the Japanese. And for the inferior fleet which was all that the British Government could then send out, the problem would have been almost insoluble. Very similar would have been the position of a Japanese fleet based on Gibraltar charged with frustrating a British invasion of Denmark.

If the British and American fleets could have combined, their united strength, with the Philippine bases to work from, might possibly have served to overawe the Japanese into abandoning their Chinese aggression. But the British and American Governments did not agree on joint action. It was election year in the United States.

That the Shanghai incident did not grow into something much worse was due mainly to the efforts of the British naval Commander-in-Chief in China, Admiral Sir Howard Kelly. He was at Batavia when the news of the landing came through, but he left at once for Shanghai. On his arrival, all foreign senior officers present in the river paid the usual visits of ceremony, except the Japanese Admiral. Sir Howard Kelly sent over to say that he would like to see him, in order to express to him the views of His Majesty's Government—or what Sir Howard thought they were or should be. The Japanese Admiral came and had impressed upon him the grave view taken by London on his aggressive conduct. He was also told that if his aircraft (from a carrier out at sea) continued to fly close over the British flagship on their way to bomb the Chinese, they would be shot down. This warning being reported to the British Admiralty, Ministers in London were aghast that a British Admiral should have taken such drastic action on his own initiative. However, the Japanese aircraft ceased to fly close over H.M.S. *Kent*.

Having made the British view-point thoroughly plain, Admiral Kelly then offered his services as a mediator to secure a cessation of the fighting and the withdrawal of the Japanese. He was determined, if he could, to get this dangerous affair settled by negotiation, though he was playing an almost lone hand in working for that end. Discretion seemed to govern the attitude of the British civilian authorities, both at home and abroad; while the senior naval officer present at Shanghai, an American Admiral, held strictly aloof from any intervention. Sir Howard Kelly therefore set to work by himself to make contact with both sides. He established friendly relations with the Japanese Admiral Nomura, who had arrived to take charge, and his civilian colleagues, Matsuoka and Shigemitsu. Similarly, by the help of the British Chairman of the Shanghai Municipal Council, he was able to meet Mr. T. V. Soong and Mr. Wellington Koo, who were both in Shanghai at this time. For a month, Sir Howard had periodical meetings with one or other of the two sides, while fierce fighting went on in the Chinese city. Under constant pressure from the British Commander-in-Chief, the Japanese were increasingly inclined to terminate the incident by withdrawing. But 'face' was an important consideration for them, and they kept on sending across more army divisions in the hope of a substantial success which would enable them to retire with dignity; but the Cantonese fought so well that they could not obtain it. Eventually, Admiral Kelly was asked by the Japanese to invite both sides to a conference, and through the British Admiral's good offices a compromise settlement was reached. One might have thought that such successful labours for the cessation of hostilities were just what the Nobel Peace Prize was intended to reward. But this prize seems to go instead to theoretical world reformers whose theories invariably break down in practice.

No preventive measures having been taken by the rest of the world, either collectively or individually, against the Japanese move into Manchuria or the attack on Shanghai, the opportunities for any such police action were thereafter to become progressively less favourable. In a little more than a year, Hitler rose to power in Germany. As his policy developed and became more clear, the conditions of the pre-1914 years began to be reproduced. With Germany increasing her armaments in Europe to the alarm of Britain, France and America, Japan could feel she had a freer and freer hand in the Far East. This time, moreover, she had no ally to worry about. Britain was not even a friend.

To make things even easier for Japan, the managers of the League of Nations obstinately refused to be instructed by their dismal impotence over the Manchurian affair. In 1935, still buoyed up by the homage of numerous hypnotized devotees, they decided to try conclusions with Italy over Abyssinia. The resulting fiasco was not only absolute but disastrous. Italy successfully defied the fifty-odd nations of the League; but the attempt to dragoon her forced her into the arms of Germany. In 1936, the Rome-Berlin Axis was born, and in the same year Germany, with British acquiescence, began to build a modern fleet.

CHAPTER FOUR

The Far East from 1936-41

*

The rapid return of Germany under the Nazi regime to the position of a fully sovereign world State with swiftly growing armaments and an expansionist foreign policy was bound to influence international power relationships all over the world. By 1937, she had successfully reintroduced conscription, reoccupied the Rhineland, and started the construction of battleships, submarines and military aircraft. As a result of the lamentable Abyssinian affair, she now had a firm understanding with Fascist Italy, and the morale of the German people was high.

In these changed circumstances, it was fairly obvious that the prospect of Britain being able to send her main fleet to Singapore in case of trouble in the Far East had not improved. If she had hesitated to take this step in 1931 and 1932, she would presumably be even less inclined to do so five years later.

This was evidently the line of argument followed by the Japanese. By 1937 they had clearly come to the conclusion that they could openly proceed with their policy of expansion in China without much fear of foreign interference; and in July of that year a full-scale invasion was launched from Manchurian territory, where the Japanese army had been installed since 1931. The Japanese calculations were justified. Neither Britain nor the United States took preventive action. As the Japanese began their operations, they announced that they had no other object than to preserve the peace of East Asia. This was by now the well-established formula with which to decorate aggressive action in that part of the world.

Some other people besides the Japanese were also taking a close interest in Britain's ability and willingness to move a fleet to the Pacific. For nearly twenty years, the Dominions of Australia and New Zealand had been content to rest their defence policies on the principle that in the event of external danger the British main fleet would hurry out to their protection, about which they had received positive and frequent assurance. They had accordingly maintained only minor defence forces of their own.

This position of primary reliance on the mother country made these two Dominions all the more sensitive to the world danger signals that were by 1937 flying in several areas. Their peoples were quite capable of interpreting these signals for themselves, and in both countries there arose a growing uneasiness as to what Britain could do to help them in the altered and worsening condition of world armaments and political alignments. The fear began to be expressed in Press and magazine articles that Britain might not now be in a position to spare a sufficiently strong fleet to come east to counter an aggressive move by Japan.

The Australian Government would, however, admit to no misgivings on this score. The Prime Minister told the House of Representatives in August 1937 that the British fleet could be relied upon to reach Singapore in time to prevent its capture or neutralization.[1] A year later, in December 1938, the Minister of Defence told the House that there had been much loose talk of the Czech crisis of a month or two before having proved that Britain would be unable to station at Singapore in an emergency a fleet strong enough to safeguard Empire interests in the East. He claimed that the crisis had indicated nothing of the sort. 'On the contrary, the Government has sound reasons for being reassured on this point.'[2] That the same feeling of confidence animated Australian Ministers in the middle of 1939 was conveyed in an article by *The Times* Canberra correspondent, who wrote that 'the Commonwealth Government are satisfied with the assur-

[1] Australian Hansard for 24th August 1937.
[2] Australian Hansard for 6th December 1938.

ances they have received repeatedly from Mr. Chamberlain and the Admiralty'.[1]

There is therefore good cause for thinking that positive pledges in regard to effective Imperial naval aid to Australia and New Zealand were being given by the British Government right up to the outbreak of war with Germany. There were certainly some most sanguine opinions being expressed in Britain in the years 1937 to 1939 by prominent politicians in England. In November 1937, Sir Samuel Hoare, a recent First Lord of the Admiralty, told the House of Commons that

> 'to-day we are justified in saying that, although we regard the submarine as an extravagant nuisance that ought to be abolished, the submarine is no longer a danger to the British Empire.'

A few months later, in the Navy Estimates debate of 1938, Mr. Churchill expressed his general satisfaction with the strength of the Navy,[2] while in the following year, at the annual dinner of the Royal Institute of International Affairs, the Foreign Secretary made the statement that the British Navy was 'unchallengeable'.

If the Japanese felt any agreement with this opinion of the British Foreign Secretary's, there was no sign of it. Instead, they gave the impression, as they forced their way into China, that the British Navy was an instrument of which they need take little account. Not content with pursuing their own interests, the Japanese were going out of their way to injure those of Britain and America and to heap insults and humiliations on British and American nationals coming into their power. At Tientsin, for instance, a Chinese city where a British concession had for long existed, British men and women were treated to unheard-of indignities, being often stripped naked and slapped

---

[1] *The Times*, 11th May 1939.

[2] 'We have had several debates in recent weeks upon defence, and I agree that, as has already been said, the gloomy feeling which was natural in many bosoms has not been particularly relieved by the course of those debates; but here to-night, on the Navy at any rate, we have a right to feel a sense of good cheer and courage. . . .'

in the face in front of the native Chinese population. These unfortunate Britons, being savaged by a set of brutal Asiatics with no hope of succour by their own Government, must have read with astonishment Lord Halifax's contemporaneous after-dinner speech.

When war broke out in Europe in September 1939, Japan remained neutral. She had been a member of the Anti-Comintern Pact, but this did not bind her to action. Moreover, the famous Ribbentrop-Molotov agreement of August 1939 had been a rough violation of this Pact and had given much offence to the Japanese, who disliked, distrusted and feared the Russians.

A general war was certainly welcome to Japan in that it might well provide her with the same opportunities as in 1914–18 for advancing her own interests without meddlesome intervention by other Powers. But it was essential to be on the winning side, and during the 'phoney war' period Japan was not sure which side that would be. She therefore tended to mark time; except in China, where her operations, though strenuously pressed, were still giving no decisive result.

The spectacular victories of Germany in 1940, whereby the whole war situation was suddenly and dramatically transformed, swung Japan over on to the German side. Such a country as this, she decided, must surely be the final winner.

The decision taken, Japanese policy was quickly orientated in the chosen direction. With France and Holland prostrate at Germany's feet and Britain thought likely to follow, now was the time for Japan to drive southward towards the oil, tin, and rubber-bearing lands of Malaya, Burma, and the Dutch and other islands of the South Seas.

The hoped-for conquest of China was far from complete. The Chinese under Chiang-Kai-Shek had put up a stout resistance, and owing to the huge size of the country and the aptitude of the Chinese for guerrilla tactics there seemed no immediate prospect of bringing the war to a successful conclusion. But if partial failure had to be accepted in China, it was imperative both for prestige and economic reasons that it be redeemed somewhere else. Provided Japan was prepared to brave the hostility of the

Western nations concerned, this could be done by expansion to the South. A move in that direction would, above all, give Japan ample supplies of that vital commodity, oil. Japan wanted oil desperately. At present she was mainly dependent on American supplies. Could she but gain control of the Indonesian oilfields, she would at last be able to snap her fingers at the hostile Republic across the Pacific.

Within three months of the fall of France, Japan had made three important moves. She had concluded a formal treaty with Germany and Italy, she had extorted from the helpless Vichy Government of France agreement to a Japanese occupation of northern Indo-China, and she had demanded of Britain the closure of the Burma road by which Britain and America were sending supplies to aid Chinese resistance to the Japanese invasion. To this demand, Mr. Churchill felt obliged to give way.

As the slogan for her coming southward move, Japan announced it to be her policy to form an Eastern Asia Co-Prosperity Sphere which, though undefined, was rumoured to include Malaya, Burma, Siam and the Dutch and other islands of the South Seas. By its title alone, it was a warning to other nations, including Britain, of what to expect.

Meanwhile, the United States had been taking preparatory steps to bring pressure to bear on a Japan which was running wild on the other side of the Pacific. The Japanese war against China had from its early stages been accompanied by blatant acts of discrimination against and injury to American interests in China. Outrages against American nationals were as frequent as against British. In the course of the hostilities against the Chinese forces, American property was often bombed and shelled, neither compensation nor apology being usually forthcoming for what there was good reason to suspect were deliberate acts. Not even the American armed forces were immune. At the end of 1937, the gunboat *Panay* was bombed and sunk by Japanese aircraft, and was not the only American warship to be attacked.

As outrage and insult mounted up, the American Government and people felt that something should be done in retaliation; and economic sanctions came first to mind. There was, however, one obstacle to any such forms of pressure in the shape of the Japanese-American Commercial Treaty of 1911. This would first have to be got rid of before action could take place. After long provocation, notice of termination was served by the State Department in July 1939. There was, however, a stipulated interregnum of six months before the denunciation became effective. This would expire in January 1940.

The American Government and Congress had waited impatiently for this date, because of then increasing irritation with the American position in respect of events in the Far East. It was felt to be absurd that the Japanese should be carrying on warlike operations against China and generally be doing their best to damage American and European interests in China with the aid, to an important degree, of raw materials actually provided by America. The latter was, in fact, supplying her hated rival with the means of attacking not only her friends but also herself. It was quite illogical, and there was rising American hostility to such a state of affairs.

No sooner was the commercial treaty safely out of the way than an American Senator introduced a resolution calling for an embargo on all war materials to Japan. So abrupt a termination of supplies was, however, considered too provocative. A more gradual squeeze was decided on and put into force. Thus, orders were made on 5th July, 26th July and 30th September 1940, for various materials to be put on the stop list: and further orders were issued in December 1940 and January 1941. The most important commodity of all, oil, remained however in free supply —anyway for the time being.

These coercive measures brought their inevitable reaction in spurring on the Japanese to greater haste in the prosecution of their southward expansion. In March 1941, they were able to extort from Vichy France the control of the Indo-Chinese rice crop and the right to occupy the Saigon airfield. This brought them within bombing distance of Singapore. Throughout April, May and June, Japanese troops in large numbers were being moved into Indo-China. Then, on July 25th, the Japanese announced a development which brought the whole Japanese-

American tussle to a climax. They said that the French had agreed to a joint Franco-Japanese protectorate over Indo-China. On hearing of this, President Roosevelt evidently decided that the time had come to force the issue. The next day, he 'froze' all Japanese assets in the United States and added oil to the embargo list. The British and Dutch at once announced that oil from Burma and the East Indies would also be denied to Japan.

The wheel that Commodore Perry had begun to turn in 1853 had now come round full circle. What his countrymen had primarily wanted, in sending him to press Japan to end her isolation and enter the international trading system, was that she should form a market for American goods; and in buying American oil Japan was carrying out the international trading rules that Perry had forced upon her. By 1941, it was America who was finding the international exchange system inconvenient and was seeking to terminate it at Japan's expense. But this time, thanks to that same system, the Japanese were not armed with bows and arrows; and, if need be, they were resolved to fight their way back to self-sufficiency. Commodore Perry's commercial samples had included a post-dated declaration of war.

President Roosevelt's imposition of the oil embargo was, in fact, the decisive step that made war inevitable. With their oil supplies from the United States and the Indies cut off, the Japanese were faced with a creeping paralysis that would eventually bring all their warlike, and many of their industrial, activities to a standstill. Nor would the final helplessness be too long delayed. Though they had built up large reserve stocks, expenditure was high and, failing regular replenishments, supplies would be exhausted in a matter of months.

Not that this danger had been unforeseen. It had undoubtedly figured prominently in Japanese strategical calculations ever since the American denunciation of the 1911 trade treaty in 1939, and had indeed been the main cause of the Japanese southward drive towards the oilfields of Borneo and the Dutch East Indies. This drive was now, in July 1941, well advanced, and powerful Japanese forces were poised in Indo-China all ready to strike. But the seizure of the southern oil lands might and probably would mean war with America and Britain, and the Japanese hesitated before taking the final step.

In the subsequent negotiations with the United States it was made clear by the latter that her terms for resuming oil shipments to Japan would include the calling-off of the China war and the evacuation of that country and also Indo-China. To have agreed to such terms would have involved Japan in the deepest of national humiliations and disastrous loss of face in the whole of Asia. She would inevitably have had to abandon all pretence of being a first-class Power and would have sunk to the position of a subordinate nation permanently dependent on the goodwill of her American suppliers of fuel oil. No people with any claim to self-respect could follow that road when there was the alternative choice of seizing the oilfields to the southward, even if that meant a war. And as the Japanese were an exceedingly proud and martial race, it was hardly conceivable that they would not risk a war to gain their economic independence of American censors and economic overlords.

Of this, the American President and State Department must have been fully aware from the beginning. They had been frequently warned by the American Ambassador in Tokyo that if Japan were deprived of oil from America she would take what she wanted in the south. It follows that Mr. Roosevelt must have had war in his mind from July 1941 onwards, since he had no grounds for thinking the Japanese would surrender to his demands. Once the oil embargo had been declared, the position was, indeed, one of unbreakable deadlock. America could not lift it without admission of diplomatic defeat. As Mr. Stimson declared, that would have been 'derogatory to the honour of the United States, a blow to American as well as Chinese morale. . . .' But Japanese honour was no less deeply involved, and Japan's future as an independent country as well.

It is true that there are said to have been moderate and liberal statesmen in Japan who were prepared to make concessions to the American view but who were overruled by the bellicose military party. Whether these liberal elements were really sincere is perhaps open to question. But if they were, they would seem to have been defeatist to the point almost of treason. To have retreated in obedience to the American oil embargo when there was a fair chance, even though the risk was great, of securing abundant oil supplies of their own would have been an act of extraordinary pusillanimity. The leaders of the military party in Japan, if it were really they who carried the issue against the opposition of the 'moderates', were making the right decision from the Japanese point of view. As the Latvian Premier had declared in comparable circumstances two years before, 'it is better to die on your feet than live on your knees'. In Britain, at times of external crisis, it has nearly always been the war party which gets its way. In 1914, 'moderate' or 'liberal' politicians who opposed the war ruined their political careers by so doing. In 1940, they were mostly locked up in prison.

In America, about the only voices raised for any concessions to Japan were those of the Chiefs of Staff. The heads of the Army and Navy, anxious to avoid or at least postpone an outbreak of war, urged a temporary arrangement with Japan whereby in return for a suitably pious formula of peaceful intention by her and a withdrawal of her forces from south to north Indo-China, the United States would resume oil supplies on a month to month basis. Though it is possible that the Service chiefs only wanted to buy time for more preparation, one is nevertheless reminded of the last-minute effort made by General Kuropatkin to avert the war with Japan in 1904. The American Chiefs of Staff had no more success. The State Department delivered instead a stiff note repeating the full previous American demands. Mr. Churchill, when consulted beforehand, had described the contemplated conciliation proposals as 'thin diet for Chiang-Kai-Shek'; which can probably be interpreted less as consideration for the welfare of the Chinese than as opposition to any *modus vivendi* with Japan. Actually, the Chinese were likely to have thin diet in any case, if not from the Japanese then from their own corrupt Kuo-Min-Tang Government; and, in the event, the rejection of conciliation was to result in some pretty thin diet for the British.

However, a policy of 'toughness' carried the day in American counsels, and a correspondingly framed communication was handed to the Japanese Ambassador in Washington on 26th November 1941. The American Chief of Naval Operations evidently regarded it as dismissing any possibility of a peaceful solution, and on the following day he sent out a war warning to U.S. naval forces in the Pacific. It amounted also to a war warning to the British Government. On November 10th, Mr. Churchill had made a public announcement that if the United States were to become involved in war with Japan, Britain would join America 'within the hour'. Let us therefore see how well prepared Britain was to take her place in a Pacific war.

CHAPTER FIVE

The Singapore Base up to 1940

*

M uch had been written and spoken about the Singapore base in the years between the wars. As a project costing a great deal of public money, as an object of recurrent political controversy, and as an important defence measure, it was a natural topic for periodical discussion in the Press and on the platform both in Britain and the Dominions. Pressmen have a noticeable, indeed an inevitable, tendency to sensationalize their treatment of defence matters. They like strategy to be highly coloured. The proper journalistic role for a new weapon is to be revolutionary, throwing all the older ones into obsolescence. The correct attribute of a fortress is impregnability. Every fortress that has come into the news in my lifetime—Port Arthur, Tsingtao, the great French defensive system of the Maginot Line—has been popularly described as impregnable before it has been attacked.

Politicians also favour impregnability for fortresses for which they are responsible, or on which they are dependent, especially those on which money is being or has recently been spent. They naturally like to convey to the taxpayers the impression that the money has been spent to the best purpose; and though they may not actually commit themselves to the word impregnable in relation to a particular fortress, they have subtle dialectical ways of engendering that idea. One way or another, it became a virtually accepted fact in Britain and the Dominions that Singapore was an impregnable bastion of Imperial security.

The public in those countries did not, of course, know details of the fortress armament. They had mostly heard of the great

1. A waterside scene in Singapore

2. Aerial view of Singapore city

3. Singapore Naval Base under construction

15-inch guns mounted there; but they could not know that they were sited and intended to deal with attack from seaward. Therefore, when Singapore was later captured from the land side, there were widespread accusations that those in authority had overlooked this contingency which, after it had happened, seemed almost blinding in its probability.

It is true that when the base was first mooted just after the armistice of 1918, the Committee of Imperial Defence was thinking mainly in terms of naval attack. The general conditions at that time were, however, appreciably different from what they became later on. Air power, though it had made great strides during the 1914–18 war, was still in its early stages of development, sea-air power in particular being practically in the experimental phase. The range of aircraft was short and their lifting power—and therefore bomb load—comparatively small. Moreover, the basic assumption which governed all plans of Pacific defence was that, in the event of trouble, the main fleet would reach Singapore within seventy days; and it was believed in London that if the Japanese were to capture the naval base within those seventy days they would have to make their attack direct against Singapore island itself.[1] Hence, the only defence forces and weapons required were those necessary to hold the island. Actually, it was also necessary to hold a small strip of the adjoining Johore State, since the naval harbour was in the inlet between the Island and the south coast of Johore. Therefore, an enemy had obviously to be kept beyond artillery range of that coast, if the warships in the harbour were to be in safety. Yet, strangely enough, it seems to have been thought for years that there was no need to defend more than Singapore island.

The assumption that the fleet would have seventy days in which to relieve an uncaptured Singapore was much too optim-

[1] Exactly when the seventy days were reckoned to start is not, so far as the author knows, on record. Presumably from the time of the decision to send the fleet east, which might well be during the period of tension before the outbreak of war. But a surprise Japanese attack being a possibility, the seventy days might have to be counted from the actual outbreak of hostilities. General Percival (Despatch para 22) says the 70 days began on the outbreak of war.

MAP 2

istic, especially on the above assumption that only the island had to be held. When the matter was put to the test, the Japanese completed the conquest of the whole of Malaya from the far north-west downwards in less than seventy days. Had there been no defending forces beyond Singapore island, as was the original and for many years the ruling policy, the Japanese conquest would have been quicker still. This could have been foreseen. In 1914, the Japanese had captured Tsingtao, a naval base with much better natural defensive positions and much more strongly fortified than Singapore against land attack, in a very leisurely siege of sixty-six days, of which only seven were devoted to the actual assault. Why, then, were seventy days accepted as being within the safety period for Singapore? Possibly because any period much less than seventy days would have knocked the bottom out of the Government's 'main-fleet-to-the-east' plan by leaving insufficient time for the fleet to get there.

The basic idea behind the Singapore defence policy can therefore be regarded as being unrealistic from the start. But realism was little in demand at the time of that policy's first inception. With world conditions as they were in 1921, Germany prostrate, France and Italy friendly to Britain, everyone in Europe suffering from war exhaustion, and the League of Nations in its first flush of popularity, there was no disposition in civilian Britain to criticize any defence scheme on the grounds of its insufficiency.

What is, however, somewhat peculiar is that no one then or later seems to have thought of the Malayan Peninsula as a territory worth protecting on its own account, apart from the naval base to be erected at its southern extremity. Yet it was a country rich in most important natural resources. It had very rich tin deposits, and its rubber output was also extremely valuable. Malaya was an area comparable in economic-strategic significance to what the West Indies had been in the days of sail, a wealth-producing region which could not be lost to the enemy without grave economic upset. Yet whereas the eighteenth-century British Governments always took great care to look after the West Indies because they were the principal sugar islands, no twentieth-century government seems to have had any thought for the tin and rubber of Malaya as Imperial assets needing protection. The naval base monopolized the ministerial outlook.[1]

Unfortunately, the politician took advantage of the state of public opinion to clamp a particularly heavy leg-iron round the Defence Services' ankles at this period. In 1923, as some guide for the planning of security measures after a great war, the Cabinet decided that there would not be another such war for ten years. It thus fixed the year 1933 as the date by which the Service departments should have their war preparations completed and up-to-date. This was reasonable enough. But an ugly qualification to the ten-year-rule was shortly to be introduced. Soon after Mr. Churchill became Chancellor of the Exchequer in 1924, the ten-year-rule became an ambulatory one. As each year passed, the 'full preparation' date did not become one year nearer, as originally intended, but receded one more year into the future. This cunning political device naturally left the Service departments almost helpless in face of a hostile Treasury, which had only to murmur the master formula 'no major war for ten years' to provide an unanswerable counter to any request for an increase in the Service estimates. Thus were the Service chiefs condemned to the endeavour to build their plans on a moving staircase.

As the years passed, the conditions governing the defence of Singapore got steadily more difficult. With the increasing range of aircraft, an enemy could bomb the naval base from airfields more and more distant, which called for such enemy to be kept further and further away, either by advancing the military defence line beyond Singapore island or by some other means. The international outlook also became less agreeable with the passage of time. Germany began to recover from her defeat. The advent of dictatorship in Italy introduced new stresses and strains into European diplomacy, and Japan, as we have seen, came to challenge the authority of the League of Nations with success. In 1933, she left the League altogether and, as she did so, the Nazis came into power in Germany.

[1] General Percival's despatch, par. 18.

In London, the Chiefs of Staff watched these developments with growing concern. The 1930 Naval Treaty had been a heavy blow to the Admiralty by its application of limitation to, and the consequential reductions in, the smaller classes of warships; and by its postponement of big ship replacement. All three Services, moreover, were still hobbled by Mr. Churchill's receding ten-year-rule.[1] Before anything effective could be done to meet the worsening world situation, this fetter must be struck off; and in 1933 the Chiefs of Staff managed to persuade the Cabinet to do so. This placed the new official date-line for a possible major war at 1943, but war actually came four years earlier.

Representations were also made to the Government about the need for strengthening the defences of Malaya. But very little was done, the principal decision being to build two new air-fields on Singapore island where there had previously been only one. Two or three others for the east coast were discussed, but no action was taken. A little later, in 1936, it was decided to fortify the island of Penang off the west coast.

The passage of the main fleet to Singapore continued to be the official master-plan for the defence of the territory. How long the Chiefs of Staff continued in the belief that this plan could be put into operation as required the author does not know. But he has reason to think that by 1935 at least they had acquired serious misgivings on the subject and had made those misgivings known to the Cabinet. Indeed, as the years went by with their record of growing German rearmament, the birth of the German-Italian axis, and the Japanese denunciation of the Washington and London naval treaties, it became increasingly obvious to even unofficial observers with some knowledge of naval affairs that the assumptions of the 1920s about sending the main fleet to the east might be out of date; and by about 1937 some of

---

[1] It can be argued that this rule was a Cabinet decision, and therefore the collective responsibility of its members. But the rule undoubtedly had its origin in the Treasury, of which Mr. Churchill was then the head, and it is well established usage in this country to link the name of individual Ministers with measures of which they are or were the departmental sponsors. Thus, it is common to speak about 'Mr. Lloyd George's 1909 Budget' or 'Mr. Bevin's foreign policy'.

these observers were beginning to question publicly in print the Government's ability to despatch more than a fraction of the fleet to Singapore in case of trouble.[1]

Similar misgivings were by then disturbing the military authorities in Malaya. The General Officer Commanding, Major-General W. G. S. Dobbie,[2] and his G.S.O.I., Colonel A. E. Percival, had come to feel that the main fleet might not, in the changed world situation, be able to reach Singapore within the promised seventy days; and that, if not, the Japanese would be in a position to undertake a deliberate operation of investment instead of the officially contemplated attempt at a quick capture of Singapore island against time. Colonel Percival set to work to think out how the Japanese would probably act in these, for them, more favourable circumstances. He concluded that they would seize aerodromes in southern Siam and north Malaya[3] in order to gain bases for the long-range bombing of Singapore. But he also thought they would still confine their main attempt at invasion to an assault on Singapore island. Doubtless for this reason, he proposed that possible landings in the north-west should be dealt with by the provision of additional air power. On the military side, he suggested only four more battalions, one for the Penang area, one for Johore, and two for Singapore island. He also proposed an increase in naval small craft for local defence.[4] General Dobbie endorsed Colonel Percival's conclusions and forwarded them to London.

In the following year (1938), General Dobbie sent home an Appreciation of his own. In it, he said that it was an attack from the northward that he regarded as the greatest potential danger to Singapore. By this time he was meaning an attack from the direction of Mersing, a feasible landing-place on the east coast of Johore about seventy miles north of Singapore and connected to it by a good motor road, rather than an attack right down the

[1] For example, Admiral Sir Barry Domvile in his book *Look to Your Moat*.

[2] Later, Lieut.-General Sir William Dobbie, of Malta fame.

[3] There was a civil landing ground in Kedah province and another smaller one in Kelantan.

[4] General Percival's despatch, Appendix A.

Peninsula. He said he was investigating an extension of the defence line some twenty to thirty miles out into Johore to meet this contingency; and in due course he began the construction of pill boxes and similar strong points in this area. This was the first indication by any high officer of a realisation that a naval harbour could not be rendered safe by holding one side of it only. That the horizon of General Dobbie's defence precautions remained limited to Johore State was due to his belief that, with the French in Indo-China as probable allies against Japan,[1] an enemy landing high up the Peninsula would be impracticable and hence that account need only be taken of carrier-based attacks on the tip of the Peninsula.

When Major-General L. V. Bond took over the command from General Dobbie at the end of July 1939, work on the defences on the Johore River line covering the Mersing road was well advanced, the sea-front defences of Singapore island had been greatly improved, and reinforcements of two infantry brigades were expected from India. Otherwise, the general scheme of defence was the same as it had been for many years; a garrison strong enough for holding Singapore island until the main fleet came out to relieve the situation.

However, the new G.O.C. had not been in charge long when this plan underwent a drastic change. Word came from London that the fleet could not now be relied upon to reach Singapore in less than 180 days. This was news of grave import. Though it might be possible to assume that Singapore island could be certain of holding out for seventy days against a Japanese attack, complacency could not be stretched to cover a period of six months. There was no doubt that the whole scheme of defence needed to be reconsidered and that the defending forces ought to be made much stronger.

The situation was actually worse than the Government was as yet ready to admit. In January 1938 there had been consultation between the American and British Naval Staffs, in which the British Director of Plans had stated that his country would

---

[1] On the assumption that the Japanese would only move in the event of a general war.

base a battlefleet on Singapore if Japan moved south.[1] It is not recorded what size of battlefleet the British Admiralty proposed to send; but that it cannot have been large is to be inferred from the development of the following year. In May 1939, when the near likelihood of war with the Axis Powers was forcing the British Government to cold realism in immediate war planning, a naval officer was sent to Washington to make the sombre confession that, owing to the need for maintaining a fleet in the Mediterranean to deal with the Italian Navy, it would be impossible to send any battleships at all to Singapore.[2] In view of the tone of confidence distinguishing Ministerial utterances in Australia at this period that we have noted in the last chapter, it must be concluded that this vitally important information was withheld from the Dominion Cabinets as well as from the Commanders in Malaya.

But hot on the heels of the official lengthening of the 'period before relief' to 180 days, came the outbreak of war in Europe. This tremendous event immediately complicated General Bond's problem in Malaya. Like everyone else, the General took it for granted that the despatch of the British Expeditionary Force to France was the prelude to another titanic struggle on the 1914–18 model. It did not therefore seem a very good moment to press for large reinforcements for Malaya.

However, as the strange quiescence on the Western European front grew longer and longer, General Bond began to feel that there was a chance, if only a fleeting one, of the claims of Malaya receiving sympathetic attention at home. In April 1940, therefore, he represented to the War Office that it was no longer sufficient to provide for the close defence of the naval base. He believed that with the greatly increased 'period before relief' the Japanese might attack anywhere on the Peninsula, and that the defending forces must be strong enough to meet such attack wherever it might come. Further, that the bombing threat from distant airfields required that the Japanese be kept beyond the frontier.

[1] Morison, Vol. III, p. 49.
[2] Morison, Vol. III, p. 49.

If this extended protection was to be provided by military means, then obviously the army in Malaya would have to be greatly increased. The holding of the frontier would be an entirely new military commitment, since it would in no way diminish the need for a strong garrison for Singapore island and Johore State. Possible landing-places on the east coast would also have to be guarded. Fortunately, they were not too numerous, as a great deal of Malaya east of the central mountain chain was virgin jungle, inimical to military operations. But some force would be required to keep watch on what there were. Nor could the possibility of a landing on the west coast of the Peninsula be altogether ignored.

General Bond therefore stated that in his view the revised requirements of Malayan defence necessitated a minimum field army of approximately three divisions, plus three machine-gun battalions and two tank regiments. A fourth division was really wanted, but the General felt, as he told the War Office, that it seemed hopeless to ask for it. If an advance into Siam was to be carried out, a further two or three divisions would be needed. and he presumed this was a still more forlorn suggestion. Though the General might be taking advantage of the military inactivity in Europe to gain a hearing for Malayan defence requirements, he knew that this inactivity might be terminated at any moment; and his common sense told him that when major fighting developed on the Western Front, the insatiable demands of the Army in France would inevitably prejudice the position of far-off places like Malaya.

Obsessed with this latent threat to the military reinforcement of his area, General Bond then went on to offer an alternative suggestion. If, he said, enough troops to meet his stated requirements could not be sent out, was it possible for the R.A.F. to be given the main responsibility (in the absence of the fleet) for the security of the territory? With the French in full and, as most people imagined, permanent control of Indo-China, which lay (with Burma) across access to Siam from China by land, a Japanese attack on Malaya would have to be entirely sea-borne; and it was a tenable proposition that a strong Air Force in

Malaya might be able to frustrate an invasion of this kind by sinking the transports at sea or during disembarkation. General Bond knew that senior R.A.F. officers in Malaya were anxious for their Service to take a larger share in the defence of the Peninsula, and that they believed that if more aircraft were available the R.A.F. could defeat a seaborne invasion by itself. The General therefore thought it proper in the circumstances to put this alternative idea of defence by air power before higher authority.

General Bond's conclusions were embodied in memorandum form and reached London by air some time in April 1940; but before they had received attention at a high level the whole strategic situation had undergone a fundamental change. France had fallen, the British Expeditionary Force had been evacuated to England with the loss of all its weapons and equipment, and Italy had come into the war against us.

These events ruled out, at all events for the time being, a life-and-death struggle in Western Europe and thus eliminated this potentially exhausting drain on the man-power of Britain. To be offset against this saving was the increased importance of the Middle East area through the presence of a hostile Italian army in North Africa, shortly to be joined by a German. But, on balance, the prospect of reinforcing Malaya with troops was probably better after the fall of France than before it.

At first, the means of augmenting the Malayan Air Force were diminished. The fall of France was rapidly followed by the Battle of Britain and that by the night bombing, for countering both of which the demand for aircraft initially exceeded supply. In the latter half of 1940 the strategical circumstances of Britain were very different from those envisaged in General Bond's memorandum, written in the early spring.

Nevertheless, the Chiefs of Staff accepted the general arguments of the memorandum. They agreed that the whole of the Peninsula must now be held and they decided in favour of General Bond's suggestion for doing so mainly by air power. The idea of basing the defence of Malaya on aircraft evidently appealed to them and they ordered that this principle should come into force as soon as the appropriate air strength had been reached. But they added that they did not think such strengthening could be completed until the end of 1941, or over a year ahead. Meanwhile, they said, extra troops would be sent out to make up for the missing aircraft. A total military force of about three divisions would be required during the intervening period but could be reduced when the air force build-up had been accomplished. There were elements of contradiction in this line of thought. What the Chiefs of Staff were saying was that the first step towards providing extra air power which was to remedy a shortage of troops was to send out more troops to compensate for a lack of air power.

The size of the then Air Force in Malaya was certainly not impressive, there being only eighty-eight first-line aircraft of all kinds, of which about half could be classed as obsolete.[1] The Chiefs of Staff stated their opinion that to implement the 'defence by air power' policy a minimum of 336 *modern* aircraft would be necessary. How they arrived at this figure is not known to the author; and one admission they made at this time does nothing to clarify their method of calculation. This was that their estimate of the strength of the Japanese air forces likely to be employed against Malaya in the event of attack was 713.[2]

The question immediately arises why they thought 336 British aircraft sufficient to deal with Japanese attackers more than double as numerous. Part of the reason is undoubtedly to be found in the opinion prevalent in British Intelligence circles that the combat worth of Japanese aircraft was well below that of their British counterparts. This Japanese inferiority was held to apply both to the aircraft and the men who flew them. On a rough comparison, the Japanese Air Force was officially placed as about on a par with the Italian and well below both the British and the German. Even so, the current estimates credited the Italians with about 60 per cent of the British efficiency, which on the same basis would have given the 713 Japanese aircraft a

---

[1] Sir Robert Brooke-Popham's despatch, para. 79.

[2] This was a curiously precise figure to advance where guesswork was the only possible guide.

relative value of 427, against the British 336. Relatively or absolutely, therefore, the Chiefs of Staff were contemplating for the British Air Force that was by itself to keep Malaya safe from Japanese attack an inferiority to the enemy they were expected to meet. As we shall see in a moment, the local commanders, working from the same data, put the British air needs much higher.

In sending their views out to Singapore, the Chiefs of Staff ordered the local commanders to forward their comments thereon, under the title of a Tactical Appreciation. This Appreciation was drawn up in October 1940, and in it the local commanders found themselves very much at variance with the Chiefs of Staff's figure of 336 aircraft for the minimum British air strength for Malaya. This the men on the spot put at 556. Remembering that Whitehall's assumption for the Japanese attacking strength was 713, the only rational conclusion, even without a knowledge of subsequent events, is that the local commanders' figure was the more reliable; again bearing in mind that it was the Chiefs of Staff's intention that the Air Force should have the primary responsibility for the defence of the Peninsula.

Nevertheless, when the Tactical Appreciation from Malaya reached London, the Chiefs of Staff refused to accept the local figure of 556 aircraft or to increase their own rival estimate of 336. Actually, it seems to have been the Air Ministry which applied the veto, since it stated the Malayan estimate of 556 to be 'far beyond the bounds of practical possibility in the light of total resources and vital requirements in active theatres at home and in the Middle East' [1]

In view of this *non possumus* attitude by the Air Ministry, it is somewhat surprising that the Chiefs of Staff persisted in their policy of primary reliance on air power in the defence of Malaya. For to override the commanders in the field as to the forces they deemed necessary to execute the official policy was a serious step for the Chiefs of Staff to take, since it inevitably implied a want of confidence in the former's judgement. It also had the effect of transferring to themselves the direct responsibility for

[1] Sir Robert Brooke-Popham's despatch, para. 79.

any failure in Malaya that could be attributed to the local commanders' requirements not being met. And these considerations received additional force from the fact that the local commanders' figure of 556 had had the endorsement of the representatives of Australia, New Zealand, India and Burma in conference at Singapore at the time, who even said it ought to have been higher.

But the Chiefs of Staff stuck to their opinion and their policy, telling the local commanders that with 336 aircraft they could do quite well enough; which was tantamount to saying either that they were alarmists or that they did not know their jobs. Whether, in fact, the Chiefs of Staff were more right than the local commanders or the local commanders than the Chiefs of Staff can never be known for certain; for in the event the Chiefs of Staff did far worse even than their own figure of 336. When the Japanese attacked at the end of 1941, there were less than half this number of aircraft in Malaya. But this, as we shall see, may not have been entirely their fault.

At this same period, the Chiefs of Staff at last gave the Commanders in Malaya the momentous information that the Admiralty had imparted to the American Naval Staff the previous year: that the fleet could not under present circumstances be spared to go to Singapore. Thus was a theory of twenty years' standing, of great use to politicians and Treasury officials during that period, officially declared incapable of execution when the danger against which it was supposed to be a certain safeguard was close at hand.

It was an admission that obviously had a profound bearing on the whole defence of Malaya, since it meant that that country would be entirely and indefinitely dependent on its military and air garrisons for its security against attack. This being so, it is additionally strange that the Chiefs of Staff, having decided to risk experimenting with the novel theory of 'defence by air power' for the protection of this vital area, should have ignored the representations of the commanders in Malaya as to the aerial garrison required for the purpose.

CHAPTER SIX

Singapore and Malaya, 1940-1

*

The War Office wasted no time in implementing the Chiefs of Staff's decision to provide more troops in place of absent aircraft. As early as August 1940, on the evacuation of Shanghai, the two battalions there were transferred to Singapore. They were joined in October and November by two infantry brigades from India. In February 1941, Australian troops began to come in, and by April two more Indian infantry brigades were in Malaya.

In November 1940, there was an important change in the Malayan High Command. This was the appointment of Air Chief Marshal Sir Robert Brooke-Popham as over-all Commander-in-Chief in the Far East. The terms of his appointment belied, however, the supremacy implied in the title. Sir Robert, for one thing, had no power over the Navy. For another, his control over the Army and Air Force was limited to strategical direction and did not extend to administration. His command was therefore one of those half-commands which can never be entirely satisfactory.

It has been mentioned that the local commanders in Malaya, at the time they were drawing up their Tactical Appreciation in October 1940, were participating in a Far Eastern conference which included representatives of the Australian, New Zealand, Indian and Burmese Governments. In March and April of 1941, there were further conferences in Singapore on a wider basis, now including representatives of the United States and the Netherland East Indies, both of which were more than likely to be involved in any Japanese warlike move in the Pacific. Plans for co-operation between Britain, the United States and Holland in such an event were discussed and several decisions were come to, the principal ones being that in case of a Japanese war the United States Asiatic fleet would retire on Singapore if and when the Philippines were invested, and would therefore be available for its defence; and that the Dutch naval forces in the East Indies would co-operate to the full with the British in the defence of Malaya. At this time, the American Asiatic fleet consisted of the 8-inch gun cruiser *Houston*, the 6-inch gun cruiser *Marblehead*, 13 destroyers, and 17 submarines.

The important announcement was made at this conference that a British Eastern fleet would after all be sent to Singapore, to arrive within about eighty days. This was very nearly a complete reversal of policy. In the space of about twelve months, the Commanders in Malaya had been told, first that the period before relief must be extended from 70 to 180 days, next that there would be no relief to the fleet at all, and now that naval reinforcements could be expected in 80 days. Superficially, the latter intimation was a return to practically the old formula that had governed the broad concept of Far Eastern defence since 1921. But there was one significant difference. The new pronouncement did not say that the main British fleet would be sent to Singapore but 'a' British fleet. The term main fleet implied, and was generally understood to mean, the bulk of the fleet, and certainly a force superior to the Japanese Navy. 'A' British fleet might be of any size. However, the natural assumption was that this fleet would be strong enough to keep the Japanese out of the south-western Pacific, as otherwise there would be no point in sending it.[1]

Negotiations had, in fact, been going on for months between the British and American Governments on this subject. The initial British endeavour had been to induce the Americans to send a portion of their battle fleet to Singapore. This they had

[1] The Australian Government seems to have held the 'main fleet' view till the last. On 23rd January 1942 the Australian Prime Minister sent a telegram to Mr. Churchill in which he said that 'we understood that (Singapore) was to be capable of holding out for a prolonged period until the arrival of the main fleet' (*Daily Telegraph*, 11th October 1950).

refused to do; and quite rightly, since such a division of their fleet would have left the Japanese with the advantage of the interior position. The British pressure did, however, cause the American Government eventually to agree, in the event of a clear threat of war in the Pacific, to send a battle force to the Mediterranean to keep the Italian fleet quiet, and thus enable British big ships to be released for transfer to Singapore. Morison says that the battleship strength of the transfer squadron was to be six.[1]

The Americans also said that they would use their Pacific fleet (not to be confused with their Asiatic fleet) offensively in order to relieve any Japanese pressure on Singapore. It had, however, been decided, under an Anglo-American agreement concluded in Washington on 27th March 1951, that in the event of Japan entering the war the decisive theatre would be held to be the European one and that the main strategy in the Far East would be defensive. It is to be remarked in passing that a defensive strategy of this kind implies or should imply a *successful* defence.

The news that British capital ships were now again to be expected at Singapore again transformed the question of Malayan defence. The planning of the past year had been based on the assumption that the Japanese would have command of the sea for six months or even permanently if they attacked Malaya. The new turn of policy brought this period back to under three months, a difference that fundamentally affected the appreciations of the previous autumn and winter. Nevertheless, there seems to have been no general revision of those appreciations or of the decisions arising from them. The 1940 Army and Air Force plans envisaging a six months' or longer period before relief remained in force, apparently without modification.

In May 1941, Admiral Sir Geoffrey Layton, the naval Commander-in-Chief of the station, who had only taken over the command the previous September, was informed from home that Admiral Sir Tom Phillips, then Vice-Chief of the Naval Staff of the Admiralty, had been given the dormant appointment of Commander-in-Chief, Eastern fleet, to become effective if and

[1] Morison, Vol. III, p. 51.

when a battle force was sent to Singapore, when Admiral Layton's own appointment would lapse. This probably meant a change of the naval command in the area just when war was breaking out, naturally a most undesirable arrangement.

By the middle of May, moreover, both the Army and Air Force commanders in Malaya had been replaced by other officers, whether from routine relief or for other reasons the author does not know. The new men were Lieutenant-General A. E. Percival and Air Vice-Marshal C. W. Pulford. General Percival was the same man as the Colonel Percival who had been G.S.O.I. to General Dobbie from 1936–38 and whose activities in that appointment we have noticed in the last Chapter. Air Vice-Marshal Pulford had started life in the Navy and had the reputation of being an excellent co-operator with the other Services. He and General Percival got on very well together and lived in the same house. General Percival describes him in his book as 'a man of my way of thinking'.[1]

The general strategic situation facing General Percival had undergone a serious change for the worse during the year preceding his arrival. When General Bond wrote his Memorandum in the spring of 1940, in which he had included the alternative of defence by air power with the Army in a subordinate role, there were no Japanese in Indo-China and Siam was still inviolate. By the middle of 1941, the Japanese not only had an army openly in Indo-China but were known to have sent numerous 'tourist' infiltrators into southern Siam where, under various commercial pretexts, they were reported to be getting airfields constructed, improving roads, strengthening bridges for heavy traffic, and collecting mechanized transport and probably petrol at strategic points much in excess of anything necessary for civil use. There was thus, by this time, a potential Japanese line of communication by land from Indo-China to near the Malayan border. The basic assumption behind General Bond's 'defence by air power' submission was therefore out of date.

General Percival decided that a further strengthening of the

[1] *The War in Malaya* by Lieut.-General A. E. Percival, C.B., D.S.O., O.B.E., M.C. (Eyre & Spottiswoode).

garrison forces was necessary. He now had to take account of a possible form of attack which could only be dealt with by military means, and although the Army had been reinforced in the previous year and was much larger than when he had last been in Malaya in 1938, he did not think it large enough. Nor was he happy about other elements of a balanced defence. There was a serious shortage of anti-aircraft artillery, not as many naval small craft as he would have wished, and no tanks. There was also much to be done in the way of training and in preparing beach defences and road obstacles, consequent on the Chiefs of Staff's new policy that the whole of the Peninsula needed to be denied to an enemy. Unfortunately, owing to a shortage of local labour, field works had largely to be constructed by the troops, which naturally interfered with training. Moreover, though it was not his direct responsibility, General Percival had grave misgivings about the size of the air force and its ability to fulfil the role the Chiefs of Staff had assigned to it; as indeed had also the Air Officer Commanding.

The latter was faced with a disquieting situation. The year before, the local commanders, backed by the Dominion and Indian representatives, had asked for 556 aircraft as their minimum. The Chiefs of Staffs had cut this down to 336. But Air Vice-Marshal Pulford did not find a force even of this latter size awaiting him, or anything like it. There were only just over 100 aircraft on the Peninsula. Nor had he any certain information that the remaining 200-odd of the Chiefs of Staff's estimate would arrive by the end of the year, as had been promised or at least implied.

However, he had to prepare for their arrival, and the task of doing so was a formidable one. There were many new airfields to be completed, each requiring hangars, living accommodation for the men, workshops, magazines, storehouses, canteens and other administrative services. These airfields, moreover, were spread out over the Peninsula, as a result of the same decision of the Chiefs of Staff that the defence of Singapore island and the vicinity of the naval base would no longer suffice. And this extension of the defensive area raised additional problems in the way of transport, recreational and social amenities, water, health, and supply generally. All this large expansion problem, too, had to be hurried along against time, and under the strain of this urgent press of work in a trying climate, the Air Vice-Marshal's health began to suffer.

Shortly after General Percival had taken over the Army Command, he was instructed to review the military strength he considered necessary for the defence of the area. Accepting the R.A.F. estimate of the scale of destruction and damage that defending aircraft would achieve amongst invasionary transports—which in the event proved to be greatly over-optimistic—the General decided that he needed forty-eight infantry battalions with ancillary troops, including two tank regiments, and he telegraphed this opinion to the War Office on August 2nd. These requirements were approved by the Chiefs of Staff, though they said they could not tell when they could make up the Malayan Army to that strength. It is to be noted that when the local commanders in their Tactical Appreciation of October 1940 (or ten months before General Percival's telegram) had asked for twenty-six battalions plus an air strength of 500-odd, the Chiefs of Staff had accepted the figure of twenty-six battalions as appropriate, while reducing the aircraft figure to 300-odd. If they were now ready to agree, even if only in principle, to the much higher battalion total of forty-eight—higher than General Bond's estimate of requirements that had caused them to turn to aircraft as the primary defence weapon in default of military reinforcement—it may be that they had by this time lost confidence in their own ability to supply the requisite aircraft. Or they may have realized that the Japanese occupation of Indo-China had invalidated previous calculations. They did not, however, cancel their decision to rely mainly on air power.

Military reinforcements continued to arrive: an Australian infantry brigade in August, an Indian brigade in September, certain other units of different arms and including divisional and corps troops in November and December, in varying stages of training and with differing adequacy of equipment.

By early December 1941 the basic fighting strengths of the

Malayan Army and Air Force, as measured by battalions in the one case and first-line aircraft in the other were as follows:

Battalions   33[1]

Aircraft   141

The Army infantry strength was well below what General Percival had said he would require. But even more striking was the shortage in the air. The figure of 141 was less than half the Chiefs of Staff's own estimate of 336 and only a quarter of that of the local commanders' 556. Indeed, it represented an even lower proportion in either case, since both the higher figures were calculated in terms of modern, up-to-date aircraft, and the 141 in Malaya were by no means that. The fighters were mainly American Brewster Buffaloes; slow, unhandy, and of short range. The night fighters were obsolescent Blenheims. The two squadrons of torpedo-bombers were of the obsolete Vilde-beeste type, with the poor speed of 100 m.p.h. There were no dive-bombers, no transport planes, no long-range bombers, no army co-operation machines and no photographic reconnais-sance units. Taken all round, the British air strength in Malaya was patently inadequate to meet Japanese attacking aircraft in the numbers that the latter might be expected to be. That Air Vice-Marshal Pulford was extremely concerned about the poor state of his command has been put on record by General Percival, who says in his despatch that 'the A.O.C. was fully alive to the weakness of the force at his disposal. He frequently discussed the subject with me and I know that he repeatedly represented the situation to higher authority.'

The scanty and senile muster in the air that was all that the busy 'appreciating' of 1940 had brought forth seems at first sight to deepen the mystery of the Malayan build-up. If the Chiefs of Staff themselves had said that 336 aircraft were neces-sary by the end of 1941, why were the equivalent of only about 100 or less provided? Such a force was obviously incapable of

---

[1] There were, in addition, certain units of local Malayan volunteers; but these were not included in the calculations of military strength made by Generals Bond and Percival referred to in this book.

standing up to the 700 Japanese aircraft of the Whitehall estimate and therefore made a mockery of the official dictum that air power should be the primary factor in the defence of the Peninsula. But in that case, what caused the Chiefs of Staff to adopt a principle that they knew must be ineffective from lack of force?

The only reasonable explanation is that they did not know; that when they ordered that air power was to play the chief part in Malayan defence, they believed that enough aircraft could be provided for this purpose. Yet, even so, their firm accompanying opinion that 336 British aircraft should suffice to deal with 713 Japanese (even if allowance, false as it happened, were made for inferior Japanese quality), was a very strange one for the highest strategical experts in the Empire to harbour. The present point, however, is why in the event they fell far short of this meagre enough figure of 336.

There is evidence for thinking that influences beyond their control may have frustrated their intention to despatch the stated number. And here it is desirable to remove any misunderstanding as to the powers and position of the Chiefs of Staff that may have arisen from previous references to that body. Those references may have fostered the idea that the Chiefs of Staff made the major strategical decisions governing the conduct of the war. But it is now clear that this would be largely a false conception. It was rumoured at the time and has since been revealed in his own writings that the powerful Minister of Defence had the main say in all forms of strategy. That he may have been ready at times to be guided by, and even bow to, the opinions of the Chiefs of Staff is to be expected and appears to be established. There were undoubtedly other times when he went over their heads or at least overbore one or other or all of them into accepting decisions which must·inevitably have been against their better judgments. And some of the decisions of 1941, having all the marks of originating with, and issuing much more from, Mr. Churchill than from the professional heads of the Services, were such as to militate against the despatch of air reinforcements to Malaya.

There was, for instance, the expedition to Greece. It is known that there was opposition to this move among many of the higher officers of the Services at the time; and to a lot of ordinary onlookers it seemed a deplorably unwise step to take. Britain's armies in North Africa were fighting under the shelter of the Mediterranean Sea, which the enemy's armies could only cross with difficulty and at great hazard. To send a British army from Africa across the Mediterranean to Greece to meet the invading German army was to turn the passage of that sea from a British asset into a liability, and meant meeting the Germans on the Continent where they could operate to the greatest advantage. In this campaign, we lost 209 aircraft and nearly 12,000 men, without counting the losses in Crete.

A month later, the Germans attacked Russia; whereupon Mr. Churchill adopted the policy of sending the utmost aid to the latter country in the way of weapons and warlike stores. The list of aircraft sent, mainly fighters, is a lengthy one. Though Mr. Churchill does not seem to give the exact total of aircraft supplied in 1941, there is mention of 645 (200 Tomahawks and 445 Hurricanes) promised, and in another place of 593 fighters actually being despatched. Taking the lower figure and adding it to the aircraft lost in Greece, it follows that had the aircraft given to or utilized for the benefit of foreign countries been sent to Singapore, the A.O.C. Malaya could by the autumn have had a total of 802 modern aircraft instead of 141 old crocks. It is true that many of the 802 would have been fighters. But more and better fighters were Malaya's principal need. And as regards bombers, Admiral Sir James Somerville was to write in his diary early in the following year when Commander-in-Chief of the fleet in the Indian Ocean, 'if I had only had out here a fraction of the hundreds of bombers that go from the United Kingdom every night to Germany, it would alter the whole picture'.

Admiral Sir Tom Phillips, while Vice-Chief of the Naval Staff in 1941, had urged Mr. Churchill to send a good supply of Hurricanes to Malaya. He had said there were plenty to spare and that if it was desired to keep the Japanese quiet by a show of force, these were the very weapons to do it. Hurricanes had an international reputation. Everyone had heard of them and knew of their power. But Brewster Buffaloes meant next to nothing to anybody and were calculated to impress nobody.

The question is, should Mr. Churchill have given preference to the needs of British Malaya over an adventure into Greece or gifts to Russia for which Stalin had not asked and for which he gave very little thanks? To answer that question, one must first ask what were Mr. Churchill's objects in each case in acting as he did.

At the time of the Greek affair Mr. Churchill told the country that, since Britain had given Greece a guarantee, British honour required that an attempt, however hopeless, be made to redeem that pledge. But Greece was not the only place where British honour was involved. The peoples of Malaya, Australia, New Zealand, Borneo and Hong Kong had been led to suppose over a period of twenty years, and in certain cases had been given specific assurances, that if they were seriously threatened in the Far East, Britain would send out forces adequate to keep them safe. British honour was therefore as much engaged in relation to the British Eastern territories as to Greece; indeed, much more so, since the guarantees given to the former counries were of far longer standing, on the strength of which the Dominions concerned had for many years planned their own defences on the assumption that British forces would come to their assistance. Greece had not, and was not even particularly keen for the British guarantee to be implemented, for fear that if the attempt proved abortive the Greek sufferings would be all the greater—as actually happened. Therefore, if any honour was gained in Greece it was at the expense of greater obligations of honour elsewhere.

As regards Russia, the plea was one of expediency. Russia having been forced into the war, it was argued that the vital thing was to aid her in every way at whatever cost. The decision to do this, said Mr. Churchill in the House of Commons on 27th January 1942, was one 'of major strategy and policy, and anyone can see that it was right to put it first when they watch the wonderful achievements of the Russian armies. . . . Moreover, if we had not shown a *loyal* effort to help our ally, albeit at a heavy sacrifice to ourselves, I do not think our relations with Premier Stalin and his great country would be as good as they are now.'

Though Mr. Churchill did not let his own countrymen know it at the time, the information he has since published shows that his then relations with Premier Stalin do not seem to have been good at all. The latter's failure to answer Mr. Churchill's personal messages for weeks, the surly note of criticism that accompanied most of the acknowledgments of help sent and offers of more are far from indicating a friendly attitude on the part of Stalin towards Britain.

Nor, although Mr. Churchill used the phrase 'loyal effort to help an ally', was there any question of loyalty owed to Russia by Britain. Russia was not an ally in the sense of there being a formal alliance between the two countries. She had not come into the war in support of any agreement with Britain or from any desire to support the British people in their struggle against Germany. Russia had been forced into the war by German aggression and nothing else. For twenty years before the war the Soviet Government had been at political daggers-drawn with the British. It had been an accomplice with Hitler in the attack on Poland that had brought Britain into the war, about which attack and that on Finland Mr. Churchill had said some very ugly things indeed. To use the word 'loyal' in relation to Russia was a misuse of the English language, a language of which Mr. Churchill is an acknowledged master.

Moreover, in this particular context, this word loyal could not avoid a comparative connotation. It implied that more loyalty was owed to Russia than to those members of the British Commonwealth and Empire who would bear the main part of the heavy sacrifices that Mr. Churchill said would have to be borne by 'ourselves' in demonstrating our Russian loyalty.

This claim for Britain to accord priority of help to Russia was insupportable. As already argued over the question of Greece,

Britain's major loyalty at this time was owed to the threatened parts of the British Empire, which she had pledged her word to defend and to which she was united by ties of blood and Imperial citizenship. The only honourable reason for diverting supplies otherwise available for Far Eastern defence to the strengthening of Russia would have been that to succour the Russian State in its fight against Germany automatically safeguarded Australia, New Zealand, Malaya and the rest. But that, of course, was not so at all. The aiding of Russia meant the hazarding, not the safeguarding, of the Far Eastern lands, since the enemy they had to fear was not Germany but Japan. Speaking in the Commons on 29th January 1942, Mr. Churchill said he submitted to the House 'that the main strategic and political decision to aid Russia . . . and to accept a consequential state of weakness in the then peaceful theatre of the Far East was sound and will be found to have played a useful part in the general course of the war, and that this is in no wise invalidated by the . . . heavy forfeits which we have paid and shall have to pay in the Far East'.

The soundness of the decision would depend on the point of view. From that of the British islander, it can be called sound in that aid to Russia made him feel safer.[1] From that of the Australian or the Malayan, it was the reverse, since the despatch of British weapons to Russia rendered him more vulnerable. Nor can it be said that if Britain went under to Germany, the Empire went under with her. Command of the sea being the prime factor in the security of Malaya, Australia and New Zealand, a victorious Germany need have been no menace to these countries had the Royal Navy got clear away, as it could be expected to do, before Britain collapsed. Even without it, the American fleet should by ordinary calculations have afforded by itself protection against seaborne attack.

The Churchillian postulates quoted above about aid to Russia were therefore only half-truths; superficially true for the European British but the reverse of true for those in the Far Eastern

---

[1] Whether it actually did make him safer is another matter, on which later chapters of this book will throw some light.

outposts of Empire. They may not even have been true in regard to Britain. It is quite possible that, on a final balance of credits and debits, she too lost more than she gained by preferring Russia to the British and Dominion territories in the Far East. Mr. Churchill himself does not seem to have thought that even the survival of the British islanders was bound up with Russian success against Germany. Writing to Mr. Matsuoka, the Japanese Foreign Minister in April 1941 (or before the German attack on Russia had begun), Mr. Churchill asked him if he really thought that Germany, without the command of the sea or the command of the British daylight air, would be able to invade and conquer Great Britain during 1941, or would even try to do so. It is clear from his book that Mr. Churchill thought not—and still thinks not.[1]

But for some reason Mr. Churchill seems to have been resolutely set against sending aircraft to Malaya, despite the repeated requests of the Air Officer Commanding, though he was willing enough to expend them for the benefit of foreign countries, sometimes without their asking. He used up a lot of them in succouring Greece. He pressed them on Russia with both hands. Even as late as November 1941, when the Japanese menace was getting rapidly worse, he was ready to send aircraft to Chiang-Kai-Shek in China in preference to Air Vice-Marshal Pulford in Malaya. Writing to President Roosevelt about the Chinese Generalissimo's call for arms, Mr. Churchill said:

'I have received Chiang-Kai-Shek's appeal addressed to us both for air assistance. You know how we are placed for air strength at Singapore. None the less, I should be prepared to send pilots and even some planes if they could arrive in time. What we need now is a deterrent of the most general and formidable character.'

Some will think that British aircraft would have been a much more formidable deterrent in the hands of the British authorities in British Malayan territory than when wielded by the nationalist Chinese. They would certainly have been a much better protection to Malaya. Mr. Churchill has stated in his book[2] that 'if the

[1] *Churchill*, Vol. III, p. 168.   [2] *Churchill*, Vol. III, p. 522.

United States did not come in we had no means of defending the Dutch East Indies, or indeed our own Empire in the East'. But we had greater means than he allowed to be provided.

Only in one respect was the British Government as good as, indeed better than, its word as given through the Chiefs of Staff to the Commanders in Malaya. They were told in April 1941 that a British fleet might not arrive at Singapore until eighty days after the outbreak of war. A British fleet did arrive at Singapore and it arrived before the outbreak. But what sort of British fleet was it?

CHAPTER SEVEN

The Arrival of the Eastern fleet and the Japanese Invasion of Malaya

*

The feeling among the naval staff at the Admiralty during the early months of the war was that serious aggression by Japan was unlikely as long as Germany and Russia were accomplices; and until well on in 1941 there was no reason to imagine that they would not so remain indefinitely.

The unexpected German attack on Russia in June 1941 naturally changed the Far Eastern outlook; and within a few days of that all-important event the Vice-Chief of the Naval Staff, Vice-Admiral Sir Tom Phillips, had initiated consideration of the formation of an Eastern fleet. In August, the Minister of Defence took a hand in the game. In a note to the First Sea Lord he proposed that 'a small but very powerful and fast force' should be sent to Eastern waters to act as a deterrent to Japanese naval aggression. The force he favoured consisted of an old battle cruiser, either the *Repulse* or *Renown*, the new battleship *Duke of York* when she was fully completed (she was then still in the last stages of construction) and one of the older aircraft carriers. The Minister said the *Duke of York* could work up to battle efficiency on her way out to the East.

The First Sea Lord replied in substantial disagreement. He said the naval staff had been studying this question for some time and that they proposed to assemble a much larger force east of Suez. This was to consist of the *Nelson*, *Rodney* and the four R class battleships, the battle-cruiser *Renown* and two to three carriers, the *Hermes* and *Ark Royal* definitely and the *Indomitable* 'in an emergency'. Of the heavy ships *Nelson*, *Rod-*

ney, *Renown* and all the carriers would act as a striking force, to be stationed either at Trincomalee on the east side of Ceylon or at Singapore, and the four R class battleships (*Revenge, Royal Sovereign, Resolution* and *Ramillies*) be used for convoy protection in the Indian Ocean, where they would be handy for reinforcing the striking force in case of need. The First Sea Lord did not like the idea of sending out one of the latest battleships and especially the *Duke of York*. He thought their best place was at home to deal with the *Tirpitz*; and he pointed out that a ship could not work up on a long ocean passage, since working up involved target practice, which could only be got where there were targets.

The Minister of Defence rejected the First Sea Lord's arguments and proposals, which he described as inherently unsound. Because the R class battleships were old he stigmatized them as 'coffin ships', though the *Repulse*, which the Minister desired to send out, was nearly as old, less heavily armed, and much weaker in armour protection. Finally, the Minister reiterated his preference for a small squadron rather than a larger one, giving the somewhat remarkable reason that it would simplify the manning question. He got his way, the professional Admiralty proposals being overridden. The ships finally selected for the East were the battleship *Prince of Wales*, the battle-cruiser *Repulse* and the aircraft-carrier *Indomitable*.

The first ship to go was the *Repulse*, commanded by Captain W. G. Tennant, C.B., M.V.O.[1] This officer had been Naval Assistant to the First Sea Lord in the first months of the war, but at the time of the fall of France had volunteered to go over as senior naval officer at Dunkirk during the evacuation. After a lively week or ten days, he and Brigadier Beckwith-Smith were the last two persons to leave the shore after assuring themselves that everyone else had been taken off.

Thence, Captain Tennant had gone to take command of the *Repulse* in the Home Fleet at Scapa. She participated in the early part of the hunt for the German battleship *Bismarck*,

[1] Now Admiral Sir William Tennant, K.C.B., D.S.O., M.V.O.

though shortage of fuel compelled her to drop out after a couple of days and proceed to Newfoundland. On the way there, she encountered a very heavy gale and only just got into harbour without running out of oil.

Repulse returned to Scapa, and during June, July and a part of August remained with the Home Fleet. In the latter month, however, Captain Tennant was sent for by the Commander-in-Chief and told that owing to the increasing tension with Japan the Admiralty had decided to send a capital ship to the Indian Ocean, and that *Repulse* had been selected.

The ship did a quick docking and then sailed with a large convoy for the Cape. At this time, the German U-boats had not arrived in the Indian Ocean, as they did later, and with Japan still at peace the *Repulse* spent a pleasant October and November, mostly visiting South African ports. At Durban, Captain Tennant heard that Field Marshal Smuts was in the vicinity and sent a message asking if he would come on board the *Repulse* and address the ship's company. This the Field Marshal did. He began on a light note by telling the men they ought to come and live in South Africa after the war, which he said was a better country than England. But he went on to make the ominous remark, as inauspicious as it was prophetic, that many of them would not live to see the end of the war. Later, in the Captain's cabin, the Field Marshal expressed the opinion that war with Japan would not be long delayed.

Late in October, the *Prince of Wales* left England to follow the *Repulse*. She was commanded by Captain J. C. Leach, M.V.O., and was a new battleship, only a few months in commission. Joining the fleet early in May 1941, she had almost immediately gone out with the detachment under Vice-Admiral L. E. Holland to search for the *Bismarck*. There had been an action with that ship, in which the *Prince of Wales* had received a certain amount of damage and in which her own turret machinery had displayed serious shortcomings. After the action, she went to a dockyard for repairs and turret modifications, and remained there for more than two months. Emerging in August, she went to Scapa for 'working up' drills and gunnery practices.

She had had quite insufficient time for these between first joining the fleet in May and going out after the *Bismarck*; and, of course, little could be done in the dockyard. However, this essential training period was again to be denied her, for at the end of August she was hustled down to Gibraltar to form part of the escort of a Malta convoy being sent through the Mediterranean. On completion of this duty, she returned to the United Kingdom to find that she was under orders for the Far East as flagship of Admiral Sir Tom Phillips, the new Commander-in-Chief of the Eastern fleet.

Sir Tom, as already mentioned, had just been the Vice Chief of the Naval Staff, a post involving the closest possible touch with the naval side of the war in all its aspects.[1] He was, moreover, an officer with a long and brilliant staff record, having previously been Director of Plans at the Admiralty, and before that principal Staff Officer to the Chief of Staff, Mediterranean Fleet, Commodore Dudley Pound. Ten years later the Commodore, since become Admiral Sir Dudley Pound and appointed First Sea Lord, took Phillips with him to the Admiralty to be the second member of the naval staff.

Sir Tom's Eastern fleet was not yet a unity. There were a few, a very few, ships of the smaller classes already in the Far East as the China squadron. There was the *Repulse* in the Indian Ocean. Sir Tom himself was now taking out the *Prince of Wales* and two destroyers, *Electra* and *Express*. The Admiralty wished to give him two more destroyers, and told Sir Andrew Cunningham, the Commander-in-Chief in the Mediterranean, to transfer two of his to Admiral Phillips's command. Sir Andrew could hardly be expected to part with his soundest ships. The *Jupiter* and *Encounter*, which he transferred, were not in fact in good structural order. One of them had something wrong with her fuel tanks, so that when completed to full capacity she took on a list of about ten degrees, which she gradually lost as she got through her oil. The other had a corrugated bottom due to too close an acquaintance with the bottom of the sea on some previous occa-

---

[1] He was relieved at the Admiralty on October 21st, four days before he sailed in the *Prince of Wales*.

sion. These two were to go through the Suez Canal and join Sir Tom Phillips's flag in the Indian Ocean.

It has been mentioned that it had been intended for the air-craft-carrier *Indomitable* to accompany the *Prince of Wales* on her way out to Singapore. But Providence stepped in to order otherwise. The *Indomitable*, a new ship, had been sent to Jamaica to carry out her essential training in the comparative peace of the West Indies. There, she had the misfortune to run ashore one day while returning to harbour. It became necessary to dock her, and she was too late to join Sir Tom Phillips's force. At this time, the small carrier *Hermes* was actually stationed in the Indian Ocean and could easily have been transferred to Admiral Phillips's fleet as he passed on his way to Singapore. But no order for this was given.

The absence of a carrier left Sir Tom Phillips's ships dependent for defence against air attack either on shore-based fighters or their own anti-aircraft armaments. The latter were quite in-adequate. Even had the training been good and the individual mountings efficient, there were far too few guns. It was already being realized in the Navy that if warships were to do any good with anti-aircraft gun-fire they needed four or five times the number of guns that they had had at the outbreak of war. Nor were the anti-aircraft crews of the *Prince of Wales* and *Repulse* well trained. They could not be: not having had the facilities for the necessary practice for a long time; the *Repulse* since leaving England for the Indian Ocean, and the *Prince of Wales* owing to her long journey out east. Unless they were to have a fairly good breathing space which could be devoted to weapon training after reaching Singapore, the Eastern fleet would have to rely for pro-tection against air attack practically entirely on shore-based aircraft.

On November 20th, the Press reported H.M.S. *Prince of Wales* as having recently put into Capetown. Ten days earlier, Mr. Churchill had made a speech at the Mansion House in which he announced that

'We now feel ourselves strong enough to provide a powerful naval force of heavy ships, with the necessary ancillary

4. Lieut.-General A. E. Percival, G.O.C. Malaya

5. Air Vice Marshal C. W. Pulford, A.O.C. Malaya

vessels, for service if needed in the Indian and Pacific Oceans.'

The Press did not fail to connect this remark with the subsequent appearance of the *Prince of Wales* at the Cape. Mr. Churchill, however, was inaccurate in referring to 'the necessary ancillary vessels' accompanying the force mentioned. The most necessary of all ancillary vessels were aircraft-carriers, and of those there were none.[1]

The battleship reached Colombo in the last week of November, where she embarked a number of Bofors guns for augmenting her anti-aircraft armament. The *Repulse* had just previously been ordered to Trincomalee on the other side of Ceylon, and while there Captain Tennant received a signal saying that Sir Tom Phillips was flying on ahead to Singapore for an urgent conference. Captain Tennant, being the senior of the two big ship captains, was therefore to take the squadron on to Singapore.

The *Repulse* met the other five ships (*Jupiter* and *Encounter* from the Mediterranean having now joined) at sea and took them on down the Straits of Malacca. They reached the naval base on December 2nd, and as the two big ships steamed up through the calm waters of the naval anchorage to their berths, they brought a sense of confidence and comfort to all those on shore who saw them come in, a feeling that was shared by the whole Colony as soon as the news got abroad. Among those watching the Eastern fleet's entry into harbour was General Percival. Even though, as a past student at the Naval Staff College at Greenwich, the General felt anxious at the incoming fleet's lack of an aircraft-carrier, he has recorded his vivid recollection years later 'of the thrill it gave us all as we watched those majestic ships steaming up the eastern channel of the Johore Strait and coming to anchor'. After twenty years of distant promise, capital ships had at last come to Singapore. But only two of them. This was not the 'main fleet' that had figured on so many staff papers since 1921.

[1] Whether 'ancillary' is the correct adjective to apply to carriers is irrelevant in this instance.

In high quarters, it seems to have been thought that words might be made to compensate for material weakness. The modern British Admiralty has no more rigid wartime rule than that of secrecy, secrecy at all costs, secrecy often carried to excess. But not so here. Before leaving England, Sir Tom Phillips had been instructed that the greatest possible publicity was to be given to his arrival at Singapore. Publicity there was. Local Pressmen, who by this time included many London and American representatives attracted by the chance of coming trouble, were assembled on board the *Prince of Wales* and supplied with all permissible details. More effective still, the voice of Mr. Churchill came on the air from London to tell the world that the '*Prince of Wales* and other heavy units' had reached the Far East.

This announcement, the form of which annoyed the *Repulse's* officers and men very much, was not of course strictly true.[1] There was only one other heavy unit. If the suggestion that there were more was made with a view to intimidating the Japanese, it was hardly likely to succeed and did not succeed. Malaya was teeming with Japanese and word soon reached the Japanese intelligence services about the composition of the British naval reinforcements.[2] The deception was therefore a dangerous one to attempt, since a Japanese discovery that the strength of the British force was being exaggerated was one from which they would draw obvious conclusions. A bluff that can readily be seen through is worse than no bluff at all. Those who would be deceived without possibility of enlightenment were, of course, the British public.

The authorities in Malaya did their best to further the London Government's policy. The naval Commander-in-Chief, Sir Geoffrey Layton, broadcast to the Malayan people, dwelling on

---

[1] So much ill-feeling between the two ships' companies arose from this cause that both Captains thought it necessary to make admonitory speeches to their men.

[2] General Percival mentions in his book a pro-Japanese wireless transmitter in Malaya that was never discovered.

the great improvement in the defence situation consequent on the arrival of battleships at Singapore. The general feeling of tension, of the possibility of a clash with Japan, nevertheless remained. The situation was one of obvious crisis. With the Japanese in virtual control of Indo-China, they were within striking distance of Malaya both from the north-east and the north-west. From Siam, into which Japanese troops might cross at any moment from Indo-China, they had only to march down through the Kra Isthmus to reach the Malayan frontier. The danger from this direction had been recognized and plans drawn up to forestall it. The Malayan Peninsula widens out from Singapore island northward till near the Siamese frontier, where it begins slightly to contract. But just over the frontier the land narrows sharply to the Kra Isthmus, which is in places only about fifty miles wide, as compared with the 300 miles of the actual frontier. For the defence of Malaya on the land side it would therefore be plainly advantageous to advance into Siamese territory so as to take up a shorter line.

Complete plans to do this were ready; and the more threatening the outlook became, the greater the desire there naturally was to put the plans into operation. It had, however, been decreed that the decision should remain one for the Government in London, a veto being imposed on independent action by the Commander-in-Chief on the spot. This was quite reasonable. An advance into Siam could well have serious political repercussions. It could be utilized to accuse Britain of aggressive action and made the excuse for hostile counter-action by the Japanese. It could also for the same reason, have unfortunate reactions in the United States. However, on December 5th the Commander-in-Chief, Far East, was informed by London that he could order the operation himself if he had information that a Japanese expedition was advancing with the apparent intention of making a landing in South Siam, or if the Japanese actually violated Siamese territory. He had previously had it impressed upon him that an advance into Siam meant war with Japan, so that a decision by him to make this advance involved issues of the gravest nature. The declaration or provocation of war is a political and not a military function, and the British Parliament is always quick to tell officers of the Services in peace-time that political decisions are none of their business. It is therefore apt to be slightly startling for an individual officer to have the supreme political responsibility of provoking a war thrust upon him at a moment of acute international crisis. It is not clear why Mr. Duff Cooper was not entrusted with this decision. He had arrived in Singapore some weeks before as the Cabinet representative in the Far East; and, as such, one would think that the political question of risking war by advancing into Siamese territory would have been one for him to settle. But that vital decision was handed over instead to the Commander-in-Chief.

On arrival at Singapore, the *Prince of Wales* went alongside the dockyard wall to fit her Bofors guns, while the *Jupiter* and *Encounter* were put into dock to have their more urgent defects attended to. At the same time, the *Repulse* was sent on a short training cruise to the southward.

Admiral Sir Tom Phillips had naturally much to discuss with Admiral Sir Geoffrey Layton when they met at Singapore. Sir Tom made no secret that he was none too happy about the condition of his fleet, which had as yet had no training as a combined force. Nor did he hide his misgivings about his fleet strength. Indeed, he had hardly arrived at Singapore when he sent a signal to the Admiralty asking that the battleships *Revenge* and *Royal Sovereign*, on convoy duty in or near the Indian Ocean, might be sent on to Singapore as soon as the latter could arrive, on about December 20th. He also wanted the despatch to the East of the *Ramillies* and *Resolution*, still in England, to be expedited. Either Mr. Churchill's earlier opposition to these ships being sent to Singapore, by reason of their age and the complication of the manning problem, had previously been overcome, or Sir Tom Phillips thought that an executive call for these ships sent from Singapore itself would be more effective than a staff paper in the Whitehall that he had so recently left. He made the further request that the battleship *Warspite*, due to pass Singapore before long on passage from the west coast of America to the Mediterranean, should be retained at

Singapore for a week.[1] Admiral Phillips clearly wanted to collect the largest muster of battleships that he could; from which it can be deduced that Mr. Churchill's principle of the value of a small force of fast ships did not make any great appeal to him.

On December 4th, the Admiral flew to Manila to confer with Admiral Hart, in command of the American Asiatic fleet. Admiral Phillips's Chief of Staff, Rear-Admiral Palliser, had by this time gone ashore at Singapore in accordance with previous intention. The Chief Staff Officer afloat was to be Captain Ralph Edwards, lately Director of Operations at the Admiralty, but this officer was proceeding to Singapore separately and had not yet arrived. The senior Staff Officer in the flagship was therefore Captain L. H. Bell, Captain of the Fleet. Admiral Phillips had not as yet taken over the naval command of the Far Eastern area, which still remained with Sir Geoffrey Layton.

While Sir Tom Phillips was away, developments of the utmost importance took place. At about midday of December 6th, an R.A.F. flying boat reported sighting just to the eastward of Cape Camo, the southernmost tip of Indo-China, two escorted convoys steering west. One consisted of twenty-two merchant ships protected by a battleship, five cruisers, and seven destroyers; and the other of twenty-one merchant ships with two cruisers and seven destroyers. A little later, there was another sighting, this time of a small convoy of one cruiser and three merchant vessels to the westward of Cape Camo, steering northwest.

What was to be made of this sensational news? That the convoys sighted were Japanese military convoys was obvious. They could be of no other nationality than Japanese and they would not be under strong naval escort unless they were troop convoys. The vital point was, where were they going?

There were two possibilities. They might be meant for an immediate attack on Malaya or they might be intended for a landing in Siam with a view to gaining military control of that coun-

---

[1] Pearl Harbour occurred before she sailed from America. She therefore had to go across the Atlantic instead of the Pacific, and she did not go to the Mediterranean.

try. The considerable naval escort, arguing the necessity for protection against naval attack, pointed to an attack on Malaya. Siam had no navy to speak of, certainly not one against which battleship and strong cruiser escort was required. Moreover, if the Japanese wished to occupy Siam, they could do so across the Indo-Chinese land border without going to all the business of a seaborne expedition. The only observable pointer to an objective in Siam was the fact that the most westerly convoy had turned north-west when it had rounded Cape Camo, which would take it clear of Malaya. This might, however, be a false course, designed to deceive aerial observers and to be discarded after nightfall.

Nevertheless, a conference between Sir Robert Brooke-Popham and Admirals Layton and Palliser resulted in a conclusion that the convoy sightings meant a move against Siam and not Malaya. Sir Robert therefore decided that the time had not yet come to exercise his discretion of advancing to a shorter line in the Kra Isthmus, in view of the adverse political results that a premature move might have. He may also have been influenced in making this decision by the strong pressure being exerted at this time by Sir Josiah Crosby, the Minister in Siam. Sir Josiah claimed to know the Siamese well, as indeed he did. He insisted that they were pro-British and anti-Japanese. If left alone, he was sure they would rise against a Japanese invasion of their country. But for this to happen it was essential that they *should* be left alone. If the British moved first, it would place the Siamese in a very embarrassing position and they might feel compelled, in order to safeguard their standing in international law, to turn against their British friends.

There was, of course, another possible line of action to meet the situation that had arisen. This was to send out the newly arrived Eastern fleet to find and keep an eye on the reported convoys and to attack them if they showed any hostile intent. This was indeed the proper treatment for a seaborne force suspected of aggressive designs. Only one escorting battleship had been reported,[1] so that the Eastern fleet should have been in

[1] There were actually two in the area.

adequate strength, as it appeared at the time, to deal with the reported convoys. But surface strength was not enough. To shadow the convoys would mean exposure to air attack if the Japanese meant business, and this was where the absence of an aircraft-carrier was so hampering; for the R.A.F. Brewster Buffaloes could not provide fighter cover far enough out at sea for a naval shadowing policy to be followed. It did not help that at this critical juncture the new Commander-in-Chief was away in the Philippines.

As it was, the best practical expedient was for aerial touch to be kept with the strange convoys, so that their destinations could be gauged as early as possible. But unfortunately this touch was not maintained. There is indeed a remarkable similarity between the events following the first sighting of the Japanese convoys and the early stages of the escape of the German battleship *Bismarck* seven months earlier. An R.A.F. reconnaissance aircraft sighted the *Bismarck* about midday on May 21st. Thereafter, for the next thirty hours there was no news, until a second air report came in at about 8 p.m. on the following day. The Japanese convoys off Indo-China were also sighted about midday of one day and again thirty hours passed in silence before another report was received about 8 p.m. As with the waiting British fleet in Scapa six months earlier, the suspense among the higher officers at Singapore became increasingly agitating. The cause of the failure to get news in the North Sea was bad weather. Off Malaya, the causes were similar, the weather conditions in the area east of Malaya and in the North Sea being much alike. It is possible, however, that one reconnaissance aircraft that did not return was shot down by the Japanese. At all events, the authorities in Singapore were left in painful uncertainty for a day and a half.

When the next news did come through, it was still not conclusive. What looked like four Japanese destroyers were seen about seventy miles off Singora,[1] steering south. Perhaps of more significance was that an R.A.F. Hudson search plane was fired on by a Japanese cruiser. In the evening (December 7th),

[1] See map on p. 123.

103

Admiral Sir Tom Phillips touched down in Singapore from his visit to Manila.

When General Percival, who had been inspecting up-country, heard of the renewed Japanese sightings, he felt sure that an attack on Malaya was imminent. In that case, what should be done about the advance into the Kra Isthmus, if he could get permission to commence it? But as he considered this, he came to the conclusion that there was no time to carry it out. He calculated that if the Japanese were to land, they might do so from midnight onwards. The British troops, if they started at once, could not be in position on the Isthmus till 2 p.m. the next day. The move forward which had been considered undesirable the day before for political reasons was now too late to make effective, and General Percival telephoned his opinion to General Headquarters to that effect.

In the early hours of the morning, the last doubts were removed. Messages came though that the Japanese were landing opposite the R.A.F. aerodrome at Kota Bharu in north-eastern Malaya. Two or three hours later, while it was still dark, bombs fell on Singapore city. Almost at the same moment of time, Japanese aircraft were swooping down on the American naval base at Pearl Harbour, bombing and torpedoing the battleships lying moored there; and when they had departed nearly the whole of the American Pacific battlefleet was out of action.

After the First World War, there were many people in England who were insistent that had the country only made its intention clear beforehand to support France against Germany, Germany would not have gone to war. When war again seemed possible after 1937, these same people revived their agitation for Britain to commit herself in advance; and the Government, as an undoubted result of this pressure, gave guarantees to various European countries and notably to Poland, which was specially likely to become embroiled with Germany. There were nevertheless those in England, and they were not few in number, who were aghast at a guarantee being given to a country which Britain would obviously be unable to help if attacked, as was proved in the event. However, the British Government was not concerned with strategy but with political gestures for 'stopping Hitler'. At the time, the Foreign Secretary uttered a solemn warning to the head of the German State. 'Halt', he said, 'Major road ahead'; at much the same time that he was saying that the British Navy was unchallengeable. But Hitler refused to be impressed by British threats. However clear Britain made her intentions, he may not have felt she represented a major road at all. Making a compact with Russia, he and Stalin marched into Poland from opposite sides and the British guarantee went up in the smoke of burning Warsaw. By the middle of 1940, there was no doubt that anyone in search of major roads would not be looking towards the north side of the English Channel.

Two years later, however, intimidation was again tried by a British Government as a means of deterring an unfriendly nation from hostile action. Mr. Churchill made his country's position in relation to Japan abundantly clear. He told her publicly in his Mansion House speech of 10th November 1941, that if she tried conclusions with the United States, Britain would join the latter 'within the hour'. The prospect for Japan of confronting such a combination as Britain and America was as daunting a one as could be provided. In what would be essentially a naval war, the Japanese Navy would be facing the two greatest sea Powers in the world. True, the British were engaged elsewhere and could not deploy their full naval strength in the Pacific. But with what they could probably provide in the East, the British and American Navies should be at least twice as strong as the Japanese. If the policy of 'making one's position clear' as a means of keeping a war-inclined nation in the ways of peace was ever likely to work, it was surely in the case of Japan in 1941. Yet it failed. The obvious conclusion is that it is just as effective to retain one's freedom of action, as in 1914, as to indulge in public threats and warnings, and leaves one far less liable to look a fool.

It is the natural assumption that it was Mr. Churchill's desire, in flashing the red light so strenuously in Japan's face, to keep her out of the war. At least, he expressed to the House of Commons later his surprise that Japan should have recklessly disregarded all the international danger signals. But, in that case, it is somewhat puzzling to read that the American higher authorities were trying to lever Japan *into* the war. Mr. Stimson has recorded of an American Cabinet meeting in November 1941, presided over by the President, that 'the question facing the Cabinet was how we should manœuvre the Japanese into the position of firing the first shot without too much danger to ourselves'.[1]

Was Mr. Churchill being kept in ignorance of this secret intention of President Roosevelt's? If so, he was being scurvily treated, and his country with him, by men he had gone to great lengths to placate. But if not, why did he make utterances calculated to keep Japan out of the war when the White House wanted her in? Can it be that the resounding threat that Britain would be in on the side of America 'within the hour' was not directed in warning at the Japanese but in encouragement at the American President and State Department? We know now from his own later confession that Mr. Churchill was hoping and praying for the entry of the United States into the war. If the President was working for war with Japan and was known or believed by Mr. Churchill to be so working, the declaration that Britain would be on his side within the hour could very well be regarded as incitement to him to persevere.

What exactly were Mr. Churchill's feelings on this subject is difficult to deduce from his book, his various references to the matter being somewhat inconsistent, if not contradictory. He shows that in his official letters he frequently expressed the hope that war with Japan might be averted. Yet every now and then one comes across passages which indicate that the hope was at least qualified. 'If Japanese aggression drew in America', he remarks on page 522 of Volume III, '*I would be content to have it.*'[2]

Odium has been heaped on Japan for her so-called treachery in attacking Pearl Harbour without previous declaration of war. But it is very questionable whether the word treachery is a legi-

[1] *President Roosevelt and the Coming of the War* by Professor Charles Beard (Yale University Press).
[2] Present author's italics.

timate one to use in these circumstances. If *The Times* of 1904 had been correct in saying that 'the cases in which a formal declaration of war precedes the outbreak of hostilities have been comparatively rare in modern history',[1] Japan's action in 1941 can hardly be regarded as an outrageous violation of recognized practice. Moreover, in view of Japan's almost identical behaviour when faced with a similar situation in 1904, the Americans had only themselves to blame if they chose to ignore that precedent.

It is, however, very doubtful if they did ignore it. There is so much evidence of official warnings to American Service commanders to be prepared for surprise attack that the expectation of such attack is established beyond question. For example, there is Admiral Stark's 'war warning' signal of November 27th to the American Navy that 'an aggressive move by Japan is expected within the next few days'. Moreover, the sighting of the Japanese convoys off Camo Point on December 6th (or nearly two days before the attack on Pearl Harbour) was known in Manila the same day,[2] and presumably was also known in Washington. The American authorities must therefore have been aware that Japan was on the move and about to attack somewhere. What seems never to have crossed their minds was that the attack would come at Pearl Harbour. But a miscalculation of this kind was hardly the fault of the Japanese; especially as the American Ambassador in Japan had previously warned Washington that this very attack was being freely rumoured in Tokyo.

No reasonably informed person can now believe that Japan made a villainous, unexpected attack on the United States. An attack was not only fully expected but was actually desired. It is beyond doubt that President Roosevelt wanted to get his country into the war, but for political reasons was most anxious to ensure that the first act of hostility came from the other side; for which reason he caused increasing pressure to be put on the Japanese, to a point that no self-respecting nation could endure without resort to arms. Japan was meant by the American Presi-

---

[1] Ibid. 24.
[2] Morison, Vol. III, p. 157.

dent to attack the United States. As Mr. Oliver Lyttelton, then British Minister of Production, said in 1944, 'Japan was provoked into attacking America at Pearl Harbour. It is a travesty of history to say that America was forced into the war.'

CHAPTER EIGHT

The Disaster off Kuantan

*

During the latter part of the night of December 7th–8th, the position regarding the Japanese landings remained inevitably obscure. At daylight on the 8th, however, air reconnaissance showed that landings were in progress at Singora and Patani on the east coast of the Kra Isthmus, as well as at Kota Bharu. At Singora, the aerodrome was seen to be in use by the Japanese, a large number of aircraft, including many fighters, being observed on the ground.

As the day advanced, reports came through to Air Headquarters from all the northern airfields of heavy Japanese air attacks. The enemy's air force was evidently concentrating on its British opposite number in the hope of crippling the defending air power at the outset. Many air combats were taking place, in which the British fighters were being both outnumbered and outclassed. It was coming as a very unpleasant surprise that the Japanese aircraft were a great deal better in every way than anyone had expected. They were of high performance and were being used with skill and determination. Against the Japanese fighters, the Brewster Buffaloes were finding themselves at an all-round disadvantage, and to make matters worse their gun-firing mechanism was giving serious trouble. Repeated bomber attacks with fighter support were coming in against the British airfields. These enemy attacks were unhappily achieving a large measure of success. The British airfield defences were poor, radar warning systems had not yet been installed on the outer airfields, and they had next to no anti-aircraft guns. They were therefore highly vulnerable to hostile air attack, and many aircraft were being destroyed on the ground while refuelling.

Except at Kota Bharu, the Army had not yet made contact with the enemy. The landing-places at Singora and Patani were some way inside Siamese territory, and since the planned British forestalling advance into Siam had not been carried out, the Japanese were now disembarking at those two spots without opposition. At 11 a.m., however, the frontier was crossed in order to gain possession of certain defensive positions inside Siam. If Sir Josiah Crosby had believed that British forbearance to infringe Siamese neutrality would swing the Siamese against the Japanese aggressor, he was mistaken. They made no attempt to turn against the Japanese. What they did do was to offer remarkably strenuous and effective resistance to the British advance; so much so that progress was slow.

At Kota Bharu, fierce fighting was taking place. The country was difficult, being much cut up into creeks, mud flats, and swamps. In this confusing terrain, a bitter struggle had been in progress since midnight between the 8th Indian Infantry Brigade and the invaders, both sides incurring heavy losses.

Only rather vague information about all this was available to Admiral Phillips on the morning of December 8th, and before he could make up his mind what action to take with the fleet it was natural that he should want to consult the other Service head-quarters, not only to obtain their latest information but to learn their trends of thought about the general position.

Accordingly, after a brief staff meeting in the flagship, the Admiral went with his Chief of Staff to the office of the Commander-in-Chief, Far East (Sir Robert Brooke-Popham). Several hours were spent there going through the situation reports and discussing possible courses of action by the Navy. It was now realized that the principal enemy landing-place was at Singora in Siam, and the discussion ranged round the question of the fleet going up there to attack the transports. One of the points that inevitably arose in this connection was that of air co-operation, and Admiral Phillips formulated his tentative requirements in this respect. Assuming that the fleet sailed that evening, he came to the conclusion that he would want three measures of air support; first, air reconnaissance 100 miles ahead of the fleet from dawn the next day (9th), while the fleet would be steaming up the coast towards Singora: second, air reconnaissance along the coast from Kota Bharu to beyond Singora from dawn on 10th, while it would be closing in for the attack on the enemy transport fleet: and third, fighter cover over the fleet somewhere off Singora from daylight on 10th. Nothing definite, however, was settled about this, and the whole question of air co-operation was deferred for later decision after the general action to be taken by the Navy had been settled.

Sir Tom Phillips returned to the *Prince of Wales*, and a signal went out for Commanding Officers to come on board after lunch. When they and the Admiral's staff had assembled in the fore cabin, Sir Tom gave the meeting the pros and cons of going out. The primary object of the fleet, he said, was to keep British territories in the East, and Malaya especially, safe from seaborne attack. That was mainly why the ships had come out. Therefore, they ought, if they could, to try to smash up the Japanese transport fleet off the northern beaches.

What were the risks? The Admiral was not much worried about enemy surface ships. So far as he knew from available reports, he had two heavy ships and four destroyers against one battleship, seven cruisers and twenty destroyers. Though he was short in the smaller classes, especially if all the enemy ships were concentrated, his two-to-one superiority in big ships should be decisive.

The danger from hostile air attack was more difficult to estimate. The Japanese were known to have air bases in Indo-China, so that heavy air attack must be allowed for. The Admiral could not yet tell what air support the fleet could expect but he would be seeing the Air Vice-Marshal in the afternoon.

The Admiral was as much concerned about enemy submarines as by the thought of air attack, if not more so. The Japanese having had the initiative in the matter of invasion, it was only to be expected that they would have placed an abundance of submarines off Kota Bharu and Singora and along the routes which British ships from Singapore would be likely to take to the north-westward in any attempt to interfere with the landings. Unfortunately, there were only four destroyers to guard the *Prince of Wales* and *Repulse* against this danger, and two of them were old and ill-equipped for the purpose.

These were the main risks, and they were not to be treated lightly. To go up the coast would probably mean running into a hornets' nest. But if the Japanese transport fleet could be annihilated, its destruction was bound to be an immense help to the defending army on shore and could conceivably involve the failure of the invasion. Other attempts might follow; but the repulse of the first one would be a severe setback for the Japanese, and British reinforcements of all kinds might arrive before a second was staged.

When the Admiral had finished his general review of the situation, he did what was an unusual thing in such circumstances. Instead of indicating any preference of his own, he asked the assembled officers what they thought the fleet should do. He told them to take into consideration that air support could not be counted on and might not be forthcoming.

There was a long silence, broken at last by Captain Tennant of the *Repulse*. Most of those present belonged to the *Prince of Wales*, and it suddenly came to Captain Tennant that they might be waiting for an 'outsider' to break the ice. So he spoke up and said that he thought the fleet could do nothing else than go out and have a try against the transports.

The first answer having thus been obtained, the Admiral then took charge and asked each officer in turn for his opinion. No one disagreed with Captain Tennant. What Sir Tom Phillips would have said had they mostly been against going out, one does not know. He might perhaps have overridden the majority.[1] As it was, he expressed concurrence and issued orders for the raising of steam.

He then gave the meeting an outline of his intentions. He would sail that evening (8th) and attack at first light on 10th either at Kota Bharu or Singora, as air reconnaissance might

[1] He had told Admiral Layton the evening before that he meant to go out.

indicate. Other details would be determined according to what air help he could obtain in the way of searches and fighter cover.

Having made his decision and outlined his plan, Admiral Phillips went back on shore with Rear-Admiral Palliser to see the Air Officer Commanding and go further into the question of air support. The Air Vice-Marshal was already acquainted with the Admiral's three requirements put forward provisionally during the morning conference with the Commander-in-Chief, Far East. He was therefore now able to say that he could definitely provide the air reconnaissance for the 9th. He was a little doubtful about the reconnaissance on the 10th; and much more doubtful about the fighter cover. Even by the afternoon of the 8th, the air situation up in the north was known by Air Headquarters to be bad, and the Air Vice-Marshal was realizing that he might have to bring the fighters down to airfields well behind the front. And if so, the Buffaloes' short flying range would probably prevent their reaching Singora or even Kota Bharu for more than very short periods, if at all. The Air Vice-Marshal had just learnt of the evacuation of Kota Bharu airfield, and with crumbling air defences did not want to promise more than he could perform. But he told the Admiral he would examine his resources afresh and give a firm answer about the two doubtful points later on. The impression carried by Rear-Admiral Palliser from this conference was that the answers given by the Air Vice-Marshal were really final but that the latter hated to have to say no to the Admiral's request for fighter cover, and was hoping against his better judgment that some providential change in the situation might enable him to reverse his negative opinion later in the day.

Sir Tom Phillips got back on board his flagship as the final preparations for sea were being made. Among those awaiting him on the quarter-deck was Captain Bell, the Captain of the Fleet, and the Admiral told him to come down to the cabin. When there, the Admiral briefly ran over his meeting with the Air Vice-Marshal about which he had come away somewhat uneasy in his mind. 'I am not sure', he told Bell, 'that Pulford realizes the importance I attach to fighter cover over Singora. I'm therefore going to send him a letter stressing this point again and asking him to let me know as soon as possible what he can do for certain.' The Admiral wrote a letter on these lines and gave it to Bell, who took it up on deck and handed it to the Chief of Staff's chauffeur on the jetty. As he stepped back on board, the brow was hauled ashore and the *Prince of Wales'* securing wires were being cast off.

The sun was setting as the ships steamed down the fleet anchorage. The flagship *Prince of Wales* led the way, followed by *Repulse* with *Electra*, *Express*, *Vampire* and *Tenedos* as screening destroyers. As they passed the Changi signal station at the entrance, a message from the Air Vice-Marshal for the Admiral was flashed across. It read 'Regret fighter protection impossible.' The Admiral shrugged his shoulders. 'Well,' he said, 'we must get on without it.'

The fleet steered out to pass round the Anamba Islands, in the belief that enemy minefields had been laid between them and the mainland of Malaya. At about 1.30 a.m., Rear-Admiral Palliser sent a confirming signal about the fighter cover. It said that this cover could not be provided. As the Air-Vice Marshal had feared, the Japanese air offensive against the northern British airfields had been so successful that they had had to be evacuated, their aircraft being brought to other airfields further south. Indeed, in the case of the fighters, they seem to have been withdrawn right down to Singapore island, apparently on instructions from Sir Robert Brooke-Popham, in order to be on hand to deal with a raid on Singapore city.

Having been aware that fighter cover might be denied him, Admiral Sir Tom Phillips had already made up his mind that, if he could not have such cover off Singora, one condition was essential if he was to proceed with the operation. He must be able to count on surprise. If the Japanese had even a few hours' warning of his approach, their transports would have time to weigh anchor and temporarily disperse, while their armed forces, air, surface, and submarine, could be organized to deal the Eastern fleet a concentrated blow. Sir Tom Phillips was ready to take considerable risks in order to destroy the enemy's transports. But he must be reasonably sure that the transports would be there to be destroyed when he appeared. To take the risks only to find the quarry vanished was not good enough.

As for the gaining of surprise, the Admiral hoped much from the weather helping him to remain undiscovered till his attack began. As previously mentioned, the conditions in this region were often very similar to those of the North Sea, where limited visibility is the rule. By sailing at sunset on December 8th and attacking at sunrise on the 10th, there would only be the daylight hours of the 9th when discovery was likely; and if the fleet took an unusual course towards its destination, it might throw off Japanese air searchers in that way. Having passed the Anamba Islands, the fleet accordingly turned north towards Indo-China instead of, as might have been expected, back towards the Malayan coast. It meant going closer to the Japanese airfields than was necessary, but this was thought a better risk than the taking of a more orthodox course up the coast of Malaya. Naturally, the great question in everybody's mind was, would they be sighted by Japanese aircraft?

Just before half-past six in the morning, a strange aircraft appeared, but to the general relief it was recognized as Dutch. The weather was fortunately favourable to concealment. As had been hoped, it was misty weather—at times even foggy—the sky was overcast with low clouds, and frequent rain-squalls were encountered. For most of the day, the fleet continued northward without any enemy sightings. But at about 5 p.m., with roughly an hour to go before nightfall, the weather suddenly cleared and three aircraft came into view. They were closely scrutinized and made out to be Japanese, and they continued to shadow till nightfall, when they were shaken off.

So the fleet had been spotted at the last moment, just before darkness would have closed in and given it sanctuary. Admiral Phillips called his staff together and discussed with them what should now be done. After this very obvious discovery by Japanese aircraft, it had to be accepted that the British approach towards Singora had been reported. In that case, was it justifiable to go on? The Admiral had from the start made the probability of surprise a condition of the attack, and now it was reasonably certain that surprise had been lost. Should they not give up the enterprise and turn back for Singapore? He thought they should, but what did the others think? All but one thought with the Admiral that the fleet must return. The one exception was the Admiral's Secretary, Paymaster-Captain S. T. Beardsworth, who was in favour of going on. Having come so near to the objective, he said it was a pity not to try their luck. But the majority against him prevailed, and at a quarter-past eight course was altered for Singapore at high speed. After they had turned, Captain Tennant signalled over to the Admiral that, if he might say so, he thought the Admiral had made the right decision.

It has been stated since the war that Japanese records show no mention of any wireless report corresponding to one from these aircraft; so that there is at least some doubt whether they did in fact report the British ships. Captain (now Admiral) Tennant has, however, a clear recollection of his wireless officer telling him at about this time of signals being made by Japanese aircraft close at hand.

In any case, the fleet's presence had already been reported to Japanese headquarters in Indo-China by another agency. In the middle of the afternoon, a Japanese submarine had sighted the British ships as they passed and had signalled their position and course. The position given (7° N., 105° E.) was very inaccurate, being 140 miles N.N.W. of the true and making the British appear that much nearer to the Japanese invasion force than they really were.

The report caused a considerable stir at Japanese headquarters. It reached there at about 4 p.m., just as the crack 22nd Naval Air Flotilla was bombing up for an attack on Singapore. Orders were at once given for bombs to be exchanged for torpedoes, but the process took about two hours to complete, by which time it was dark. So alarmed were the Japanese authorities, however, at the threat to the invasion transports that a night air attack was determined on. But the aircraft, possibly misled by the erroneous position given for the British ships and ignorant of their having turned back, made no contact.

Meanwhile, Admiral Phillips was steaming south through the night. He had had to detach the destroyer *Tenedos* at half-past six to return to Singapore on account of her fuel shortage; and he told her when she parted company that next morning, when well away from the fleet, she was to report that it would be returning to harbour sooner than expected.

At 11 p.m., a signal was received from Rear-Admiral Palliser at Singapore, giving a sombre account of the day's happenings. It told of loss of ground and the evacuation of aerodromes in the north, spoke of heavy concentrations of Japanese bombers in south Indo-China, and said that the Commander-in-Chief, Far East, was thinking of devoting all air efforts to the defence of Singapore. This latter piece of news may conceivably have led Admiral Phillips to suppose that his Chief of Staff's previous signal about fighter cover not being available now applied to the whole Peninsula as well as Singora. This present signal certainly made it clear that the situation ashore was bad.

This signal had hardly been digested when another came in from Admiral Palliser. In his office at the Naval Base the Chief of Staff had been grappling with the many rumours and alarms that are the inevitable accompaniment of a hostile invasion. Reports of fresh landings were especially frequent after dark, but it was certain that many of them were false and all needed to be treated with critical reserve before being acted upon. Presently, Kuantan on the east coast was named as the scene of another landing. This was one of the more credible reports. Kuantan was about half-way down the east coast and had one of the best airfields on that side of Malaya. This airfield had been heavily bombed a few hours before, so badly that its aircraft had been withdrawn to Singapore; and the attack might well have been the prelude to a landing. With Kuantan in their hands, the Japanese would have an excellent short-range air base for bombing Singapore. And there was another feature of Kuantan attractive to invaders. From it ran one of the few and much the best of the lateral roads towards the west coast of Malaya, offering an inviting means by which the Japanese could threaten the main British communications running up the Peninsula to the fighting lines. Kuantan was therefore to be regarded as a likely spot for a new Japanese beachhead.

Nevertheless, Rear-Admiral Palliser wanted to be sure before making a signal. He therefore asked Army headquarters for confirmation that the report was genuine. After a pause, their reply came back. They had made further inquiries, they said, and felt sure it was a true report. Firing was said actually to be going on. The Rear-Admiral felt that this was good enough, and he passed the news out by wireless to the Commander-in-Chief in the *Prince of Wales.*

Sir Tom Phillips at once perceived the significance of the signal. For reasons similar to those that had influenced his Chief of Staff, he thought Kuantan a natural enough place for a landing. He was some way north-east of Kuantan at this time but he made up his mind to investigate the report next morning. The fleet's course was altered accordingly and its speed again increased. Once more, the Admiral entertained hopes of surprise, since the Japanese ought not to know that he had turned back after dark.

Sunrise came at six, when they were sixty miles from Kuantan, closing the shore at twenty-five knots. By 8 a.m. the coast was in sight, but binoculars showed no sign of enemy transports. To make quite sure, the Admiral ordered the destroyer *Express* to go right in and report. In under an hour she was back and signalling that all was quiet on shore. It was clear that the report of a landing had been false.[1]

Before, however, resuming his course to Singapore via the Anamba Islands, Admiral Phillips first went to look for some small vessels, apparently in tow, that had been sighted on the horizon as the fleet had been approaching Kuantan. It was just possible that these were invasion craft, and the Admiral thought

---

[1] That its falsity was not reported by Rear-Admiral Palliser when he discovered it is to be explained by the fact that, in all the early confusion of the invasion, he did not discover it till after the *Prince of Wales* and *Repulse* had been sunk.

he would like to examine them before finally departing. But the suspicious vessels were never sighted, as other events supervened.

About 10 a.m., there came a report from the destroyer *Tenedos* that she was being bombed. She had, it will be remembered, been detached from the fleet the previous evening to return to Singapore owing to her low fuel endurance. She was now, at 10 a.m. on the 10th, about 140 miles to the southward of the battleships. As she had previously reported being sighted by a Japanese aircraft, this news of her being bombed was nothing out of the ordinary and did not necessarily imply danger to the battleships further north. However, at 10.20 a.m., a shadowing aircraft was sighted from the *Prince of Wales*.

The attack on the *Tenedos* was actually a bad shot for the main portion of the fleet. The latter had, in fact, been sighted by a Japanese submarine during the night, who reported it was moving south and apparently returning to Singapore.[1] The signal had reached Saigon at 3.15 a.m. and at daylight the Japanese sent out nine reconnaissance aircraft to search the most likely area of sea. These were followed an hour later by a striking force of thirty-four bombers and fifty torpedo aircraft. A few of the bombers became detached and it was these that bombed the *Tenedos*.

Admiral Phillips knew nothing of the submarine report of his return southward, and when the reconnaissance aircraft came in sight he assumed it would be some hours before any attack developed. But actually, as the striking force was already in the air, it came much sooner than he expected. A few minutes after eleven a formation of approaching aircraft was sighted. They were nine in number, flying at about 10,000 feet; and as they got nearer they were seen to be making for the *Repulse*. Both heavy ships opened anti-aircraft fire and the sky near the bombers began to be dotted with the shell bursts. But owing to previous lack of practice, the shooting was admittedly not good.

The hostile bombers flew on in good formation. Then from the *Repulse* could be heard the sound of falling bombs. It grew

---

[1] It was not the same submarine as had reported the fleet the afternoon before.

rapidly louder, and those on deck hardly had time to realize that the bombs were coming very near when the whole ship shook to a number of heavy explosions and huge splashes shot towering up close on both sides. As the spray subsided, smoke was seen amidships and there came a ring at one of the bridge telephones. It was Commander Dendy reporting a bomb hit on the armoured deck beneath the hangar. Fortunately, no penetration and no serious damage.

One thought at once came to the minds of the senior officers in the British ships. Those who had been previously saying, and they included the Intelligence people, that the Japanese were no good as airmen were plainly wrong. This was not the Italian standard of bombing but something much more formidable.

A lull of perhaps twenty minutes. Then another approaching formation, and much lower than the first lot had been. The newcomers looked like being torpedo aircraft, and this was what they were. This time both ships received attention. Captain Tennant of the *Repulse* maintained a steady course till the attackers had reached the torpedo dropping position, and then put his wheel over. By this means he found himself, as he had hoped, combing the torpedo attacks and was able to dodge them all successfully. Fortunately, the tracks showed up very clearly in the calm sea.[1]

The *Prince of Wales* was not so lucky. There was a heavy detonation on the port side aft, and from the *Repulse* a very tall column of water was seen to go up. It is now thought that two torpedoes may have gone off simultaneously in much the same place. Anyway, the effect was pronounced. The ship rapidly heeled over 11°, her speed fell off from near 30 knots to under 20, and steering became erratic. Counter flooding was ordered and brought the ship back a degree or two; but after twenty-five minutes the port side of the quarterdeck was awash and the list had put most of the heavy anti-aircraft guns out of action.

---

[1] To everyone's surprise, the Japanese aircraft dropped their torpedoes from anything up to 300 or 400 feet, instead of coming down to 20 or 30 feet as was the practice in the British air services. Nevertheless, the Japanese torpedoes seemed to run quite well when dropped from these heights.

It was now three-quarters of an hour since the first bombing attack, and so far as Captain Tennant knew no signal had been sent off by the flagship to tell the Singapore authorities that the fleet was under assault. Had the Commander-in-Chief sent off such a signal it should have been intercepted in *Repulse*; but nothing of that kind had been received. Nonplussed, Captain Tennant could only assume that some unknown factor was preventing the flagship making this obviously needed signal. He therefore had it made himself at 11.50. Ten minutes later it had reached Air headquarters at Singapore, and Air Vice-Marshal Pulford immediately ordered a squadron of fighters to the spot. Within a few minutes they were in the air and speeding towards Kuantan.

Hardly had Captain Tennant sent off the signal when another attack developed against *Repulse*. As with the first attack, it was by high-level bombers. *Repulse* was steaming at high speed and manœuvring sharply. Even so, the bomb-dropping was remarkably accurate; and although the ship was not hit, all the bombs fell very close.

By this time, the two ships were some distance apart. Noticing, however, that the *Prince of Wales* had the not-under-control signal flying, Captain Tennant took the *Repulse* over towards her to see how she fared and if he could help. Seeing the *Prince of Wales's* list, he signalled over to the Admiral to ask about the flagship's damage and whether her wireless transmission was in order, in case the Admiral had any urgent signals which *Repulse* could send. But no reply came back, and almost at once another enemy wave was seen coming in to the attack.

From their low height it could be deduced they were torpedo aircraft. There were about eight or ten, and they attacked in a most determined manner. First they came along all together from the starboard bow. When about three miles away, one party separated from the remainder and flew to pass down the *Repulse's* port side as if to attack the *Prince of Wales* on her quarter. The first batch of aircraft on the *Repulse's* bow pressed in to just over a mile and then dropped their torpedoes. To comb them was not difficult. The *Repulse* had only to alter course a little to starboard. But this was evidently what the other flight was waiting for. Being then abreast the ship's port bow, they suddenly swung round and aimed their torpedoes at her from the port beam. It was a skilful attack plan. The *Repulse* could not have altered round to comb the new tracks, had there been time, without presenting her broadside length to the first torpedoes. She was bound to be hit on one side or the other, and Captain Tennant decided he might as well go on as he was. Fortunately, the torpedoes dropped on the port side were not too well aimed, but there was one coming in from this direction which they could all see was bound to hit; and with a roar it exploded opposite the after funnel. The *Repulse* stood up to the hit well, remained under control and continued to steam at twenty-five knots.

Again, the *Prince of Wales* came off worse. She, too, was under attack from other aircraft, and having been slowed up and rendered unable properly to steer by the earlier torpedo or torpedoes, was easier game. She received either three or four hits.

More Japanese aircraft appeared almost at once. It will be remembered that on the strength of the submarine report during the night, a large force had been sent out from Saigon about an hour after daylight. It was organized in flights of nine aircraft each, and these were attacking as they arrived over the vicinity of the ships.

Several flights now seemed to come in at once and from various different directions. Up to now, Captain Tennant had found the game of trying to outwit the Japanese torpedo droppers and afterwards of spotting and combing their torpedoes an absorbing and rather fascinating one. This time, however, there were too many flights attacking at once for much dodging to be possible. Torpedoes came streaking in from several bearings together and there was no hope of avoiding them all. One torpedo hit well aft just by the gun-room. It evidently jammed the rudders, because the ship could no longer steer. Three more hits came quickly, two on one side and one on the other.

It was obvious that the *Repulse* was doomed. She was listing rapidly and slowing up. No captain likes to give the order for abandoning ship, but Captain Tennant now reached the painful conclusion that the time for this distressing order had come. Fortunately the loudspeaker system was still working, and through it he told all men below to come up and begin casting loose the Carley floats. The men came streaming up. From the bridge, those assembling on the forecastle deck could best be seen, the men collecting quietly up to the rails on the high side of the ship, waiting for her last roll over. Captain Tennant went

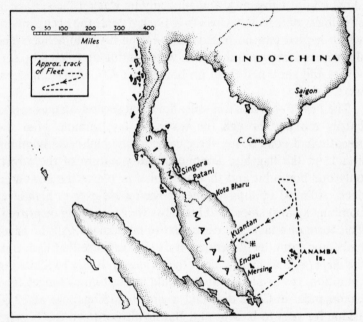

MAP 3

again to the loudspeaker. He told all hands that they had done all that was possible, he thanked them for their efforts and wished them luck, A minute or two after he had spoken, the ship capsized.

As she heeled rapidly over, Captain Tennant clambered over the side of the bridge on to what had previously been a vertical surface and was walking unsteadily along it when the sea seemed to come up and engulf him. The ship must have rolled right over on top of him, for everything at once became pitch dark, telling him he was a long way down under water. The defeatist part of the mind that we all possess whispered to him that this was the end of all things and that he might as well take in water and get it over. But another part of his brain bade him react against this advice, and he decided to hang on to life as long as possible; though he wondered if he could possibly hold his breath long enough to come up again. Lumps of wood hit him in the darkness. After what seemed a long, long time the water began to show a faint lightening, and suddenly he was on the surface in swirling water, luckily close to a Carley float, the occupants of which hauled him on board still wearing his steel helmet. The destroyers *Vampire* and *Electra* were coming up to pick up survivors and soon had them on board. But 427 officers and men were lost.

The *Prince of Wales* was still afloat, but severely damaged and hardly moving through the water. A few minutes after the *Repulse* had gone down, there came a new high-level bombing attack on the flagship. Despite the easy nature of the target, only one bomb hit and that one failed to pierce the armoured deck. Admiral Phillips had never been a believer in high-level bombing against ships, and his views were not being disproved. This form of attack had done next to no damage. All the harm had come from the torpedo aircraft. It was these that had sunk the *Repulse*, and had reduced the *Prince of Wales* to a sinking condition. It was plain that she could not last much longer. The Commander-in-Chief did send a signal to Singapore at 12.50 asking for tugs to be sent out. But he also ordered the *Express* alongside to take off the wounded. The later hits, by letting water into the ship the other side, had practically removed the list; but the stern was under water, and it was inconceivable that the ship could survive. At twenty minutes past one, the *Prince of Wales* also rolled over and disappeared. The time and date, 1.20 p.m. on 10th December 1941, are worth particular note, since they form a landmark in the history of the British people; indeed of the world.

The *Prince of Wales* had hardly disappeared when the fighters from Singapore appeared on the scene. They found some watching Japanese aircraft, who immediately made off, and the three British destroyers engaged in picking up survivors. Altogether, 90 officers and 1,195 men out of a total of 1,612 of the flagship were saved. But Admiral Sir Tom Phillips and Captain Leach were not among those picked up.

CHAPTER NINE

Inquest on the Disaster

*

The immediate cause of the loss of the *Prince of Wales* and *Repulse* was a lack of air cover over the ships off Kuantan, this in turn being basically due to the extreme shortage of fighters in the British Air Force in Malaya. Had there been enough of them to meet the foreseeable requirements of Malayan defence and had they been of the high quality which was possible, the story of the first few days of the Japanese invasion would assuredly have been a different one. With sufficient fighters to look after Singapore Island and the outlying airfields as well, the Japanese would not have had the walk-over they did in the north, the Malayan airfields near the frontier ought to have remained in British operation much longer, Kuantan airfield would hardly have been evacuated at the first attack as actually happened, and Admiral Phillips would not have had to be given the chilling message that he could expect no air protection. What the effect of that message was on his mind is mainly conjectural. It seems, however, a reasonable assumption that had the Admiral been assured that fighters would be on call at Kota Bharu and Kuantan whenever he should want them, he would not have hesitated to signal for their assistance as needed. As it was, he had pressed for air cover in the north before leaving harbour, but had been twice told that he could not have it; and the subsequent message that fighters were being concentrated for the defence of Singapore island made it possible for him to conclude that air cover would not be forthcoming at all.

For that or some other reason, the Admiral did not again ask for cover on the morning of December 10th when air attack was a likelihood—was indeed developing. The first warning of hostile bombers being in the vicinity came from the *Tenedos* at 10 a.m. Had the Admiral taken this initial danger signal as the moment for communicating with air headquarters ashore, fighters could just have been on the spot before the first torpedo air attack began. It is conceivable, however, that as the *Tenedos* was a good many miles from the heavy ships, Admiral Phillips hoped that her discovery by the enemy would not necessarily lead to his own and was therefore reluctant to break wireless silence lest his flagship's position should thereby be given away. He is known to have been from the start extremely sensitive to this danger in the use of wireless. It was one that had for some time been something of a fetish in the British Navy.

What is difficult to understand is why the Admiral never made an attack report at all, neither when an enemy reconnaissance plane appeared over the main portion of the fleet at 10.20 a.m. nor when the attacks began just after 11 a.m. No convincing reason is known for this omission. There is just a chance that any signal ordered at this time might have been lost in transmission through a special mishap. The first torpedo (or torpedoes) that struck the *Prince of Wales* is known to have flooded the wireless cypher office, where all signals were being handled. In the ensuing hurried evacuation of this office it would have been easy for even an important signal to fall by the wayside.

That the need for such a signal cannot have entered the mind of the Admiral at all is improbable. He was not alone on the bridge. There were various officers with him, including Captain Leach and his own signal officer, whose duty it would be to jog the Admiral's memory, if necessary, about essential signalling. Unfortunately, neither of these officers survived the ship, so that what was discussed with the Admiral in these last hours may never be known.[1] But there is the possibility that has already been discussed that previous signals from the shore may have led the Admiral to think that any signalling by him would be a

---

[1] The Captain of the Fleet, Captain L. H. Bell, was sent down to the conning tower when the first bombers were reported coming, to prevent a congregation of the whole senior staff in one spot.

waste of time. Nevertheless, the desirability on general grounds of keeping shore headquarters apprised of attacks on the fleet is unquestionable.

In the same way, there is no doubt that the Admiral should have signalled his intention of returning southward while he was being shadowed by Japanese aircraft on the evening of December 9th. With those informers overhead, wireless silence no longer mattered much,[1] and it was a good opportunity to tell the shore what the fleet's movements were likely to be. It would be the Admiral's last innocuous chance of making a wireless report before dawn next day at the earliest, since any signal made during the night might betray the fleet's change of course to the southward after—it was hoped—the air shadowers had been given the slip. But Admiral Phillips did not take it.[2]

One cannot tell what effect the news that the fleet had turned back might have had on the air dispositions for the next day. Air Vice-Marshal Pulford might or might not have sent some fighters to Kuantan airfield to be nearer at hand if the fleet wanted sudden help on its way home. But without that information (except for the very vague signal sent by *Tenedos*), Air headquarters was left in the dark about what was happening at sea. There was no one more acutely distressed at the loss of the big ships than the Air Vice-Marshal, an ex-naval officer and a boyhood friend of some of those who had just lost their lives. 'My God,' he said to Captain Tennant that evening, 'I hope you don't blame me for this. I had no idea where you were.'

It has been suggested since the war by Mr. Churchill that Admiral Phillips falsely believed himself to be beyond the reach of Japanese torpedo aircraft off Kuantan, Mr. Churchill saying that there were sound reasons for the Admiral's belief.[3] These reasons are given as being that 'the distance from the Saigon airfields to Kuantan was 400 miles, and at this date no attacks

[1] It still did matter to this extent: that the fleet's position as deduced by wireless cross bearings might well be more accurate than as given by aircraft whose own positions might be a long way out.

[2] Though he did order the departing *Tenedos* to inform Singapore next morning that the fleet was coming back early.

[3] Churchill, Vol. III, p. 551.

6. Admiral Sir Tom Phillips (right), Commander-in-Chief, Eastern Fleet, and Rear-Admiral Arthur Palliser, his Chief of Staff, at the Singapore Naval Base

7. H.M.S. *Prince of Wales* coming alongside the jetty at the Singapore Naval Base

by torpedo bombers had been attempted at anything approaching this range'.

But why had they not? Because the British torpedo bombers which had done this attacking did not have the performance to operate at more than 200 miles from their base. It is possible that an able man like Admiral Phillips could so completely have misunderstood these mechanical limitations to torpedo air warfare in the previous part of the war as to imagine that Japanese torpedo aircraft with a known operational range of 500 miles could somehow not attack at more than 200–300; though it seems rather unlikely. But if he had made that mistake, if he did believe that a torpedo air attack at over 400 miles could be discounted, it then becomes difficult to appreciate why he should have been so anxious for air cover off Singora, since the flying distance from Saigon thither is also over 400 miles. Moreover, the distance from Saigon to Singora is within twenty or thirty miles of that from Saigon to Kuantan, and it is surely beyond credence that so small an extra mileage would make the difference between a sense of acute danger and of comfortable immunity in Sir Tom Phillips's mind. If the Admiral thought himself less exposed—anyway for a period—to torpedo plane or any other form of air attack off Kuantan than off Singora it is surely more reasonable to conclude that it was because he believed his appearance off Kuantan would be unexpected. He did not know that a Japanese submarine had seen him steering south during the night.

Not that the Admiral's look into Kuantan brought him unduly close to the Japanese air bases. On the contrary, his course on the previous day after passing the Anamba islands had taken him nearer to those bases than he would have been off Singora, which he thought it too dangerous to approach. It hardly looks, therefore, as if he were placing a great deal of reliance on keeping outside enemy air range. What he is known to have hoped much from was the weather; that rain, mist, and low cloud would keep him hidden from air discovery. It can, of course, be held that in going to sea at all without the assurance of air support Admiral Phillips was showing insufficient awareness of the gravity of air attack. It is equally possible that he had determined that, in all the circumstances of the case, he must go out whatever the risk. That certainly had been the feeling among the officers whose opinions he had invited at that meeting in his cabin on December 8th.

If it was wrong for Admiral Phillips to go out to the attack in the way that he did, what else should he have done? There are those who have contended that (without an aircraft-carrier and being denied the assurance of shore-based air cover), he should have retired to Ceylon to await the arrival of the delayed *Indomitable*. Such a retirement was, however, surely out of the question. For twenty years it had been well understood by all the parties concerned, in Whitehall, the Dominions, and Malaya that in the event of any threat to British territories in the Far East a British fleet would come out to Singapore and provide the necessary protection. Such a threat had now arisen and a British fleet had just come to Singapore to deal with it. Had this fleet, at the first attack, turned round and steamed back into the greater safety of the Indian Ocean (or Australian waters), it is highly probable that all those in Malaya who knew about it would have felt basely abandoned and that the ships' companies of the fleet would have considered themselves indelibly disgraced.[1] The position would have been slightly better had the ships been stopped at Ceylon and not been sent forward till reinforced: but not much better. An enforced wait in the background while Malaya was being invaded would have thrown a great strain on the ships' companies and might have had unlooked-for effects.

Since the ships had reached Singapore, inactivity in the face of a Japanese attack was virtually unthinkable. As it was, there were signs of restlessness in some of the messes of the Eastern fleet during the forenoon of December 8th because the ships were still in harbour while a hostile landing was taking place. The fleet was almost bound to have taken offensive action, and

---

[1] Nevertheless, the First Sea Lord in a memorandum to the Minister of Defence dated 28th August 1941 said that if war broke out his proposed Singapore squadron (*Nelson*, *Renown*, and an aircraft carrier) would have to 'retire to Trincomalee'.

to have done so even had it come out east under cover of full wartime secrecy. But the blaze of publicity that attended its arrival at Singapore made such action inevitable. After all the broadcasting, newspaper reporting, and speech-making about the *Prince of Wales* and other heavy units coming out to restore the situation in the Far East, the fleet could only have refrained from all attempts to interfere with a Japanese landing at the expense of becoming an international laughing-stock. There is a ray of consolation to be derived from the fact that Sir Tom Phillips never got his ships back to Singapore in the thought of the excruciating decision that would then have faced him as to what to do next. If there are any regrets to be felt, they are perhaps that his Secretary's opinion was not followed of going on to Singora so that, if they were sunk, the ships might at least have taken something with them.

Mr. Churchill records in his book a different idea still as to what the fleet should have done. He says the *Prince of Wales* and *Repulse* had been despatched to the Far East 'to exercise that kind of vague menace which capital ships of the highest quality whose whereabouts is unknown can impose on all hostile naval calculations'. He describes a meeting, 'mostly Admiralty', in the Cabinet war-room on the night of December 9th at which there was 'general agreement' that the proper strategy for the two ships was to disappear among the islands. Mr. Churchill does not say which Admiralty officers were present, but of those most likely to have been there the then First Sea Lord is dead and so is the Assistant Chief of the Naval Staff. That there was, however, general agreement in a meeting that was 'mostly Admiralty' about this hiding strategy for the Eastern fleet entitles such a plan to careful consideration.

In seeking to evaluate its strategical content, the first point to be clear about is the major object of the Eastern fleet, whether in hiding among the islands or not. Was it to exert 'a vague menace'? No, because that is not an object but a course of action (or inaction). About the correct object there is no real room for doubt, and it has already been referred to more than once. As the situation stood on December 9th, it was the defeat of the

Japanese seaborne invasion of Malaya. *This was one of the main reasons for the existence of the Navy: to protect British territories everywhere against seaborne attack.*

What could the Eastern fleet do to achieve this object? Again as previously mentioned, its most promising course of action to this end was to destroy the Japanese invasion convoys, preferably before they could reach the disembarkation points, but otherwise after reaching them.

Where would the Japanese convoys be found? No laborious guesswork was required to divine their route. They would naturally hug the Indo-China coast down to Cape Camo to keep as close as possible to their own airfields. From Cape Camo they would steer for Kota Bharu or Singora either by the shortest line or by a detour up into the Gulf of Siam for greater safety. In both cases, air cover could be available all the way across, so that any attacking fleet would be open to torpedo plane and bomber attack by day, and submarine attack, too.

To give protection during the night and in bad flying weather by day, the Japanese could be expected to provide a strong surface escort of, say, three battleships or two battleships and a carrier or anyway a reasonably superior force to the British ships in hiding. There were quite enough Japanese ships for this to be done, especially after the Pearl Harbour striking force had got back.

With their convoys thus protected, it would have mattered little to the Japanese that there was a vague menace of the *Prince of Wales* and *Repulse* somewhere among the islands. To do any harm, the British ships must have left their hiding-places and gone to the convoys, where the escorting warships and protective aircraft could expect to give them a warm reception.

Such must have been the general prospect as viewed by Admiral Phillips and his staff had his ships been in hiding. They would have had to realize that, if the fleet were to help Malaya, it would have to operate close up to Indo-China or in the entrance to the Gulf of Siam; in more or less the same region, in fact, to which Admiral Sir Tom Phillips did take his fleet.

Either the Eastern fleet was strong enough to take such action or it was not. If it was, then what did it gain from hiding among the islands? Clearly nothing. Possible island hiding-places were no nearer to the Japanese convoy routes than Singapore, but actually a good deal farther away. And that being so, there was everything to be said for using Singapore. It offered the protection of anti-submarine nets, minesweeping flotillas, anti-aircraft guns and fighter squadrons, none of which would be at the fleet's disposal when hiding among the islands. There, the ships would be at the mercy of any submarine which happened to find them at anchor, and would be dangerously exposed to hostile air attack. Nor would the concealment be any too promising, with Japanese reconnaissance aircraft ranging the islands in search of the British heavy units.

Why take all these avoidable risks when the Singapore base was not only closer to the operating ground but, as well as giving far greater safety to a fleet inside it, was stocked with all kinds of naval supplies, including oil, ammunition, stores, victuals, together with repair shops and docks? Indeed, it was the very difficulty of operating modern expensive capital ships without rather elaborate naval bases to guard and service them that had led to the heavy outlay of £20 millions for such a base at Singapore. To suggest that this great base, now completed, was not to be used by the ships for which it had been constructed, and which should instead go away to hide among undefended islands, has an odd sound. And for the battleships to behave thus while a strong land and air garrison in Malaya fought for the security of a deliberately unoccupied naval base at Singapore would have been highly paradoxical.

But if, on the other hand, the Eastern fleet under Sir Tom Phillips was too weak to make any attempt on the Japanese convoy route, could it do anything for the preservation of Malaya by vanishing from the vital area? Nothing whatever. Unless attacked, the Japanese convoys would just go on running. In that case, was there any merit in hiding among the Islands? Very little, since a threat that never materializes is a damp squib.

The hiding fleet might, it is true, have snapped up a few Japanese merchantmen here and there. But this would not have affected the major issues of the moment; nor was it proper work for capital ships, their basic function being to fight for the command of the sea by giving open battle to the capital ships of the enemy. For centuries, the British Navy has been the foremost practical exponent of this principle, so that it became a proverbial matter in the fleet that the battlefleet's job was to seek out and destroy the battlefleet of the enemy. There could be no greater antithesis to this principle than the idea of a battlefleet going into hiding, which converts what should be a front-line fighter into a guerrilla relying on stealth. There are classes of ships specially suited to this second role, but they are not battleships. Submarines and disguised raiders are the true guerrillas of the sea.

In the previous war, the German armoured cruisers *Scharnhorst* and *Gneisenau* had been lost for long periods among these very South Pacific islands; but the effect of their 'vague menace' had been very small. It had not prevented the Admiralty, then under Mr. Churchill, from organizing amphibious expeditions against the German islands; even though, in at least one case, the German squadron was suspected of being in the neighbourhood of the objective in superior force to the expedition's escort. The 'vague menace' of heavy ships in hiding did not deter Mr. Churchill, and equally should not have deterred the Japanese.

Nevertheless, it would appear from his book that it was with Mr. Churchill that the 'vague menace' idea originated, for we find him pressing it upon the First Sea Lord in a memorandum of 29th August 1941.[1] If the First Sea Lord showed this memorandum to his Vice Chief of the Naval Staff, Sir Tom Phillips, the latter does not seem to have taken its message to heart. For when he later found himself in command of the Eastern fleet in a war with Japan he made no attempt to become a vague menace but went straight out to attack the enemy. Perhaps Sir Dudley Pound did not mention the theory to him: or, if he did, may have expressed private disagreement with its basic principle. Mr. Churchill does not record any favourable Admiralty reply to his

[1] Churchill, Vol. III, p. 773.

'vague menace' memorandum, which he might well have been tempted to do had one been received.

If the Eastern fleet was too weak to give battle, could it have been stronger than it was? We have seen in Chapter Seven that it could. The Admiralty had wanted to make it much stronger and had prepared definite proposals for so doing. It was Mr. Churchill who had insisted on keeping it weaker than it need have been. It was a peculiar insistence on his part; as was also his strong desire to have one of the latest battleships for despatch to the east, and his opinion, as expressed to the Dominion Premiers, that she would be 'the best deterrent' to the Japanese.

It is likely that politicians feel a peculiar attraction for modernity in any form, since it gives them the polemical safe-guard of following 'the most progressive policy' or of having employed 'our very latest' this or that. There is, moreover, to some minds and especially those given to imaginative enthusi-asms, something a little hypnotic about the newest weapons, replete with the latest equiment, and fashioned with the aid of the most up-to-date thought, which induces a tendency to credit them with magical qualities that they do not possess. Mr. Chur-chill had once already given evidence of such a tendency in the exaggerated expectations he had placed on the participation of H.M.S. *Queen Elizabeth* with 'her enormous guns' in the Dar-danelles campaign of 1915. It can be thought that he was being similarly carried away by optimism about the capabilities of the *Prince of Wales*. For no one not so affected could conceivably have believed, as Mr. Churchill did, that she and the old *Repulse* could by their mere appearance in the Indian Ocean have 'a paralysing effect on Japanese naval action'.[1]

It is not too easy to trace Mr. Churchill's exact mental atti-tude towards this question of Far Eastern naval warfare. At one moment (August), he was writing to the Admiralty that

'A (*Prince of Wales* class) battleship in the Indian Ocean would . . . exercise a vague general fear and menace at all

---

[1] Churchill, Vol. III, p. 768. It is noteworthy that in the House of Com-mons debate of 29th January 1942, Mr. Churchill referred to the Prince of Wales as 'this vast ship'.

points at once. It appears, and disappears, causing immediate reactions and perturbations on the other side.'

This was a strategy of hiding and guerrilla warfare. At another time (November), he was assuring Stalin that

'We are sending our latest battleship, *Prince of Wales*, which can catch and kill any Japanese ship, into the Indian Ocean. . . .'

This is not a doctrine of evasion but of the direct offensive. 'Catch and kill' indicates seeking battle with a full hope of destroying the enemy. 'Appear and disappear' suggests almost the exact opposite. It is hardly to be thought that Mr. Churchill would be trying to deceive a war associate like Stalin with bold words which he did not mean. The adverse effect in loss of confidence by the associate should the exaggeration be exposed by events would be too serious to make it worth while. The challenging broadcast early in December about the arrival of the *Prince of Wales* 'and other heavy units' at Singapore is also hard to reconcile with the statement that only a week later a meeting, 'predominantly Admiralty', thought the *Prince of Wales* and *Repulse* should go into hiding. Surveying Mr. Churchill's various pronouncements about these ships, it is difficult to fit them all into any coherent strategy.

The major error into which he seems to have fallen is indicated by his obvious obsession, noticeable in most of his minutes, memoranda, and telegrams during this period, with the idea of raids by individual ships and not engagements between squadrons. He thought in terms of the Japanese raiding the British communications in the Indian Ocean and of the British Far Eastern ships raiding the Japanese communications somewhere else, though he did not say where. He clearly failed to realize that the main issue at stake was an organized struggle for the command of the sea. What we should and did have to face in the south-west Pacific were not the sorties of so many Japanese *Bismarcks* but the embattled challenge of a superior Japanese fleet.

CHAPTER TEN

The Loss of Malaya

*

Even in the midst of the greatest war in history, the news of the sinking of the *Prince of Wales* and *Repulse* made a great sensation throughout the world. Only a few days before, the arrival of these ships at Singapore had been given world-publicity as securing the British Far Eastern possessions against Japanese attack. The Japanese had attacked almost at once, and the British 'heavy units' which had allegedly restored the situation had been disposed of in less than three days.

There at once arose a clamour of propaganda among the professionally air-minded that the loss of the ships by air attack conclusively proved the superiority of shore-based aircraft over the heaviest surface ship. It proved, of course, nothing of the kind; but only that battleships with practically no anti-aircraft defence could be sunk by air attack—quite a different thing. On subsequent occasions, when battleships had suitable anti-aircraft protection, they retained their operational value. Three months after the loss of the *Prince of Wales* and *Repulse*, the German heavy ships *Scharnhorst* and *Gneisenau*, well protected by fighters, steamed up the Channel and got back to Germany without a single bomb hit, despite attacks by over 200 British bombers. In 1944, British battleships with good fighter cover lay for weeks off the Normandy beaches.

In Malaya, there was little inclination for theoretical arguments as to whether aircraft could or could not always sink battleships. The people there were much too vitally affected by the loss of the ships to take any but the most directly practical view of the disaster. To them, the news brought a shock of dismay. They had felt greatly reassured when the big ships had arrived. For many years, the arrival of a British fleet had been held out to them as the official guarantee of their safety from attack. And now suddenly, at the very outset, the shield had disappeared. The Eastern fleet had been annihilated and the command of sea had passed to the Japanese. It is generally agreed that the naval catastrophe sent a wave of depression over the Peninsula; and it is probable that the feeling that the sea was in enemy control adversely affected the garrison, even if unconsciously, throughout the campaign.

With the death of Sir Tom Phillips, there became no naval Commander-in-Chief. Admiral Layton had officially handed over the command at 8 a.m. that day and had embarked for passage to England during the forenoon. He had not sailed, however, when the bad news came through, and he went back on shore. The Admiralty naturally told him to resume the command.

Sir Geoffrey succeeded to a situation that was out of control. A large fleet of transports was anchored off the coast at Singora and Kota Bharu, discharging men and stores to the beaches. Little could be done against it by surface craft, since what had happened to the *Prince of Wales* and *Repulse* showed what other surface vessels could expect in the vicinity of the Japanese landings. A number of cruisers arrived at Singapore within a few days of the sinking of the capital ships, having come in from various directions, including Australia. But any force Admiral Layton might have tried to use on the east coast would have had no air cover, and would have been open to the same and even heavier air attack than that experienced by Admiral Phillips.

Moreover, the Japanese could always have met a British naval force with a superior one. When, later on, they staged a landing at Endau, the then Senior Naval Officer did send two of the older destroyers against it. But, running into a larger Japanese covering force, one ship was sunk and the other had to retreat damaged to Singapore. In any case, other commitments were claiming the bulk of Admiral Layton's surface ships. From the early stages, both Sir Robert Brooke-Popham and General Percival laid stress on the importance of the safe arrival of reinforcement convoys from the southward; and their escort and protection kept all the cruisers and newer destroyers fully occupied. The only hope of making any impression on the invasion fleet was by submarine. Unfortunately, there were no British submarines on the station. But the Dutch naval authorities at Java at once sent their seven submarines up to Singapore. These vessels went on to attack the Japanese shipping and did so with so much gallantry and determination that they suffered somewhat severe losses. However, they accounted for a number of transports. It had previously been hoped that the seventeen American submarines based on the Philippines would have become available, but instead of falling back on Singapore as planned, they moved down to Java. They were also initially handicapped by orders not to attack escorted shipping.

By the end of the second day, our troops in the north were beginning to retire under heavy Japanese pressure; and the retreat continued without an appreciable break during the next two months. The Japanese troops used for the invasion were picked ones, who had been specially trained for the purpose, and the men were animated by an eager enthusiasm for their task, which they had been taught to regard as of primary importance to the Imperial Japanese cause, as indeed it was. Everything had been carefully planned and special equipment was devised for the tropical conditions that would be met. A stratagem much employed was to utilize the physical similarity of the Japanese to the local inhabitants. By dressing the troops in cotton singlets and shorts, they were made extremely hard to distinguish from the ordinary Malays and Malayan Chinese. By this means, bodies of the enemy were able to pass unsuspected through the British lines and launch attacks from the rear. This infiltration was particularly trying to the defenders, who were fighting with the unpleasant feeling that the enemy might all the time be getting past and behind them.

Frequent use was also made by the Japanese of outflanking movements by sea. Their main advance being down the west side of the Peninsula where the best communications lay, it was there that such outflanking was mainly practised. On this side, the Japanese did not enjoy surface command of the sea, since they could not get their ships into the Straits of Malacca through the channel between Singapore and Sumatra. Water transport for military outflanking purposes was therefore a problem for them; but they solved it by the use of native boats[1] and by transporting a number of their own landing craft across the northern part of the Peninsula by road. In these, parties of Japanese soldiers would embark, pass south round the British flanks and land in the rear, where they would operate against communications and generally do their best to create confusion and uneasiness in the British front line.

Such moves by the Japanese were difficult to counter. All Admiral Layton's cruisers and destroyers were employed on convoy duty and were none too many for that purpose; though the old destroyer *Scout* did operate for a short period in the Malacca Straits. Rear-Admiral Spooner, to whom Admiral Layton had delegated the local naval defence of Malaya, had to do what he could with improvised craft; with converted yachts and harbour craft, private motor boats, and other similar vessels. Occasionally the minesweepers were drawn upon for special purposes, such as coastal bombardments of enemy positions, but at the expense of their own essential work. The principal need was for high-speed motorcraft with good offensive power, but these were lacking. In 1940, Admiral Layton had asked the Home authorities for three flotillas of motor torpedo boats; but no reply had ever been received. The non-appearance of the promised American destroyers from Manila also left an unexpected gap in the defence.

If the Japanese did not possess the surface command in the Straits of Malacca, they had something equally effective. Admiral Spooner's scratch flotillas had the savage obstacle to contend with of a complete Japanese air superiority over the Straits in the neighbourhood of the land fighting. This soon put

[1] It is probable that, in the endeavour to safeguard their property, native boat-owners hid them up the creeks, where they were found by the advancing Japanese.

a stop to naval movement by day; and for effective patrol by night most of the vessels were too slow. It was, indeed, not long before air attack had disposed of them all. Even six fast Eureka boats which arrived from America in December were wiped out by enemy aircraft almost at once. With unchecked air power in their support, the Japanese could make use of seaborne landings more or less as they pleased.

Throughout December and January, the British Army in Malaya was steadily forced back. It was outnumbered, harassed in flank and rear, faced with enemy armour while having none of its own, and battered by Japanese aircraft who were virtually unopposed. By the middle of January the defence line was as far south as Johore, the State immediately north of Singapore island. A long retreat is not stimulating to the morale of any army. In addition, the Indian troops were adversely affected by the disturbing discovery that the forces of the great British Empire could find themselves engaged with a far better equipped enemy.

Meanwhile, the Home Government, impelled to emergency action by the steady Japanese advance, was making efforts to send in reinforcements. The Japanese having air control of the Malacca Straits, that route was impassable, and all convoys had to go through the Sunda Strait between Sumatra and Java and thence north and north-west to Singapore. With British aircraft in southern Malaya, Japanese warships were not venturing south of Singapore, so that the approach route from that direction was still open.

The Commander-in-Chief, Far East, and the G.O.C. and A.O.C. were soon made aware that help was on the way. Unfortunately, they were also aware that help could not come quickly. Except from India, troop convoys could not reach Singapore till about the middle of January; and though it was just possible to fly bombers and other large aircraft direct to Singapore via north Sumatra, the all-important fighters had not sufficient range and would have to come in by ship, either crated or carrier-borne.

The first reinforcement to arrive from the westward was an Indian infantry brigade on January 3rd. It was newly formed and incompletely trained. The next relief convoy came in on January 13th, bringing a British infantry brigade group (53rd), a heavy anti-aircraft regiment, an anti-tank regiment and fifty Hurricane fighters. The infantry had originally been destined for the Middle East but had been diverted to Singapore; and when they arrived had been nearly three months embarked. They could hardly, therefore, be in prime physical condition, and it would take some time to harden them up, quite apart from their lack of experience of jungle warfare. With the fighting going against their own side, these were both important handicaps. The brigade group was also without its guns and transport, but substitutes were provided on the spot.

The Hurricanes were crated and had to be unpacked and assembled. But this was done quickly and the machines were air-borne in a day or two. Though a considerable improvement on the Brewster-Buffaloes they were unfortunately fitted with special gear for desert flying, which reduced their speed below that of the Japanese Navy Zero fighters at most levels. The Japanese pilots had, of course, by this time had over a month's experience of the special conditions of Malayan air fighting, to which the new-coming British airmen were unaccustomed. At first, the surprise of the Hurricanes' appearance gave them some success. But the Japanese soon adjusted their methods, and the wastage from air fighting, accident, and destruction on the ground was fairly rapid. At this stage of the campaign, a 'penny packet' of fifty Hurricanes, especially with a speed handicap, was too small to make much difference.

In the last week or ten days of January, convoys came in more frequently; on the 22nd with an Indian infantry brigade, very raw, and 7,000 Indian assorted troops of such poor quality that the G.O.C. did not think it worth moving them beyond the reinforcement camp: on the 24th with an Australian machine-gun battalion and a draft of about 2,000 Australians who were almost untrained. On January 29th, the British 18th Division (less one infantry brigade group and certain ancillary units[1]) arrived and disembarked. Like the 53rd Brigade group before it,

[1] These arrived a few days later.

it had been many weeks on shipboard and could not possibly be in fighting condition.[1] And time was now short. Almost as the division landed, the British Army withdrew across the Causeway to Singapore island.

The same convoy that carried the 18th Division brought a light tank squadron from India. These were the only tanks to arrive in Malaya. At about the same time, forty-eight modern Hurricanes were flown in from H.M.S. *Indomitable* on the other side of Java. But most of them did not remain in Malaya but were evacuated to Java and Sumatra. Those few that did stay were employed on Singapore island and operated under miserable conditions, the pilots living in the open with no shelter against the tropical rainfall except the wings of their aircraft, and their airfields under periodical rifle-fire.

By the time the 18th Division was ashore, the situation for the defenders was critical. The original garrison was exhausted after a long fighting retreat with little sleep, and had become dispirited by the unequal weapon conditions under which it was having to fight. And the whole army of eighty-odd thousand men was now crowded into the comparatively small Singapore island.

The Japanese paused for just over a week, making their preparations for the final assault. On February 8th, the attack began, and in a matter of a few hours the enemy had secured a lodgement on the island.

There is no need to describe the final tragedy in detail. Under incessant bombing from the almost unopposed Japanese Air Force, under heavy gun-fire, the air black with the smoke of the burning naval oil tanks, with native labour non-existent, civilian services failing, water giving out, the garrison fought on for another week. On February 15th, General Percival capitulated.

The surrender caused little surprise anywhere, the outside world having seen it coming for some time. In England, the people received the bad news with their usual steadfastness. About the only sign of panic manifested in public came from Lord Addison in the House of Lords, who made a violent and

[1] It had actually been disembarked in India for a fortnight, but had otherwise been at sea since October.

vulgar attack on Sir Robert Brooke-Popham, in the course of which he called the Air Chief Marshal 'a nincompoop'. Lord Addison was of the political party that had worked the hardest against adequate defence preparations in peacetime. Perhaps an uneasy conscience on this latter point contributed to his Lordship's deplorable indulgence in personal abuse.

For it was unnecessary to search any further for the causes of the loss of Malaya than the lack of means to defend it. The Army was short-handed and was gravely handicapped by an absence of tanks until the very last moment, when the few light tanks arrived. For months before the Japanese attack, the latest and best quality British heavy tanks were being shipped to Russia. But none ever reached British Malaya. The Air Force was ludicrously short for the part it had to play, whether that part was regarded as principal or co-operative. With so few and such inefficient fighters, with an inadequate radar warning system, with next to no anti-aircraft gun defence for the airfields, air superiority was a gift to the Japanese; and with the British Air Force driven from the skies, the Army was subjected to the gruelling disadvantage of constant exposure to enemy air attack. General Percival has estimated that the attacking Japanese aircraft initially numbered nearly 700. The local commanders in Malaya had asked for between 500 and 600 but were given less than 150. As for the Navy, its insufficiency for its task under the operating conditions forced upon it was dramatically demonstrated within three days.

There have been those who have alleged that the defence of Malaya could have been more stubborn; and that, if it had, the more substantial reinforcements just beginning to arrive towards the end of January might have been in time to hold the enemy some way up the Peninsula. Such critics have clearly failed to grasp that the decisive factor in the struggle was the command of the sea. When that command passed to the Japanese, the Army's position, even had it been stronger than it was, became almost hopeless. For with the trump card of sea supremacy in their hands the Japanese could confidently count on winning the rubber. Even if the British held enough of the sea command to the south of Malaya to go on getting their troop convoys into Singapore, the geography of the situation was against them. The Japanese main islands were under 3,000 miles by sea from Malaya; the British Isles (via the Cape) 12,000 miles. Calcutta (via the Sunda Strait) was as distant as was Japan; Sydney and Melbourne more distant. Moreover, in both India and Australia the Japanese entry into the war had raised urgent political and military questions of home defence, many of the first-line troops of both countries being already in the Middle East.

In the vital matter of reserves, the Japanese had all the advantages. They had a nearby advanced base in Indo-China. They had a large and seasoned army in China, and a very big home population of high fighting quality and long military tradition, among which training to arms had been extensive. Despite the war in China, the Japanese undoubtedly had much greater reserves of men, munitions, and shipping available much closer to Malaya than had the British, and were therefore in a position to meet British reinforcement with greater reinforcement, should it be necessary. As it was, all went well for them from the start. But General Percival estimates that they landed three reinforcing divisions and one tank regiment after the first assault, and it cannot be doubted that they could have sent more, had they wished.

Whether any greater efforts could have been made in defending Malaya is a question on which anyone is at liberty to speculate. But it can be stated with reasonable certainty that Napoleon himself would not have altered the final result, which was a foregone conclusion from the moment the command of the sea was lost. Malaya's fate was sealed on the morning of 10th December 1941, when the *Prince of Wales* and *Repulse* disappeared beneath the waves.

The Japanese did not possess the command of the sea in the Gulf of Siam when they landed. But to have landed there at all, they must have counted on gaining that command. They took a tremendous gamble in attacking the American fleet in Pearl Harbour. But after their success there they can have had no more qualms about Malaya. For with the American Pacific fleet *hors de combat*, the Japanese Admiralty was in a position to reinforce the Malayan area to the point of overwhelming superiority. If the two British heavy ships had survived the air attacks of December 10th, their ability to operate in the Gulf of Siam could not have lasted much longer in any case.

Wherever the Japanese, in the initial weeks of their invasionary flood, were reasonably sure of the command of the sea, there they succeeded. Nothing and no one was able to stop them. General MacArthur, later to become one of the great leaders of the war, was no more successful in the Philippines than General Percival in Malaya.

As well as enjoying the command of the sea, with all that this meant, the Japanese had important advantages on the land side of warfare as well. Once they could gain a footing on shore in Malaya, they would have the benefit of fit and eager troops as compared to a Malaya garrison that was neither war-experienced nor in the best moral condition due to being in too quiet an area in time of war. In peacetime, troops remain reasonably efficient whether at home or on tropical stations abroad. In war-time they do not deteriorate out of contact with the enemy provided they are training for offensive action. But there is undoubtedly some psychological ill that attacks an army waiting inactively outside the war area while their fellows are fighting elsewhere. For one thing, there will be a constant restlessness on the part of the more bellicose officers and men at being out of the battle and a natural tendency for ambitious and enterprising officers to get themselves transferred to the battle zones. There is certain also to be a steady process of withdrawal, as there was from Malaya, of experienced officers and non-commissioned officers for training new armies at home. In these ways, a subtle poison begins to spread in an idle force. It happened in Malaya. The Germans experienced it in France before the Allied invasion of 1944. In the 1914 war, the German High Seas Fleet deteriorated so much in the prolonged safety of its harbours that it eventually broke out into mutiny rather than go to sea. Morale can be recovered if and when war comes to the area, but not immediately; and for a time the invading enemy will have an advantage. The only solution is a frequent exchange of war-tried formations with those in waiting under peaceful conditions. But this was omitted in the case of Malaya, possibly through the general shortage of shipping making a systematic flow of units through Malaya difficult to operate.

A question of importance, and one that was freely discussed at the time, is whether the landing of reinforcements in Malaya was rashly prolonged beyond the point of prudence, some contemporary critics averring that the last troops to arrive, and notably the 18th Division, virtually marched off their ships straight into a prisoner-of-war camp. There is, of course, no more difficult problem in war than to know how long to continue reinforcing a garrison that might in the end be defeated. As long as there is a chance that reinforcements might turn the tide, they will naturally be sent. But there may come a time when the final issue becomes doubtful, whatever is done; and this in turn may pass to the stage when defeat appears probable. Most men being reluctant to envisage failure before they must, the tendency will be for the mental acceptance of ultimate defeat to be delayed as long as possible, and therefore for the despatch of reinforcements to a beleaguered area to be stopped, if at all, too late rather than too early.

With this tendency in mind, can it be said that the disembarkation of troops at Singapore almost till the last moment was ill-judged and unfortunate? Clearly, to have gone on landing men after reasonable chance of holding the Peninsula had disappeared would have been a waste of men and bad strategy. The question is, when did that chance evaporate? Though it is next to impossible to assign an actual date to such a nebulous turning point, there is at least evidence for saying that it came before the 18th Division reached Singapore. In his despatch, General Percival quotes a telegram from the War Office on January 20th asking for his 'personal assurance that, if the worst came to the worst, nothing of military value would be left intact for the enemy on Singapore island'.[1] No one drafting such a telegram can have failed to have in mind the fear that all Malaya was about to be

---

[1] General Percival's despatch, para. 414.

lost to the enemy. The 18th Division did not reach Singapore till nine days later.

The decision to allow the division to land appears even more perplexing in the light of the official object for which the defending forces were fighting. This was the preservation of the naval base.[1] But before the 18th Division had gone ashore or even arrived at Singapore, it had become quite certain that it would not be possible to hold any part of Johore and that the retreat would be continued across the Causeway on to Singapore island. This meant that the Japanese would soon arrive on the north shore of the naval harbour, after which no British warship would naturally be able to lie there. The war in Malaya would then be officially lost by the British, since their strategical object of protecting the naval harbour and base would be no longer attainable.[2] That being so, the logical thing to do, once it had been decided to abandon Johore and retreat into Singapore island, was to start getting the surviving troops away by sea. Instead, we find General Percival being subjected to intense pressure by the Home Government, acting through the Supreme Commander, to fight to the bitter end.[3]

What was the reason for this harsh order? Twenty months before, the British Expeditionary Force, cornered at Dunkirk, had been got away by sea, to the British Government's enormous relief. At the same period, the British Channel Islands were evacuated before they had been attacked. Why, then, should General Percival's army, cornered in Singapore island, have been told to remain and fight to the last? If the conditions for evacuation were worse than at Dunkirk, nevertheless a lot of men could undoubtedly have been removed during the week the Japanese were preparing for the assault on the Causeway. For such as had been, there was urgent employment waiting in at least two areas close at hand. The Supreme Commander himself

---

[1] General Percival's despatch, para. 18.

[2] It was distinctly ironical that a desperate struggle had been waged for the previous seven weeks to save a major naval base from which there were no major war vessels to operate.

[3] The appointment of the Supreme Commander (General Wavell) is dealt with in the next chapter.

was organizing the defence of Java. Even more important was the defence of Burma, which the Japanese were now invading from the south-east. Troops were desperately wanted to contest their advance and to battle for the security of India, if Burma could not be held. What, then, led to the men crowded on Singapore island, with no apparent object of a material nature left to fight for and with other nearby regions thirsty for reinforcement, being told to continue the struggle until driven into the sea? The answer was, for a long time, not easily discernible.

Light has, however, been thrown on this hitherto obscure question by Mr. Churchill's fourth volume. He has revealed that he himself began to doubt the wisdom of further reinforcement of Malaya some time before the end and while the 18th Division was still at sea; so much so that he came to feel that the Division should be diverted elsewhere. He was terribly anxious about the Japanese invasion of Burma, where the enemy was already threatening Rangoon, and he thought the 18th Division could best be used to save that city and oppose the further Japanese advance towards India; a pretty plain indication that he believed Malaya to be as good as lost.

Mr. Churchill had, however, reckoned without the Australians, at this time in a state of mounting alarm at the Japanese successes. The whole scheme of Commonwealth defence that for the last two decades had rested on the great naval base at Singapore, reputed to be impregnable, was fast melting away before the increasingly agitated gaze of the Australian people; and in the sudden onrush of this fearsome crisis for which they were both materially and morally unprepared, they were saying that they had been basely deceived by the authorities in London and left in the lurch.

Mr. Churchill was unduly hopeful if he thought that the Australians would take kindly to a proposal to divert the 18th Division from Singapore to Burma—if indeed he meant to tell them, about which there is some doubt.[1] It is true that Australia was now in the American sphere of responsibility, this having been concerted between Mr. Churchill and the President at their

---

[1] They got to hear about it in roundabout fashion.

recent meeting in Washington. But however handy such a transfer was to those on the Olympian heights of the supreme war direction, it did not look quite the same to the Australian Government, the members of which did not readily appreciate the twenty-year-old British guarantee being so easily got rid of. The Australian Prime Minister telegraphed that his country had received many promises of protection by a main fleet based on Singapore and that his Cabinet expected everything possible to be done to fulfil those promises by defending Singapore to the last, failure to do which would be regarded as an 'inexcusable betrayal'.

The Australian Government's insistence on the 18th Division being sent to Singapore was actually ill-judged, because the situation there was by this time beyond being saved. The time to agitate for more effective measures for the defence of Malaya was at any period during the twenty years up to 1941. Now it was too late. But it is fair to remember that the Australian Government was facing an emergency even more disturbing than the Dunkirk crisis of 1940 which had caused Mr. Churchill to make the anguished offer of common citizenship with the French. A certain blurring of perspective on the part of the Australian Cabinet in January 1942 cannot therefore be thought exceptional.

Mr. Churchill should have stood firm against the Australian Government: as firm as he was telling the Malaya garrison to stand against the Japanese. Instead, he capitulated; and the 18th Division went on to Singapore and useless sacrifice. Thus, the object of the Malay garrison changed in the last days. From being the protection of the naval base, it became that of saving the British Government from criticism by the Australian. Whether this was an adequate object on which to expend a division of troops and to hazard the destruction of a city like Singapore is a matter of opinion.

It is possible that the strong language used by the Australian Prime Minister to Mr. Churchill may have shaken the latter into a radical change of outlook on the subject of Empire defence. At all events, by April 1942 he seems completely to have reversed the views on strategical priorities that he held in January, only three months before. In the latter month, it will be remembered, he told the House of Commons that 'anyone could see it was right' to give aid to Russia priority over the defence of Singapore. In April, however, Mr. Hopkins and General Marshall arrived in England as envoys from President Roosevelt to urge on Mr. Churchill the need for a landing in France early in 1943, or even late in 1942, as a means of drawing off German pressure on the Russians. In his book, Mr. Churchill comments on this proposal as follows:[1]

'In planning the gigantic enterprise of 1943 it was not possible for us to lay aside all other duties. *Our first Imperial obligation*[2] was to defend India from the Japanese invasion, by which it seemed it was already menaced. . . . To leave 400 million of His Majesty's Indian subjects, to whom we were bound in honour, to be ravaged and overrun, as China had been, by the Japanese would have been a deed of shame.'

The obvious deduction from the above passage is that by April 1942 Mr. Churchill had been converted to the idea that Empire defence took priority over aid to Russia. The extent of the conversion is indicated by a somewhat significant omission from this same passage in Mr. Churchill's book. He said that it would be a deed of shame to leave 400 million of His Majesty's Indian subjects to be ravaged and overrun by the Japanese, 'as China had been'. It is true that China had been ravaged and overrun, but only partially. On the other hand, by April 1942, Malaya, British Borneo, and Hong Kong had been overrun wholly and completely. Why, then, should Mr. Churchill have made no reference to these latter territories, for which he was responsible, but mention only China, for which he was not? Conceivably because he could not advance the cases of Malaya, British Borneo, and Hong Kong, better examples though they were, in support of his argument that the defence of India should have priority over aid to Russia without inviting the question why he had previously insisted so emphatically on giving aid to Russia priority over the defence of Malaya, British Borneo, and Hong Kong—and also Australia and New Zealand.

[1] *Daily Telegraph* of 27th October 1950.   [2] Present author's italics.

The Loss of Malaya

When Singapore fell, General Percival went into captivity with his troops. The day before, Rear-Admiral Spooner and Air Vice-Marshal Pulford had escaped with a number of officers and men in a motor boat. By ill luck, they met a Japanese destroyer when half-way to Java. Their motor boat was destroyed but the party got ashore on an uninhabited island, where eventually most of them died of disease and starvation, including the two senior officers. The rest of the Malaya garrison went into prison and concentration camps and on to the Burma Road.

CHAPTER ELEVEN

The Loss of the Dutch East Indies

*

While Singapore was still holding out, while the campaign in Malaya was even in its middle stages, thought was being given in high allied quarters to the defence of the Dutch East Indies, and advance preparations were being made therefor. It was a foregone conclusion that if the Japanese were to complete their conquest of Malaya and the Philippines they would attack the Dutch Islands. It was mainly lack of oil that had driven them into making war, and the Dutch Indies possessed important oilfields. Moreover, the long chain of Dutch islands from Sumatra to Java and beyond formed a natural strategic frontier which the Japanese were certain to want to acquire. Of this chain, Sumatra and Java were the two islands of chief significance, Sumatra because it was rich in oil and Java because it was the seat of government and possessed naval bases and arsenals; and it was expected that these two would be made the first objects of attack.

Accordingly, a general concentration of allied forces began to assemble in the Dutch islands, and mainly in Java, as the Japanese invasions of Malaya and the Philippines made progress. If, in addition to its economic assets, the Dutch island chain was attractive to the Japanese as a strategic outpost line, it was equally important to the Allies as a screen covering northern Australia and commanding the passages into the Indian Ocean.

As early as December 22nd, preparations were ordered for moving an R.A.F. maintenance unit from Kuala Lumpur to Java. By the middle of January it was decided to speed up the transfer of air units from Malaya to the Dutch East Indies, and a number of successive withdrawals took place. On January 19th, the Dutch fighter squadron left, followed three days later by the Dutch bombers. On January 23rd, the British squadrons began to go to Sumatra and Java; and by the end of the month only three Swordfish and a few Hurricane fighters were left on the Malayan Peninsula.

There was also a gathering of naval vessels. When forced away from the Philippines in December, the American Asiatic Fleet had collected in Java, mainly at the naval base at Sourabaya at the eastern end, instead of going to Singapore as promised. The British naval forces employed on escort duty continued to be based on Singapore until early in January. By then, reinforcement convoys were known to be getting close to Malaya, and so much stress was placed by military headquarters on their safe arrival that Admiral Layton determined to shift his own headquarters to Java, in order the better to organize convoy protection. He accordingly left Singapore on January 5th, taking with him Rear-Admiral Palliser, whom he appointed as Senior Naval Officer at Batavia, at the west end of Java, for convoy direction duty. All the convoy cruisers and destroyers were thereafter based on Batavia,[1] until after Singapore had fallen.

It was a period of intense organizational activity in London and Washington. Much high-level improvisation was being hurried along to meet a situation going from bad to worse, and changes in the national and inter-allied higher commands were frequent, almost bewilderingly so. At the end of December, General Sir Henry Pownall relieved Sir Robert Brooke-Popham as Commander-in-Chief, Far East, having been appointed before the outbreak of war. He, however, retained this post for only a few days; for Mr. Churchill had gone to Washington to consult the President, and it was agreed between them to set up an Allied Supreme Command in the south-west Pacific. The officer selected was General Sir Archibald Wavell, then Commander-in-Chief in India. Mr. Churchill has revealed that the selection of this officer was proposed by the Americans. With the Allied defences steadily disintegrating, it was not unnatural for the Americans

[1] Or, to be exact, on Tanjong Priok, the port of Batavia.

to want to avoid the odium of chief responsibility for final defeat. On the more promising occasions that were later to occur, they were not backward in desiring the supreme command for an American.

General Wavell arrived at Singapore on January 7th, and made General Pownall his chief of staff. Both Generals proceeded to Java, where the Supreme Headquarters was set up at Bandeong. The chief command of the Allied naval forces was given to the American Admiral Hart, though the Dutch Admiral Doorman, with whom British officers got on very well, was made the Commander of the combined fleets. Admiral Hart had arrived in Java tired and ill, and he told Admiral Layton that his appointment was not of his seeking and little to his liking. What he wanted was a rest. He also insisted on having Rear-Admiral Palliser as his Chief of Staff. Admiral Layton had therefore to find another Senior Naval Officer, Batavia, and he selected Captain J. Collins, R.A.N., with the rank of Commodore, to whom Captain L. H. Bell, formerly of the *Prince of Wales*, was to act as Chief Staff Officer.

The Japanese were wasting no time in the prosecution of their main strategy. In one of the rapidest series of invasions in history, they had started to overrun Borneo and Sarawak and other adjacent islands without waiting for either Singapore or the Philippines to fall. With amazing speed and following what must have been an extraordinarily complete and bold plan of action, they flooded southward. By the end of January they had control of the Macassar Strait. The day before Singapore capitulated, they seized the southern end of Sumatra. Admiral Doorman, with an allied cruiser squadron made an attempt to interfere, but heavy Japanese bombing forced him to turn back. By the fourth week of February an attack on Java was clearly imminent.

Admiral Hart had now gone home and the Dutch Admiral Helfrich (previously head of the Dutch naval forces) had succeeded him as Allied Naval Commander. The ships at his disposal consisted of a mixed collection of cruisers, destroyers and submarines of Dutch, British, Australian and American nationality.

At this juncture, the imposing edifice of a Supreme Allied Command in the south-west Pacific with nicely balanced international sub-structures that had been organized at Washington fell to pieces. The Supreme Commander informed the Allied Governments that Java could not be defended against a Japanese attack and was ordered back to India; and there he flew, taking the U.S. Army Air Force with him. Other members of the High Command also dispersed to distant destinations. General Wavell was, of course, quite right. Without command of the sea, Java was as much at Japan's mercy as Malaya. But it was only a fortnight before that he had told General Percival at Singapore he must fight to the last.

Java being Dutch, the Dutch higher officers decided to fight. They could still count on the Allied navies,[1] although the latter knew that if the enemy behaved with ordinary competence they were due for annihilation. They had not long to wait.

On February 25th, Allied scouting planes sighted two escorted Japanese convoys making towards Java, one seemingly coming down for the east end of Java, and the other for the west. It could be worked out that they would arrive either on the 26th or 27th. Rear-Admiral Doorman went out to look for the easternmost convoy with five cruisers and eleven destroyers. The cruisers were the *Java* (flag) and *de Ruyter* (Dutch), the *Exeter* (British), *Perth* (Australian) and *Houston* (American). The *Houston* and *Exeter* were 8-inch cruisers and the remainder 6-inch. Of the destroyers, three were Dutch, three British, and five American. It was a scratch international force in which there had been no time to concert more than very elementary signal arrangements. Tactically, the ships were capable of little more than following each other in line ahead. The cruisers were without their own spotting aircraft, which had been left behind on shore.

Just after 4 p.m. on February 27th, enemy ships were sighted ahead; and as the forces got closer two heavy cruisers and a large number of destroyers were made out. The heavy cruisers opened fire almost at once on the *Exeter* and *Houston* from the

[1] And a few American and British aircraft.

very long range of 28,000 yards. The Japanese had spotting aircraft up, which gave them an immense advantage at this great distance and also later when firing over smoke-screens.

Admiral Doorman steered to get closer, and after a time the action became general. At the end of about three-quarters of an hour, the *Exeter* received a bad hit in a boiler room. She came down in speed and swung round to port to avoid a collision with her next astern. But the latter and the ships following her thought this was a formal manœuvre and they altered course as well, resulting in temporary disorder. The Japanese seized this opportunity to deliver destroyer attacks and there was much confused fighting and smoke-laying during which the British destroyer *Electra* was sunk.

The battle went on. By half-past five, the *Houston* was running out of ammunition. There were torpedo attacks by both sides, but none took effect. The Japanese Admiral seemed inclined not to press the action too strenuously but instead to prefer to cover his transports. Admiral Doorman kept pressing in to get at them but was seriously handicapped by his lack of spotting aircraft and the unintegrated nature of his force, and was embarrassed by the enemy's great superiority in destroyers. The fight was still indecisive when contact was lost at nightfall.

Admiral Doorman had to guess what course to steer for intercepting the convoy during the night. Unhappily, the course he chose caused him to steam over a minefield laid by his own side that afternoon. Here the British destroyer *Jupiter* was blown up. The American destroyers had by this time parted company for Sourabaya, while the Dutch destroyers had become dispersed, and one of them had been sunk.

At 11 p.m. the two Japanese heavy cruisers were sighted in the moonlight and an ineffective exchange of fire went on for perhaps half an hour when the Japanese ships fired torpedoes. Luck was with them. Both the *de Ruyter* and the *Java* were hit almost simultaneously and both sank, Admiral Doorman going down with his flagship. It is, however, thought by some that the two cruisers were blown up on another of their own Dutch minefields. Of the remaining three cruisers, the damaged *Exeter* was already making for Sourabaya, and the *Houston* and *Perth* for Batavia.

Meanwhile, Commodore Collins had despatched the cruisers *Hobart*, *Dragon* and *Danae* and the destroyers *Scout* and *Tenedos* to see what they could do against the westerly enemy convoy. They had, however, orders to search for twenty-four hours only and afterwards make for the Indian Ocean through the Sunda Strait.

They set forth and steamed north for the allotted period, but found nothing. It is rather curious to note why they did not. Their approach was seen by Japanese aircraft, but these estimated all the British ships to be one class larger than they really were, reporting three battleships and two cruisers.[1] The Japanese escort commander, highly alarmed, therefore turned the whole convoy northwards to withdraw from this unexpectedly strong enemy force. Despite all their recent triumphs, the Japanese nerves were none too strong.

Having sighted no enemy, the British force followed its instructions and proceeded out into the Indian Ocean. The Japanese convoy it had been seeking lost a day in retreating from its exaggerated menace and then turned back for Java.

The few remaining survivors of the eastern battle[2] had also made up their minds to escape into the Indian Ocean, if they could. The *Houston* and *Perth* left Batavia after dark to slip through the Sunda Strait unobserved. As luck would have it, the western Japanese convoy, having recovered from its alarm at the report of approaching British heavy ships, had just anchored in Banten Bay, on the east side of the Sunda Strait, as the *Houston* and *Perth* were leaving Batavia. The two Allied cruisers, creeping along the shore to escape notice, ran slap into the fleet of anchored Japanese transports. For an hour or less, there was a brilliant display of battle fireworks. Making the most of their opportunity, the two ships poured salvoes into the enemy troopships. Defending cruisers and destroyers came rushing in from round about to protect their military charges, and with probing

---

[1] We shall find this misreporting from the air frequently recurring.
[2] Later given the name of the Battle of the Java Sea.

searchlights, dazzling gun-flashes, and the flickering of flames in burning ships, there ensued a fierce dog-fight at close quarters. The *Houston* and *Perth* were, however, greatly outnumbered and were soon heavily damaged by gun-fire and torpedo hits. The *Perth* sank just after midnight. The *Houston* lasted another half-hour and then, shot to pieces and with dead and dying all over her decks, she too rolled over and disappeared.

The *Exeter* from Sourabaya had a few hours longer to live. With the British and American destroyers *Encounter* and *Pope*, she was also trying to make the Sunda Strait. But after daylight they ran into a greatly superior force and all three ships were sunk.

The Japanese invasion proceeded unchallenged from the sea and practically so from the air. Java lasted a fortnight and then capitulated; and the silence of conquest descended over the East Indies.

In the endeavour to ward off the invasion of Java, which the Supreme Commander had already given up for lost, from which he had departed, and from which most of the Allied air forces had flown, five allied cruisers and fifteen destroyers were sacrificed in vain. That, materially at all events, it was bound to be a vain sacrifice can be judged from the fact that the Japanese covering force for the invasion of Java consisted of four battleships and four aircraft carriers. It is true the Japanese Admiral left the actual fighting to be done by cruisers and destroyers. These, in the event, sufficed for the job. But they had the advantage of knowing that there was overwhelming force behind them. And if the Allied forces did not possess precise knowledge of this overwhelming force, they will have fully expected that Japanese capital ships would be somewhere in the vicinity. The Allied fleet was not engaged in a forlorn hope. It had no hope at all of anything but honour, which no one will refuse it. Whether honour was a sufficient object in such circumstances is an arguable point. The Allied global shortage in cruisers and destroyers, and especially destroyers, was at this time acute; and the ships lost in the hopeless defence of Java could have been used only too well elsewhere. However, as the Dutch had at once sent their submarines (and air squadrons) to defend Malaya in December, the employment of British cruisers and destroyers to defend Java in February cannot be criticized, if the Dutch wished to fight to the death. Perhaps we shall learn in due course what views, if any, the Supreme Commander expressed on the question of a naval last stand before he flew away to India. It was not the happiest of chances that led the American Secretary of the Navy, Mr. Knox, to take this particular moment to broadcast his opinion that the south-west Pacific was a secondary theatre of war.

8. H.M.S. *Repulse* leaving Singapore for her last voyage

9. Captain Tennant of H.M.S. *Repulse* (left) on board rescuing
destroyer after being picked up

10. H.M.S. *Prince of Wales*, just before sinking, taken from
destroyer alongside

CHAPTER TWELVE

The Naval Situation in the Indian Ocean, January to May 1942

*

While the Japanese were still fighting their way down the Malayan Peninsula, the Admiralty and Government in London saw looming up in the not too distant future one of the ugliest prospects imaginable. If the Japanese captured Singapore, as it could be seen that they might, they would be in temporary command of the sea over wide stretches of adjacent ocean, west, south, and east.

South and east would, by geography and previous agreement, be mainly the concern of the Americans. West was the province of the British, and an alarming problem was now facing them there. Using the naval base at Singapore, made for them at great expense by the British taxpayer, the Japanese would be able to strike far into the Indian Ocean; and spread about that ocean were a number of British interests of absolutely first-class importance. With Singapore in Japanese hands, the whole east coast of India would be open to seaborne invasion; and if India were so invaded, who could predict the political repercussions in that sub-continent?

Should the Japanese go on to capture Ceylon, an infinity of mischief would be within their reach. They could stop the flow of oil tankers coming down the Persian Gulf to give mobility to British and Allied ships and aircraft. They could sever the newly opened southern supply line to Russia through Persia. Seaborne communication between India and the outside world could be cut off. Nor was this the worst they could do. Along the east coast of Africa ran the main British supply route to the Middle

East. By it came all the reinforcements of men, tanks, guns, ammunition, lorries, and all the numberless other things needed by the Desert Army. This, too, would be vulnerable to Japanese sea power; and if it were successfully attacked, our whole Middle East position was imperilled, including our naval influence in the Mediterranean. For with its communications cut, the Desert Army could not avoid defeat, Rommel would reach Cairo, the Mediterranean fleet base at Alexandria would be overrun, the overland route to Iraq, Persia, and India would be at the German disposal, and the Suez Canal would become an enemy waterway. The havoc that the Japanese could do to the British war effort if they used their command of the sea to strike westward was incalculable and would probably be catastrophic. These dire possibilities contingent on the loss of Malaya accord so ill with Mr. Churchill's persistent policy of reinforcing almost anybody, British or foreign, other than the Malayan garrison, as to suggest that the Minister of Defence cannot have understood the real importance of the Singapore naval base and what might happen if the base were lost.

The sudden uprising of this harshly menacing situation jolted the home authorities into a hurried search for counter-measures. The Ministerial idea that there was merit in fewness was abandoned and ships were scraped up from all possible quarters for despatch to the Indian Ocean. There were no more hesitations about the R class 'coffin ships'. The *Ramillies* and *Resolution* were sent off under Vice-Admiral Sir Algernon Willis to join the *Revenge* and *Royal Sovereign* in the Indian Ocean. The *Warspite* was also to go there, instead of to the Mediterranean as previously planned. The carrier *Indomitable* was already in Eastern waters, and the carrier *Formidable* was ordered there, too. The small carrier *Hermes* had been part of the East Indies squadron for some time and was at Trincomalee, though it was proposed to send her to Australia later on. With her were a number of cruisers and destroyers, some belonging to the station and some that had escaped from the Java Sea defeats. Thus, a force of five battleships, two (and temporarily three) carriers, and smaller classes was in process of formation as the new Eastern Fleet.

The size of this force is the more significant in the light of the exceptionally heavy casualties among the Navy's big ships that had lately been occurring. On November 12th, the carrier *Ark Royal* had been torpedoed and sunk in the Mediterranean. A week or two later, the battleship *Barham* suffered the same fate. In the following month, the battleships *Queen Elizabeth* and *Valiant* in Alexandria harbour were heavily damaged by charges placed under their bottoms by Italian 'frogmen'. With the *Prince of Wales* and *Repulse*, the Navy had thus in the last two months of 1941 lost two battleships, one battle cruiser, and one large fleet carrier sunk, and had had two more battleships put out of action for long periods. It was against this background of disaster that the constitution of a new Eastern fleet was proceeding.

With Singapore going or gone, the question of a base for the new Eastern fleet became of primary importance. First consideration, both at the Admiralty and on the spot, was given to the emergency base at Addu Atoll that had for long figured in the secret Admiralty plans for moving the main fleet to Singapore. This consisted of a lagoon ringed by coral islands out in the ocean south-south-west of Ceylon.

Alternative bases existed in Ceylon itself, at Colombo on the west coast and at Trincomalee on the east. Colombo had the drawback of being the main commercial port-of-call and therefore was usually crowded with merchant shipping. It had the advantage of being contiguous to the city of Colombo and having certain repair and supply facilities. Trincomalee was a better and more commodious naval harbour but had little else to offer and was cut off from easy contact with other parts of the island.

The prospective value of the Ceylon bases if Singapore should fall caused the Admiralty in mid-January to direct Admiral Sir Geoffrey Layton, then in Java superintending the establishment of the naval headquarters there, to proceed to Ceylon to make advance preparations for the use of the island by the fleet to be assembled in the Indian Ocean.

For the eventual command of the new Eastern fleet, another

admiral had been selected. This was Sir James Somerville, who for the previous two years had been commanding Force H based on Gibraltar. He had carried out several operations inside the Mediterranean and had taken part in the chase of the *Bismarck*, during which it was the aircraft from one of his ships, the *Ark Royal*, that had given the decisive blow that had slowed the *Bismarck* up. Sir James had actually been invalided from the Navy just before the war, but after its outbreak his vivid personality and well-known ability had soon obtained him a sea command, in spite of his medical disability. Now he was chosen to direct the operations against the victorious Japanese on which, for all the Admiralty could tell, the whole outcome of the war might depend. He was still ranked as a Vice-Admiral on the retired list.

Sir Geoffrey Layton had not been long in Ceylon before he found himself appointed by the Government as Commander-in-Chief of the island, a post for which his forceful character admirably suited him. There was much for him to do. If Malaya had been insufficiently defended against attack, Ceylon had practically no defences at all, material or otherwise. There was an air-raid organization, but it had seldom if ever been practised. Labour conditions were thoroughly unsatisfactory, with the result that a score of ships were lying at anchor outside the harbour, at the mercy of Japanese submarines, owing to the slowness of unloading the ships inside. The railways were in a bad state and had only three days' reserve of coal.

Sir Geoffrey Layton took all this in hand with vigour. He insisted on improved payment for dockers, with immediate benefit to the clearance of ships. He instituted large-scale relaying of the permanent ways and commandeered a collier in the harbour to ease the fuel crisis. To meet the urgent need for more aerodromes, he requisitioned the Colombo race-course and golf-links, and in three weeks had rolled them flat enough for use by aircraft, the process involving the demolishing of the houses of the Chief Justice and the General Officer Commanding. He had to build many storehouses and magazines for ammunition. He even found himself compelled to import cattle from Australia and set up a stock farm on the race-course at the hill station of Newara Eliya.

Most serious of all was the lack of armaments. The military garrison was confined to the local volunteers. There were no anti-aircraft guns and no radar warning system. The only aircraft were a few old Blenheims and flying-boats. The worst deficiency was in fighters. Without these, the island would be at the mercy of any Japanese bombers that might make their appearance. The Admiral decided on drastic measures. H.M.S. *Indomitable* was at this time on her way to fly off two squadrons of Hurricanes for the defence of Java. Believing Java to be as good as lost and therefore regarding the despatch of these aircraft thither as a probable waste of good material, Admiral Layton ordered their diversion to Ceylon, where they duly arrived: much to the indignation of the Air Ministry when it heard the news. But it was a providential act of piracy, as we shall see.

Java fell on March 9th. On March 24th, Admiral Sir James Somerville, the Commander-in-Chief of the new Eastern fleet, arrived at Colombo in the carrier *Formidable*, and at once went into a series of urgent conferences with Admiral Layton, Commodore Edwards transferring to Admiral Somerville's staff.[1]

The principal and most vitally important point for discussion was what the Japanese were about to do. Since the fall of Java a fortnight before, they had made no overt move and there was no way of telling where next they would strike. Their most likely courses of action were broadly three. They might move eastward in the Pacific, say in an attempt to capture Pearl Harbour and the Hawaiian group. They might move south against Australia. Or they might come west into the Indian Ocean. A westerly move was what most concerned Admirals Somerville and Layton, and the possibility of it happening was one to cause them the liveliest

[1] It has previously been mentioned that Sir Tom Phillips's Chief of Staff afloat was to be Commodore Ralph Edwards from the Admiralty, who had however not arrived when the *Prince of Wales* and *Repulse* went out for their last sortie. He was then designated as Chief of Staff to Sir James Somerville; but having already arrived in Ceylon he first of all acted in that capacity to Admiral Layton.

concern. For, as has been shown, if the Japanese made a serious advance westward, the damage they might do was enormous and could be fatal to the Allied cause.

To the British officers at Colombo there seemed good reason to anticipate that the Japanese were about to come west. The Japanese invasion of Burma pointed that way. So did the enemy's occupation of the Andaman Islands in the Bay of Bengal on March 23rd, the day before Admiral Somerville reached Colombo. And four days after he had arrived there and begun his survey of the situation on the spot, there came an intelligence report that a Japanese carrier-borne air attack on Ceylon was about to be staged.

Sir James Somerville immediately decided to go to sea to meet the challenge. After weighing up the possible enemy directions of approach, Sir James realized that these were subject to such wide variation that he could not hope to cover them all. He therefore decided it would be best for him to choose the enemy's most likely approach line and place himself on that. He estimated it would be from the south-eastward.

He was far from happy at the possibility of having to fight an action so soon after his arrival. The enemy would inevitably consist of a well-drilled force. His own was not only not well-drilled, it was not drilled at all. He had not yet seen the R class battleships, which were now moving across the Indian Ocean making for Addu Atoll. A fleet can be made up of individually efficient ships and still be a mediocre instrument if it has not been exercised as a whole. This was the position of the Eastern fleet. However, they must do their best. Transferring his flag to the battleship *Warspite*, which had arrived from America on the 26th, Admiral Somerville sailed with her, the *Formidable*, the cruisers *Enterprise*, *Cornwall*, *Dragon*, *Caledon* and six destroyers on March 30th.

Next day, the small carrier *Hermes*, the cruiser *Emerald* and two destroyers joined the flag, and a little later they all sighted the R class battleships, who had with them six more destroyers, the latter squadron making a junction a few hours later. Getting the combined force into cruising disposition without the previous distribution of tactical instructions proved a lengthy proceeding involving much signalling, and showed how raw the fleet was as an integrated force.

On the morrow, as there was no news of the enemy, other than a number of reports of his submarines, the Commander-in-Chief was able to put in a very useful day of fleet manœuvring. On the following day, April 2nd, still no news of the main enemy and more fleet exercises; though, of course, weeks if not months were needed to get the fleet up to a high standard of combined efficiency. The destroyers, which were now getting short of fuel, oiled from the cruisers *Cornwall* and *Dorsetshire* and from the oiler *Appleleaf*. This should have set the fleet up for several more days at sea, but for another shortage which now proclaimed itself; that of fresh water. The R class battleships were old. They had been built for warfare in the North Sea where the distances are short. Hence, their water distilling plant was not adequate for long voyages in tropical seas in a temperature which inevitably sent up the consumption of fresh water. They were now running low. In any case, after four days at sea without news, the Admiral was beginning to think the Japanese attack was a false alarm, and in view of the fuel and water shortage he decided to go back to base to fill up.

But what base? The three at his disposal were Colombo, Trincomalee and Addu Atoll. They were really only two, since Colombo was usually full up with merchant shipping. Sir James Somerville had no difficulty in choosing Addu Atoll, although he had not been there. It was the recognized emergency base for a Japanese war, and it was comfortably clear of Ceylon. If he took the fleet to Trincomalee, they might be caught in harbour by the threatened Japanese attack; with the grave risk, in view of the poor state of the Ceylon defences, of suffering a Pearl Harbour. Sir James therefore made for Addu Atoll. But first he detached the cruisers *Cornwall* and *Dorsetshire* to Colombo and the carrier *Hermes* to Trincomalee. The two former had defects to be made good and the latter was to pick up certain stores before proceeding to Australia. There was a measure of danger in sending them to Ceylon, but unless they went 1,000 miles up to

Bombay, there was nowhere else but Ceylon where the ships could get repairs done; and Admiral Somerville wanted to be able to concentrate them quickly if need be.

The fleet's arrival at Addu Atoll brought home to everyone the unwisdom of relying on paper schemes nicely tucked away in Whitehall safes and never tested in practice. Addu Atoll was a forsaken spot, its ring of barren, burnt-up, coral islets not even

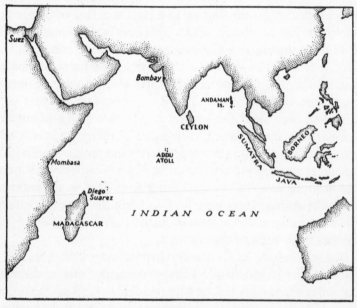

MAP 4

providing a secure haven inside them. Some of the gaps in the ring had been given an extempore guard of anti-submarine obstructions of some kind, but there was nothing to stop enemy submarines sitting outside and firing torpedoes through the holes.[1] Also, the fleet was fully exposed to gun attack from ships out at sea. His first visit to the emergency base convinced Sir James Somerville that this was no place for his fleet.

But for the moment he had no time to dwell on its shortcomings, for hardly had his flag officers arrived on board for

[1] As, indeed, they did at a later date.

consultations than a signal came through from Ceylon that a large Japanese force had been sighted from the air 350 miles to the south-eastward, the very direction that Admiral Somerville had anticipated. The fleet had just started fuelling and could not be fully ready for sea for a good many hours; but Sir James determined to get away that night with the *Warspite*, the two carriers, and some smaller vessels, and leave the R class battleships to come on later. It was bad luck that they should have been caught like this on the wrong foot.

All night, the leading force (known as Force A) steamed east at nineteen knots, with the intention of seeking battle. Just before nine in the morning, Colombo reported being bombed. Admiral Somerville knew that the *Cornwall* and *Dorsetshire* had already been sent to sea and he signalled them a rendezvous. Reports of an enemy battleship force to the northward came through, but air reconnaissance from the carriers found nothing.

At 2 p.m., a garbled message was received from *Dorsetshire* mentioning a shadowing aircraft; and shortly afterwards Force A's radar screen showed a formation of aircraft on Dorsetshire's bearing. No other signal came through from the cruisers, and as their silence lengthened, anxiety began to be felt for their safety. This mounted steeply when an aircraft report was intercepted about an hour later of much floating wreckage and large numbers of men in the sea in roughly the cruisers' last reported position. It looked as if calamity had overtaken them; as, in fact, it had. It was learnt later that they had been attacked by a cloud of enemy carrier aircraft and that both had been sunk.

About seventy Japanese carrier planes had attacked Colombo. They bombed the shipyards and ships in harbour, though without great success. They would have done much more damage had it not been for the presence of the Hurricanes so fortunately and wisely purloined by Admiral Layton some weeks before. These were late going up, and in consequence suffered losses on the ground. But they nevertheless accounted for perhaps twenty-five of the attackers.

Out at sea, Sir James Somerville from time to time received reports of enemy formations of heavy ships but failed to get contact with them. Nor was he himself sighted, though the radar showed many traces of enemy air reconnaissance being about. The numerous enemy reports and the fate of the two cruisers were bringing it home to Sir James that his own force was in some danger, divided as it was. He therefore decided to rejoin his Force B (the R class battleships) and turned back accordingly. In fact, his previous decision to push on ahead with one battleship and two carriers only, though gallant and forceful, was distinctly rash. The events of recent months had demonstrated the possibility of a strong Japanese force being present, and for Sir James Somerville to divide his fleet was therefore basically unsound.

The junction of the two forces took place early next morning, and the whole fleet then set course to the eastward again. The Commander-in-Chief had meanwhile been undergoing a drastic revision of outlook. Though he had started off from Addu Atoll with offensive intent, he had been forced to the conclusion from the previous day's occurrences and the current intelligence reports that the Japanese fleet was much superior to his. It appeared to consist of four battleships and five carriers, with plenty of cruisers and destroyers. Sir James had five battleships, but four were old, slow, and unmodernized. He had only two carriers against five, a serious inferiority in this increasingly important and possibly decisive class of ship, made worse by the poor quality of the aircraft his own ships carried. Their obsolescent Albacores stood little chance against the Japanese Zero fighters, now known to be dangerously good machines. Admiral Somerville was gradually realizing that if it came to an engagement, he was more than likely to get the worst of it.

On shore in Ceylon, Admiral Layton was even more certain about it. Having first access to the air reconnaissance reports which came from his shore-based aircraft, he knew the composition of the Japanese naval forces in the vicinity rather better than Sir James Somerville, and was aware that, in addition to the main Japanese force off Ceylon, there was another up in the Bay of Bengal, which included at least one carrier, that was attacking shipping in that focal area. He made up his mind that the situation was desperately serious. If there were an action, he believed that Sir James Somerville's force would be destroyed; and his mind fully grasped all the ugly possibilities contingent on such an event. He also knew that the novel role of inferiority would not come naturally to any British admiral and especially one of the type of Sir James Somerville, and he determined to make it as easy for that officer as he could to take the uncongenial course of avoiding battle. Sir Geoffrey Layton had no authority over Sir James, and could not therefore give him direct orders, even had he wished to. But he made a signal to the Admiralty, which he knew Admiral Somerville would take in, that a strong Japanese force was looking for the Eastern fleet and that the latter was facing immediate annihilation.

With this vehement signal to reinforce his own reflections, Sir James Somerville decided that the risk of defeat was so great and its probable consequences so damaging to the Allied prospects that it was now his painful duty to make the preservation of his fleet his primary object. But there was one secondary consideration he would not abandon. Like Sir Richard Grenville who refused to desert his men 'lying sick ashore', Sir James Somerville had not forgotten the survivors of the *Cornwall* and *Dorsetshire* whom he knew to be in the water away to the eastward. After discussing the matter with his staff, Sir James came to the conclusion that instead of following the obvious way of escape by bolting to the westward, he might put the enemy off the scent and at the same time achieve his subsidiary object of rescuing the cruiser survivors by taking the very unlikely course of steering eastward towards them. This he did, sending on ahead the cruiser *Enterprise* and two destroyers to start the rescue work. This calculated boldness was completely successful. The rescue ships rejoined the fleet with 1,200 survivors, who had been on rafts and boats or just floating in the water by their lifebelts for thirty hours. Nor was the fleet sighted by enemy aircraft, though all day long air reconnaissance tracks on the radar screen showed the enemy searching to the westward for the fleet's position. For the Admiral, his staff, and the senior officers of the fleet it was an extremely anxious day.

That night the fleet turned west; and by next morning, April 7th, the Admiralty had evidently decided that the Eastern fleet was in a perilous position, for it signalled that ships must not go to Ceylon as being too exposed to air attack. It also suggested that the R class battleships should proceed to East Africa. This was practically telling the Commander-in-Chief that he was too weak to engage the present enemy. Sir James decided that a general retirement was unavoidable, though he must first fuel at Addu Atoll in spite of reports of enemy submarines hanging around it. But where he was then to go was a problem to which he and his chief of staff found it hard to find an answer. Ceylon was Admiralty barred, Bombay was too small, and Addu Atoll too dangerous. They were eventually reduced to studying a pocket atlas of the Indian Ocean in search of inspiration. From this source, the choice came to lie between the entrance to the Persian Gulf and Mombasa in East Africa, and the final winner was Mombasa.

Thither Force B departed on April 9th. Sir James Somerville intended, disregarding the Admiralty's prohibition, to make a swift visit to Colombo with Force A for an urgent meeting with Sir Geoffrey Layton. But on the way thither he heard that there had been a carrier-borne raid on Trincomalee. It was also learnt that the *Hermes* had been hustled out to sea without any fighter aircraft when the raid warning was first obtained. She was therefore defenceless when discovered by the Japanese carrier planes and fell an easy victim to them, together with the destroyer *Vampire*, which had gone out with her. They would have been better off under the air umbrella inside Trincomalee; where also, if they were sunk, most of their crews could have been saved. The surviving Hurricanes went up again, and once again accounted for a substantial number of Japanese. A little later that day, Sir James Somerville received a report of four enemy carriers and other heavy ships off the east coast of Ceylon coming south. This decided him to abandon his projected visit to Colombo, and he steered instead for Bombay.

Fateful issues had been at stake during the previous five days. Had Sir James Somerville's force been sighted, brought to action and—as Admiral Layton feared—annihilated by the Japanese fleet, the subsequent course of the war might and probably would have been different. The moral effect of a heavy naval defeat is always impressive and in this case must have been stupendous. One British Eastern fleet had been destroyed by the Japanese in December, and Mr. Churchill has recorded that it gave him the worst shock of the war. Had a second and much larger British Eastern fleet been similarly disposed of in April, the shock not only to him but his countrymen would have been much more than twice as heavy; so severe, in fact, that Mr. Churchill's political credit could hardly have survived it. The British Minister of Defence may or may not have known on 6th April 1941, that his office, his future, and his place in history were that day waiting on the toss of a heavenly coin whether or not the many questing Japanese aircraft would catch a glimpse of the British fleet.

If fortune was against the Japanese that day, they had invited its disfavour. Centuries of naval history, and particularly British naval history, had demonstrated that the master-stroke in naval warfare is the destruction of the enemy's battle-fleet. The Japanese knew that Admiral Somerville's fleet was somewhere in the area. They had a total force of six carriers and four battleships in or near Cinghalese waters, a force so superior that the destruction of the British fleet should have been assured, had its destruction been the main object of the Japanese. But, instead, they allowed themselves to follow the secondary objects of bombing Colombo and Trincomalee and sinking merchant ships in the Bay of Bengal. It was a misuse of highly trained naval aircraft to employ them in bombing harbours whence the vital warships had departed, an error for which a heavy price was exacted by the shore-based Hurricanes in the shape of forty or fifty Japanese naval planes shot down. The attack on Pearl Harbour by naval aircraft was sound strategy because the American fleet was inside. The attack on Colombo and Trincomalee was bad strategy because the British fleet was at sea. The minor successes of bagging the *Cornwall*, *Dorsetshire* and *Hermes* did not compensate for the major mistake of missing the main fleet through failure to concentrate on its discovery and destruction from the start.

On the British side, all pretence of disputing the control of the eastern side of the Indian Ocean was now abandoned. The R class battleships went off to Kilindini harbour near Mombasa, and though Force A[1] made an occasional visit to Ceylon and spent much time at sea between it and Africa, it was recognized that if the Japanese chose to send an amphibious expedition to seize Ceylon or make a landing on the coasts of India, the Eastern fleet could not stop it.

Thus was once again exposed, as history had often recorded before, the futility of the 'fleet in being' theory. An inferior fleet in being might conceivably have a certain value in very special circumstances, but hardly in open sea warfare. In the ordinary way, an inferior fleet cannot artempt to interfere wirh the operations of a superior without becoming liable to destruction, as Sir James Somerville found on this occasion. For general purposes, there is no escape from the old rule of 'superiority at the decisive point'. This rule had stood the British Navy in good stead in past times, and the present endeavour to ignore it had been swiftly disillusioning.

On April 11th, the Commander-in-Chief, Ceylon, sent a signal that the enemy had withdrawn; and another one next day that they had apparently returned to Singapore. The great question remained, what would they do next? Would they return? Would there be a seizure of Ceylon, which it was now clear could not be prevented? If Ceylon went, the Japanese would have two naval bases in mid-Indian Ocean. Should their strategy be pointed westward, they would probably have designs on another base over by the African coast. Following on the precedent of Indo-China, French Madagascar with its good harbour of Diego Suarez stood out as their likeliest choice. The British Government determined to get there first,.if it could.

A week passed without further enemy activity. In the middle of the following week, the Admiralty signalled that it expected the next Japanese attack would be against Ceylon. British pre-

---

[1] Less *Formidable*, who had stripped a gear box.

parations for the seizure of Diego Suarez were being hurried forward as far as possible, but it would be some days before the operation could be started. More days went by and still the Japanese made no reappearance; and on May 5th the British descent on Madagascar took place and was brought to a successful conclusion in three days. There was no enemy reaction. If the Japanese were intending to dominate the whole of the Indian Ocean, they could be expected to have shown their hand by now. But at this very time things were happening 6,000 miles away to the eastward.

CHAPTER THIRTEEN

The Coral Sea Battle, May 1942

*

The Japanese were on the move again; but fortunately it was not to the westward. Their next serious objectives were in the Pacific instead of the Indian Ocean. The bombing of Ceylon and the raid on shipping in the Bay of Bengal were apparently no more than demonstrations meant to give the British something to think about and keep them quiet while other business was proceeding elsewhere.

Much as the Japanese had already gained in the Pacific, their programme of expansion was still incomplete. Indeed, this programme was expanding as it went along. The astonishing success and small cost of their high-speed conquest of the bulk of the British, Dutch, and American possessions in the south-west Pacific had given them the urge to press on to further triumphs while the going was good. Gazing victoriously over the whole spread of the Pacific Ocean, the Japanese High Command decided to drive onwards over a wide arc from north-east to south-east.

With the exception of the tiny acreage on Bataan where the Americans were still holding out, the Japanese now possessed an unbroken chain of islands from the northernmost of the Kuriles off the tip of Kamchatka, down through the Japanese main islands, the Ryukus, Formosa, the Philippines, to Borneo and the former Dutch Indies. They were also established at Rabaul in new Britain, on the island of Bougainville in the Solomons, and on the north side of Papua, the south-east spur of New Guinea. On the southern side of Papua lay the excellent harbour of Port Moresby, an Australian naval and air base which looked out over the Coral Sea towards the north-east coast of Australia. The Japanese had been trying to reach it overland from the north coast, but jungle and the intervening mountain ridge had defeated that attempt.

In Australia and New Zealand, there was, as has already been mentioned, the tensest anxiety as the Japanese came steadily closer. These countries had lived for many years in the belief that the British fleet would keep them safe against external menace. Now, when the time had come, they found to their enormous consternation that the British fleet had failed them, and they were left virtually defenceless before a ferocious enemy pouring southward with extraordinary speed. But help came from another quarter. The Americans sent troops, ships, and aircraft, and in March General MacArthur arrived in command.

The Japanese were well aware of this American move. Their present programme of expansion envisaged an extension of the above-mentioned island chain at both its extremities. In the south-east, they proposed to capture Port Moresby from the sea, since they could not do so overland, and then push on through the Solomons to occupy New Caledonia, the Fijis and Samoa. This, they hoped, would sever the line of communication between the United States and Australia, and leave the latter Continent at their mercy should they later want to invade it.

In the north-east, almost as an extension of the Japanese Kuriles, were the American-owned Aleutian Islands, which ran in a convex curve across the top of the Pacific right up to the coast of Alaska. These chilly, gale-swept, fog-bound, and mostly mountainous islands formed a series of natural stepping-stones between Asia and America—or so at least they looked on the map. But their strategic significance depended on their physical accessibility and value for sea- and air-base purposes; and not all of them came up to specification in this respect. The Americans, however, had a fairly good base at Dutch Harbour at the eastern end of the chain. The Japanese were now intending to seize one or two of the more westerly of the islands, partly to give themselves jumping-off bases in case of a further easterly move in the future and partly to deny them to the Americans, who might conceivably use them for bombing Japan.

When the Japanese had got what they wanted here and in the southern islands, they would possess a continuous line of islands running in an immense curve from the far north-east past the east coasts of Siberia, north and south China, Indo-China and Malaya to the far south-east beyond Australia and New Zealand. But this was not enough for them. Inside this huge crescent were a multitude of smaller islands, many of them typical coral formations. Some, indeed most, of them were divisible into recognized groups, of which those known by the names Caroline, Marshall, Palau, Mariana and Bonin were the nearest to Japan and had been in Japanese possession since 1919; while the Gilbert group south-east of the Marshalls had just been captured from the British. But there were also single islands scattered here and there over the Pacific, too isolated to be included in a definite group, one of which, Wake Island, north of the Marshalls, had been seized from the Americans in December. Many of these small islands, whether in a group or not, were possible sea and air bases, and since they filled up the space inside the main crescent, it was the Japanese policy to use them wherever desirable for the construction of a screen of defensive positions far out in the Pacific. It was hoped that these screening islands, if given suitable military and air garrisons, would in conjunction with the Japanese Navy keep the enemy well away from the Co-prosperity Sphere for long enough time for its consolidation.

The next group eastward of Wake Island, mentioned above, were the Hawaiian Islands, still in American hands and containing the major naval base of Pearl Harbour, where the American Pacific fleet had received that crippling blow on December 7th. At the western end of this group—or the end nearest to Japan— was a coral island known as Midway. On this island the Japanese had their eye. With its capture, they would have a footing in the next group towards America, along which group their outer defensive perimeter might perhaps be extended if matters continued to go well with Japanese arms.

Grandiose as was this Japanese programme in the Pacific, it had two weaknesses. So enormously long a defence line, stretching right up and down the Pacific Ocean, would be highly vulnerable to piecemeal breaching from outside. Moreover, the programme itself was essentially defensive and its pursuit involved the discarding of the offensive opportunities now offering in the Indian Ocean.

What risk there was in a westward offensive did not lie in the Indian Ocean itself, where the Japanese, if they deployed naval forces well within their means, could probably eliminate the British Eastern fleet without much difficulty and thereafter utilize that Ocean at their pleasure. The deterrent was the American fleet in the Pacific, which was now beginning to recover from Pearl Harbour. Sporadic attacks by American carrier Task Forces were already being made on some of the conquered Japanese islands and the Doolittle raid on Tokyo had just taken place. It was natural for the Japanese to feel anxious about such American activities in their own Pacific Ocean and to wish to have their main naval forces at hand to deal with them.

Nevertheless, if the Japanese could have brought themselves to take some chances in the Pacific, an offensive to the westward might have paid them the greater ultimate dividend. The destruction of the British Eastern fleet under Sir James Somerville and the strategical harvest that could have been reaped therefrom could either have knocked Britain out of the war or have forced the United States to send its remaining naval forces eastabout to restore the situation in the Indian Ocean, thus relieving the Japanese from the hostile attentions of those forces in the Pacific. The security of the Co-Prosperity Sphere might thus have been better achieved by attacking the British enemy where he was weak than by attempting to erect a maritime Maginot Line against the American foe in the Pacific.

Admiral Yamamoto, the Japanese naval Commander-in-Chief, was aware of the basic weakness of his Government's Pacific programme and wished to include in it an offensive element. As we shall see in the next chapter, he proposed to utilize the projected attack on Midway, scheduled to take place in

June, as a means of provoking a battle with the American fleet. He realized that Japanese security could not be guaranteed by an island defence line, however far distant, but only by maintaining a Japanese naval supremacy over the American fleet. This might or might not be possible as a permanency; but the longer it could be continued the better the chances of the consolidation and survival of the Co-Prosperity Sphere. Periodic battles of attrition by which America's growing naval strength could be pared down were necessary for this purpose, and Yamamoto proposed that the Midway operations should provide one such occasion.

First in order of time, however, was to be the seaborne attack on Port Moresby in New Guinea, with which was to be coupled the occupation of Tulagi in the Solomons close to Guadalcanal. These twin operations were planned by the Japanese to take place early in May, and preparations for them were actively in progress in Rabaul from the latter part of April.

By the cracking of Japanese cypher signals, the Americans were able to get advance warning of what was afoot and were thus able to take timely counter-measures. The British had done the same to German signals in the early part of the previous war and so had managed to have intercepting forces at sea when German naval sorties were taking place. It is naturally an immense advantage to know more or less what your enemy is about to do before he does it. The Americans did not learn the whole Japanese plan. But they did know by April 17th that a Japanese expedition would enter the Coral Sea in the first days of May escorted by one light and two large carriers, with cruisers and destroyers also present.

To meet this threat, Admiral Nimitz, the new American Commander-in-Chief in the Pacific, organized an Allied force for the Coral Sea to consist of the carriers *Lexington* and *Yorktown*, accompanied by five American cruisers plus one American and two Australian cruisers which were to be brought up from Sydney by Rear-Admiral J. G. Crace, R.N., who was to command the whole eight after the junction. The overall commander of the combined force, which also included destroyers, oilers and other auxiliaries, was to be Rear-Admiral F. J. Fletcher, U.S.N., with his flag in the *Yorktown*. They were all to be in the Coral Sea by May 1st. In addition, there were shore-based aircraft available at Port Moresby, and at Townsville and other places in Australia, but these were under the command of General MacArthur.

The principal Japanese naval forces consisted of a striking force made up of a carrier group under Rear-Admiral Hara, consisting of the large carriers *Shokaku* and *Zuikaku*, just returned from the Indian Ocean, plus two heavy cruisers under Vice-Admiral Takagi. There were also two close support groups for the convoys, one composed of the light carrier *Shoho* and four heavy cruisers under Rear-Admiral Goto, and the other of one seaplane carrier, two light cruisers, and four gun-boats. These were in addition to destroyers and auxiliaries.

At 8 a.m. on May 3rd, the Japanese Tulagi expedition, sailing from Rabaul, arrived off the beaches and started to disembark. This becoming known to the Americans by aerial observation, there ensued several days of intermittent fighting (known later as the battle of the Coral Sea) which marked the first clash in history between rival carrier forces. Possibly for that reason, the operations are hardly to be regarded as models of their kind for either side.

When the two American carriers had met on May 1st, Rear-Admiral Fletcher had ordered the combined force to complete with fuel. This was apparently expected to take four days, but Admiral Fletcher's *Yorktown* finished oiling on May 2nd. Receiving news that enemy forces might be on the move, the Admiral thereupon took his *Yorktown* Task Force off westward in order to carry out air searches; which resulted next morning in his being 100 miles distant from Admiral Fitch's *Lexington* group and the latter not knowing where the *Yorktown* was.[1]

It was not till the evening that Fletcher received a shore-based air report of the landing at Tulagi, upon which he started off northward with a view to attacking next morning with *York-*

---

[1] Each carrier, with attendant cruisers or destroyers, formed a separate Task Force. Rear-Admiral Fitch commanded the *Lexington* T.F.

town alone. He had known from previous intelligence that the Japanese would probably have one light and two large carriers in support of their operations, so that by advancing to the attack with the *Yorktown* without waiting to pick up the *Lexington*, he was taking a fair amount of risk. But the two big Japanese carriers were at this time out of reach to the north of Bougainville Island; a strange covering position, seeing that any American interference would almost certainly come from the southward. Goto's light carrier and cruisers had accompanied the transports to Tulagi, but had started back for Rabaul the same day, so that when Fletcher arrived within striking distance the next morning, he found no air opposition.

The *Yorktown* flew off a strong force of dive-bombers and torpedo planes shortly after dawn from about 100 miles to seaward. When these reached the Japanese landing area, they found two enemy destroyers but otherwise only minesweepers and other auxiliary warships. The American airmen mistook them, however, for more important vessels. The human instinct to exaggerate danger makes such false identification a very common mistake in war. The first sightings at Jutland were between British light cruisers and German destroyers. The Germans in their wireless reports promoted their opponent vessels to armoured cruisers, while the British stepped the enemy destroyers up to light cruisers. Airmen are naturally even more prone to such nautical enlargement than professional sailors who live in closer contact with warship classes. The Japanese airmen, as we have seen in Chapter 11, behaved thus in the Java Sea.

The minor Japanese vessels found at Tulagi were subjected to a series of heavy air attacks lasting nearly all day. Seventy-six half-ton bombs were dropped and twenty-three torpedoes, but the total bag was one destroyer damaged and beached, three minesweepers, a patrol craft, and four landing barges sunk. The Americans fancied they had disposed of a light cruiser, three destroyers, a seaplane-carrier, and four gun-boats. Three American aircraft were lost.

This prolonged aerial bombardment obviously gave away the proximity of an American carrier force, and rendered desirable the early reinforcement of *Yorktown* by *Lexington*, the latter having finished oiling the day before. But for some reason, Rear-Admiral Fitch steamed south-east during the day, thereby increasing his distance from *Yorktown* to the north of him. The Japanese large carriers, as soon as they heard the news of *Yorktown's* attack, hurried south towards Tulagi, but had not quite got within striking distance by nightfall. Their faulty positioning on the wrong side of Tulagi had lost them the opportunity of dealing with the American carriers in detail.

Admiral Fletcher took the *Yorktown* south during the night and met the *Lexington* and her group next morning. The next two days (May 5th and 6th) were spent in fuelling by both sides, but reports of the sailing of the Port Moresby invasion force continued to reach the American Commander; and on the evening of the 6th, Fletcher set the course of the fleet north-west to reach an intercepting position. He did not then know that the Japanese carriers had entered the Coral Sea and had actually got to within seventy miles of him. Nor were the enemy carriers aware of the proximity of the Americans. As both sets of carriers fuelled at different times during the 6th within easy striking distance of each other, it was as well for the peace of mind of the respective commanders that they remained in ignorance of each other's whereabouts. On completion of his own oiling and before proceeding north-west for the night, Admiral Fletcher ordered his oiler *Neosho* with her attendant destroyer *Sims* to proceed to the next fuelling rendezvous about 100 miles to the southward, which they reached early next morning.

At daylight on May 7th, Admiral Fletcher's force was a little over 100 miles due south of Rossel Island. About 200 miles due east of him were the two Japanese large carriers, intending to come north-west to cover the Moresby expedition that Fletcher's force, unknown to the Japanese, was proposing to attack. Before setting off, however, the Japanese carrier admiral thought he would search to the southward in case any American carriers were in that direction. The search planes went off, and an hour and a half later there came from them a most welcome signal that one carrier and a cruiser were in sight. This was a stroke of luck, and Rear-Admiral Hara gave orders for an immediate strike.

The Japanese airmen had, however, imitated the behaviour of their American opposite numbers of four days before at Tulagi in viewing the enemy below them through a mental magnifying-glass. The carrier and cruiser were none other than the oiler *Neosho* and the destroyer *Sims*. At intervals during the next four

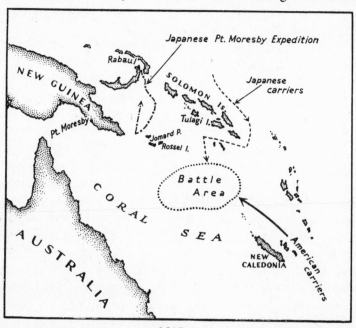

MAP 5

hours, death and destruction rained down from the skies on the wretched pair. Never realizing the mistake they were making, the Japanese bombers made attack after attack against the almost defenceless ships. The *Sims* was hit in the middle and sunk in two halves. But though sorely smitten and helplessly drifting, the *Neosho* remained afloat for four days until the surviving members of her crew were taken off and she herself was sunk by an American destroyer.

While the make-believe American carrier was being shattered by the Japanese, Admiral Fletcher's aircraft were busy with a real carrier further north. In the early morning, the Admiral had ordered Rear-Admiral Crace's cruisers to press on ahead to try to destroy the Port Moresby expedition, estimated to be about to enter the Coral Sea through the Jomard passage. Fletcher wished to keep his own carriers for possible action against the Japanese carriers, whose position he did not yet know.

It will be convenient at this point to follow the fortunes of Crace's cruiser force. This sped on north-westward and was duly sighted by enemy airmen. Its appearance and evident purpose caused such anxiety to the Japanese Commander-in-Chief that he ordered the Port Moresby expedition to turn round and come northward again. The Crace force itself soon came under repeated heavy bombing and torpedo attacks by Japanese shore-based aircraft, but fortunately without being hit. A gratuitous final infliction was an attack, also unavailing, by three of General MacArthur's shore-based Army bombers. The Japanese paper score in these attacks was one battleship and one heavy cruiser sunk, and one battleship torpedoed. That of the American Army bombers, one cruiser hit. After sweeping north-westward all day and half the night without sighting the enemy, Crace retired southwards.

Having sent Crace's cruisers off on their separate mission, Admiral Fletcher decided to carry out an air search. At 8.15 a.m. an exciting report came in from a *Yorktown* plane of two carriers and four heavy cruisers a little over 200 miles to the north-north-eastward. This was evidently the Japanese main striking force, and preparations were at once made for a full-scale attack by the aircraft of both American carriers. By 10.30 a.m., 93 planes were in the air and starting off for the reported enemy.

It was, as the reader may by now have come to expect, not the main Japanese carrier force at all. Instead, it was a small support group of two old light cruisers and a few gunboats. This time the mistake was a double one. Just as Admiral Fletcher's striking force was disappearing into the distance, the reconnaissance aircraft that had sent the reporting signal arrived back in the carrier, when it was discovered that the coding of the signal had given a wrong composition to the enemy, which was meant to be described as two heavy cruisers and two destroyers, but was in reality the smaller classes mentioned above. Admiral Fletcher therefore realized to his embarrassment that the main Japanese carriers were somewhere else and that he would have nothing to attack them with for some time.

The mass of American air power flew onward and eventually attacked a different target still. It was lucky enough to come across Rear-Admiral Goto's covering force of the light carrier *Shoho* and four heavy cruisers. Here, at all events, was a carrier of some sort, and the American airmen swooped down on her from all directions. There was no avoiding such a multitudinous onslaught. Hit time after time by bombs and torpedoes, the *Shoho* lasted but a few minutes before she sank.

The American carriers had actually been shadowed for some time before their striking force flew off; but fortunately they had not been attacked before their aircraft had got back and refuelled. Should the latter now be used to locate and attack the main Japanese carrier force? Though it was hardly 3 p.m., Admiral Fletcher decided not. He would wait till the morning.

In the Japanese carriers, however, Rear-Admiral Hara was more enterprising. He sent off a bomber and torpedo plane force to find and attack the American carriers. In the circumstances, luck should have been with them; but the perverse lady turned her face the other way. The aircraft did not find the American carriers, but passed near enough for the American fighters to have a brush with them and shoot down nine. A further eleven Japanese aircraft were lost in night landing.

The following morning of May 8th found all combatants out of the ring except the two heavy-weights, who were intent on getting at each other. The American carriers had one great advantage in that they possessed radar, which the Japanese did not yet have. This technical asset gave the Americans warning of the approach of hostile aircraft while they were still fifty miles or more away, whereas the Japanese had to rely on visual sighting. The Americans could also direct their fighters by radar on to the enemy, while the Japanese could not.

The Coral Sea Battle, May 1942

Both sides sent off early morning searches, and the striking forces followed in due course at much the same intervals. Of the American attackers, the *Lexington's* aircraft had some difficulty in finding the enemy and the bulk of her dive-bombers failed to do so altogether. All *Yorktown's* aircraft got in their attacks, but without great success. The torpedoes were dropped from too far off and all missed. But the dive-bombers secured two hits on the *Shokaku*, neither of them serious except that the flight deck was so damaged forward that the ship could no longer fly off aircraft, though she could recover them. The *Lexington's* torpedo planes with four dive-bombers came in just after the *Yorktown* attack and also made for *Shokaku*. These torpedoes were likewise long shots and also made misses. One more bomb hit was obtained, but the damage was moderate. As, however, *Shokaku* could not now operate aircraft, Admiral Hara detached her to return to Japan for repairs, and her aircraft eventually landed on *Zuikaku*.

While this was going on, the Japanese aircraft were giving their attentions to the *Yorktown* and *Lexington*. Radar warning was received by the American carriers just before 11 a.m. and the ships went on to high speed and sent up more fighters. In a few minutes, the Japanese aircraft came roaring in to the attack. As they had done against the *Prince of Wales* and *Repulse*, their torpedo planes flew in on the *Lexington* from more than one direction and pressed close home before releasing their torpedoes. Avoidance was thus rendered most difficult and the *Lexington* was hit twice on the port side. A simultaneous attack developed from Japanese dive-bombers, and amid the rising screams of their approach, the barking of the anti-aircraft guns, the piercing wail of the ship's siren which had jammed on, and the roar of torpedo explosions, two bombs found their mark.

The *Yorktown* was undergoing a similar ordeal but was more fortunate. Torpedoes were dropped on one side only and were all avoided. From the dive-bombers she received one hit which, though it went deep into the ship and killed many men, did no great structural damage.

Surprisingly, no attempt was made by either side to repeat

the attacks. This may possibly have been due to the optimistic stories brought back by the airmen of what they had done. Admiral Hara was apparently led to believe that both American carriers were under water, and Fletcher was told that one Japanese carrier was settling fast. Still, there was the other; and in any case, a liberal allowance is needed in air warfare for enthusiastic over-reporting.

As it was, fortune worked in the Japanese carrier commander's favour. The torpedo hits on the *Lexington* had caused an escape of petrol fumes. About an hour after the action was over, these somehow became ignited and a terrific internal explosion occurred. From that moment the ship was doomed. Enveloped in smoke and flames and with further explosions going off every now and then, it became evident that despite every effort of the ship's company and assistance from other ships she could not be saved. After some hours, she was abandoned and she sank just after nightfall.

The first carrier duel in history thus ended to the advantage of the Japanese. Of the two large carriers on either side, one American had been sunk and one slightly damaged against one more seriously damaged and one untouched.

While the fighting was in progress, two other American carriers, *Hornet* and *Enterprise*, had been speeding down towards the Coral Sea to reinforce the *Yorktown* and *Lexington*. But after news of the ending of the battle had reached the American Commander-in-Chief at Pearl Harbour, they were recalled. These two reinforcing carriers had just returned from the raid on Tokyo, and could not have been sent earlier. Had they not gone to Tokyo, where they had no military effect on the war, but been sent instead to the Coral Sea, they could probably have converted an American reverse into a Japanese annihilation.

As well as recalling the *Hornet* and *Enterprise*, Admiral Nimitz ordered the *Yorktown* to make all haste back to Pearl Harbour and repairs. He had information about a coming Japanese attack on Midway Island, to be backed by the enemy main fleet, and he wanted as many ships as possible to be ready to meet it.

The Coral Sea Battle, May 1942

Yorktown took eighteen days to cover the 3,500 miles to Pearl Harbour, arriving there on May 27th. Admiral Fitch estimated that her damage from bomb and near misses would take three months to make good. But Admiral Nimitz, like Lord St. Vincent after the battle of the Nile, had other ideas. He had reason to fear that the next Japanese attack was coming within about a week and he would allow *Yorktown* no more than two days to be got ready. As she arrived, she went straight into dock, and swarms of workmen poured on board. Working continuous shifts they had patched up her injuries and she was afloat again in forty-six hours. It was a fine effort, and it was just as well it was made.

CHAPTER FOURTEEN

The Battle of Midway

*

'When contemplating battle,' said Napoleon, 'it is the rule to concentrate all your forces and neglect none. One battalion often decides the day.' Admiral Yamamoto was contemplating battle with the American fleet, and very sensibly. No amount of defensive outposts would keep Japan permanently safe unless the American fleet could be kept down to an inferiority. Half of its battleships had been put out of action for longer or shorter periods in the previous December. But there was still the other half and there were all the carriers, which latter had escaped the Pearl Harbour holocaust through being at sea. If Yamamoto could force a battle on the Americans, he might be able to destroy more American ships. Then, perhaps, he would be strong enough to stifle the construction and assembly of others by carrier raids on the American west coast shipyards and the Panama Canal, and thus ensure that the Pacific remained a Japanese lake; for an attack east-about from the Atlantic would be a very difficult operation for the Americans now that Singapore had fallen. Admiral Yamamoto's desire for a naval action was sound.

There was good prospect of success. Under cover of their extreme peace-time secrecy, the Japanese had gambled heavily on the ascendency of the aircraft-carrier and had built themselves ten of these ships by 1941, whereas the Americans had only. seven, of which there were, in early 1942, only five in the Pacific.[1] There was therefore a good chance of Admiral Yamamoto being

[1] The recent loss of the *Lexington* had reduced this to four, and of these four *Saratoga* was in dockyard hands till the end of May.

able to eliminate the American carriers in battle, provided of course that he observed the Napoleonic maxim mentioned at the head of this chapter. There was every reason for him to do so. American resources in shipbuilding, engineering, and raw materials were greatly in excess of the Japanese, and if given time the Americans could undoubtedly redress the setback of Pearl Harbour and build up a naval strength that the Japanese could not hope to match. Japan's survival depended on her making the very utmost use of her temporary opportunity.

It is therefore strange that Yamamoto or the Japanese Admiralty should have given so little heed to the principle of concentration for the decisive operation. A month before the selected time, three of the all-important Japanese carriers, two large and one light, had been used for the support of the Port Moresby invasion, which enterprise could perfectly well have waited till later and which in the event was not successful. The result was that the one light carrier was sunk, one large carrier too badly damaged to be ready for the Midway affair, and the other, though she escaped direct hits, was not ready either.

Midway Island was a good choice of objective for the contemplated operations. It was a desirable acquisition for its own sake, the Americans having done much to make it attractive. They had cut a channel into the central lagoon. They had built an airfield, gun defences, a wireless station and the requisite housing and recreational amenities. It was, in fact, a ready-made air and submarine base, and since it was 1,000 miles beyond Wake Island, the farthest-out Japanese base in the north-central Pacific, it would be useful in both capacities. To the Americans, it was valuable as a covering outpost for Pearl Harbour, and a threat to it could be expected to draw their fleet out to its succour. Its seizure should therefore satisfy both the two Japanese objects of extending their defensive perimeter and bringing on an action with the American fleet.

The plan was to send against Midway an invasion force of troops, covered and escorted by two battleships, a light carrier, eight cruisers, destroyers, minesweepers and other ancillary vessels. Operating separately from the invasion force, there was to be a Carrier Striking Force under Vice-Admiral Nagumo of four carriers plus attendant battleships, cruisers and destroyers, intended to give the main punishment to the American fleet, if it could be brought to battle. Some way behind the carriers would be the Commander-in-Chief with the three latest battleships, including the new *Yamato*, the largest warship in the world, mounting 18-inch guns. These latter were to have a light carrier and destroyers with them.

The chief blow against the American fleet, should it appear, was thus to come from four large carriers. As this was not the full number of carriers available to the Japanese at this moment, where were the others? The large carrier *Zuikaku* had recently returned from the Coral Sea operations, in which it had received no hits. It should therefore have been as ready as the *Yorktown*; more ready. But for some reason it did not sail with the remainder. The light carrier *Zuiho* was accompanying the invasion convoy. The light carrier *Hosho* was with the main battleship force.

Two other light carriers, the *Ryujo* and *Junyo*, had been allocated to a diversionary operation in the north. This was an attack on certain of the Aleutian Islands. The plan, in brief, was to make a bombing attack on the American base at Dutch Harbour on June 3rd, the day before the assault on Midway Island, in the hope of drawing American carrier forces away from the latter and thus facilitating its capture; though any expectations of this kind were actually nullified by an Intelligence leakage which reached the Americans that Midway was the main enemy objective. There was also to be a seizure of the Aleutian Islands of Kiska, Addu and Atok. But even had the Americans obtained no hint of coming events, the division of the Japanese carrier strength between the Aleutians and Midway was a source of weakness, since any American carriers that were drawn off temporarily towards Dutch Harbour could be expected to return hotfoot towards Midway as soon as the attack on the latter developed.

It would therefore have been quite possible for the Japanese to have augmented their carrier striking force at Midway by at

11. Admiral Sir Geoffrey Layton

12. Air Chief Marshal Sir Robert Brooke-Popham (left) and General Sir Archibald Wavell

least four light carriers, and they committed a serious blunder in not doing so. They may have thought they had sunk both *Lexington* and *Yorktown* in the Coral Sea, but they did not know. It was therefore prudent to allow for at least one of these to be available a month later, as in fact one was. There was also the carrier *Saratoga*, recently under modernization on the west coast of America, which for all the Japanese could tell, might now be at sea—and *was* at sea while the Midway operations were in progress.[1] Hence it was a reasonable assumption that four American carriers might be encountered, if not more than four. But whether two, three, four or five, it was to the surpassing interest of the Japanese on this crucial occasion to present as great a superiority in this class of ship as they could; and by raking in every such vessel able to operate they could have produced four to five large and four light carriers to set against a hypothetical four and actual three large Americans. The consequences of the Japanese failure to observe the principle of concentration at the decisive point we shall see.

As at Coral Sea, the American high command had warning from decyphered signals of the enemy's intentions, and so could prepare the necessary counter-measures. The defences of Midway Island were stepped up, extra aircraft sent there, and troops and supplies poured in. With advance knowledge of the date of the attack, the fleet could also be got into a suitable position at the right time. In this way, there was good reason to hope that the inestimable benefit of surprise might be stolen from the Japanese and enjoyed by the Americans. It would be difficult to exaggerate the value to the latter of the Japanese backwardness in cypher technique.

The various Japanese forces left their different bases during the last week of May, and began their long steam to their allotted areas of operation. The Japanese did not suspect that the other side had wind of their intentions and assumed that they would have a day or two to capture Midway Island before the news of their appearance brought an American fleet to the scene. The

---

[1] She was on the way to join the main American carrier force, but was not in time.

first duty therefore assigned to Nagumo's carriers was to carry out air bombardments of Midway Island with a view to beating down the local American air power and smashing up the airfield and other defences.

Apart from submarines, which both sides had placed where they thought was most useful, the American naval Commander-in-Chief was relying solely on his carriers for dealing with the

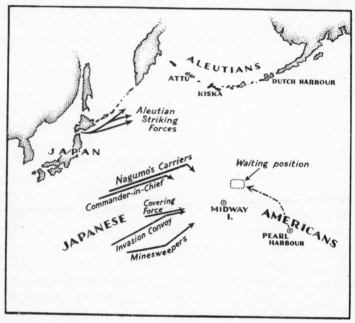

MAP 6

oncoming enemy. Though some of the battleships damaged at Pearl Harbour were now repaired, he deliberately left them behind. The American carriers were organized into two groups, each with a guard of cruisers and destroyers. One group (Task Force 16) contained the carriers *Hornet* and *Enterprise* under Rear-Admiral R. A. Spruance. The other (Task Force 17) had the *Yorktown*, flying the flag of Rear-Admiral Fletcher, back from the Coral Sea, who was in overall command of both groups.

On June 2nd, the American carriers reached a position about

300 miles north-easterly from Midway Island, the various Japanese forces then being rather more than half-way to Midway. The Japanese transports with their escorting warships and the minesweepers were approaching the island from the south-west. Six hundred miles to the north of them was Nagumo's carrier group, steering north-east well clear of Midway and meaning to make its final approach on a south-easterly course. In between but behind (or west) of the carriers was Admiral Yamamoto with his battleships.

The Americans, fully on the alert, were sending out shore-based air searches from Midway far to the westward towards the approaching enemy. The first sighting was made about 9 a.m. on June 3rd, when a Midway aircraft sighted the invasion convoy approaching from the south-west. The officer in command at Midway Island at once ordered a bombing attack by nine Army aircraft. They found the Japanese invasion group in the late afternoon and dropped their bombs without hitting, but came back to report having damaged two battleships or heavy cruisers and two transports. Next, four Catalinas (Navy sea-planes) made a moonlight attack with torpedoes in the early hours of June 4th and hit an oiler, but she kept her place in her group.

Admiral Fletcher had naturally been given these enemy reports. His previous Intelligence information had been that Nagumo's carriers would send in a bombing attack against Midway at dawn on June 4th from a position north-west of the island. Fletcher therefore decided to move in towards Midway to be nearer the probable position of the enemy. He meant to try for a strike at the Japanese carriers while their aircraft were away attacking Midway. Accordingly, during the night he steamed towards the island from the north-east. Nagumo, whose programme was exactly what Fletcher believed it to be, was approaching it from the north-west.

At first light on June 4th, and when about 240 miles from Midway, Admiral Nagumo sent off his island attacking force of 36 bombers and 36 dive-bombers with an escort of 36 fighters. This mass of aircraft was picked up by the Midway radar while nearly 100 miles distant and all preparations were made to receive it. Bombers were got into the air and told to fly clear, and the 20 Brewster Buffalo and 6 Wildcat fighters advanced to meet the incoming horde. There was an air battle out at sea, in which the Buffaloes and Wildcats, as well as being outnumbered, were seriously outclassed by the Japanese fighters, and all but two were either destroyed or heavily shot about. The Japanese aircraft swept on to Midway and delivered their attack; but though much damage was done to unimportant buildings, the airfield remained usable and the American bombers, being already in the air, were not affected.

Of these latter, 6 Navy and 4 Army planes all armed with torpedoes, had already started off to attack the enemy carriers, whose position had by now been reported by search planes. They were sighted by the Japanese carriers at about 7 a.m., who flew off extra fighters to deal with them; and nearly half the American planes were shot down before they could release. The remainder did no good, all their torpedoes going very wide. But the surviving Army planes claimed three hits and the Navy planes one.

Nagumo had just received a signal from the leader of the Midway attacking force to say that another strike was needed. When sending off the first, he had made allowance for the possible proximity of hostile carriers by retaining over ninety aircraft armed with torpedoes ready to be flown off against ship targets. By the time the above signal had come in, closely followed by the American Midway-based torpedo attack, the Japanese search planes on the look-out for enemy ships had sent in no report. Nagumo was therefore faced with a tricky decision. It would be about an hour before his attacking force against Midway would be arriving back and landing on. It would also take about an hour to re-arm his ninety reserve aircraft with bombs instead of torpedoes. If he started this latter process at once, a second striking force against Midway could just about fly off before the first got back, which would save at least an hour on using the original aircraft a second time. On the other hand, it would also mean having no anti-ship striking force for about two hours.

Nagumo made the fateful decision to risk enemy carriers being in the vicinity, and he gave orders for the squadron to re-arm the reserve aircraft with bombs. So down they went on the lifts.

A quarter of an hour later, a slightly disturbing report came in from a Japanese search plane of ten enemy ships about 170 miles to the east-north-eastward. Being without details of the classes of ship sighted, the signal was irritatingly vague. Admiral Nagumo, having just decided on one course of action, did not want to change it without good reason. Yet if perchance there were carriers in this unspecified enemy group, he might be in grave danger if he went on with his programme of another strike against Midway.

The Admiral thought about it for a quarter of an hour, obviously with increasing uneasiness. Then he began to hedge. He signalled to his carriers that the change-over from torpedoes to bombs was to be suspended for any planes that had not yet been dealt with, and he wirelessed to the search plane to ascertain and report the types of the enemy ships. The more or less reassuring reply which came in after twenty minutes was to the effect that the enemy consisted of five cruisers and five destroyers. Ten minutes later, however, a further signal was received from the search plane which must have given Admiral Nagumo an unpleasant jolt. She could now, she said, see one enemy carrier.

An hour had passed since Nagumo's change-over order had been given and the planes affected were still in the hangars. Moreover, the fly-on of the first attacking force was due to begin at any moment. In ten minutes, its planes were already circling the carriers and the direction of the wind forced Nagumo to continue on as he was for the forty minutes of the landing on. For him it must have been a period of almost insupportable anxiety. He could not range up and fly off an attacking force against the American carrier or carriers and recover his Midway aircraft at the same time. Nor could he complete this recovery without being chained to his previous course and thus making it easier for enemy aircraft to find him; and soon he had the ugly news from his search planes that American carrier aircraft in large numbers were coming in his direction. Leaden minutes dragged by while his own returning aircraft continued to come down on their carriers' decks. At last, at 9.17 a.m., the nerve-racking process was over and Nagumo immediately altered the squadron's course 90° to port. But before he could bring up a striking force on deck, a group of enemy torpedo planes came in sight.

The early search from the American carriers that morning had gone out from the *Yorktown* at 4.30 a.m. These aircraft saw nothing; but enemy reports soon began to come in from the Midway aircraft. The first was received at 6 a.m., which placed enemy carriers and battleships about 200 miles west-south-west of the American ships. As *Yorktown* had her search planes to recover, Admiral Fletcher signalled to Admiral Spruance to attack with the two other carriers.

The latter's first idea was to close in some distance on the enemy since 200 miles was too far for the torpedo planes with their radius of about 175 miles. But when the news of the Japanese strike on Midway came through shortly afterwards, it occurred to Spruance and his Chief of Staff that a chance had opened out to catch the enemy carriers when they were embarrassed with the recovery of the Midway force. Calculations suggested that from this point of view the best time of attack was round about 9 a.m., which necessitated launching at about 7 to 7.30. It meant a dangerously long fly for the torpedo planes, but it was decided they would have to take their chance.

Launching from *Hornet* and *Enterprise* began at 7 a.m. and took some time to complete. All available planes were sent, Admiral Spruance believing in the principle of the concentrated blow. Each ship sent off about 14 torpedo planes, 33 dive-bombers, and 10 fighters; a dozen or so of the latter being kept for protection of the carrier. Admiral Fletcher kept *Yorktown's* aircraft on board for nearly two hours longer and then sent off only half of them. Apparently, he did not believe in concentration.

While the carrier aircraft were flying over the sunlit sea towards their enemy, the American Midway planes were making further attacks. Just before 8 a.m., sixteen Marine Corps dive-bombers went in against the Japanese carrier *Hiryu*. They were counter-attacked by Japanese fighters, who shot down eight and damaged six others beyond repair, leaving only two fit for further action. About ten bombs were dropped but all missed. At just about 8 a.m., came fifteen Flying Fortresses for a high-level bombing attack. They believed they had obtained four hits but actually got none. They were swiftly followed by eleven Marine Corps Vindicator bombers, which likewise scored no hits. The shore-based aircraft had thus achieved nothing. What would the carrier planes do?

It was the torpedo planes that first found the enemy. Those of the *Hornet* and *Enterprise*, after separately reaching the estimated enemy position and seeing only an empty circle of sea, had to search around for some time before being rewarded with a sighting. The *Hornet's* group went in first at about 9.30 a.m. Fiercely attacked by Japanese fighters, they were shot to pieces and all destroyed. A few minutes later, those of the *Enterprise* met much the same fate. Eleven were shot down and the torpedoes of the other three all missed. A little later, the *Yorktown's* group appeared. Though starting long after the others, they had taken a shorter line towards the enemy. Only two survived and there were no hits. The torpedo attacks had been a complete failure, and the aircraft very nearly annihilated.

There remained the dive-bombers. If these had no better success than the torpedo planes, the outlook for the Americans would be black indeed.

All the *Hornet's* dive-bombers missed the enemy altogether Admiral Spruance had sent off no search planes, and no one as yet knew about Admiral Nagumo's recent turn to the northeast. Most of the American aircraft therefore flew to the calculated position of the enemy along his previous south-easterly course. Not finding him there, the *Hornet's* dive-bombers turned south-east towards Midway Island. They naturally sighted no enemy and eventually either landed on the island or fell into the sea.

There were now left only the dive-bombers of *Enterprise* and *Yorktown*. But a dramatic change of fortune was now to occur.

Both groups were successful in sighting the enemy and, by pure chance, both happened to arrive over him at practically the same moment, though they had started from their respective carriers with an hour and a half between them. Moreover, their appearance was as fortunate in its timing as in its conjunction. The last of the torpedo plane attacks, which was still in progress as the dive-bombers approached at 19,000 feet, had drawn all the Japanese fighters down to near the water-level. Being without radar, the Japanese can have had no long warning of the dive-bombers' coming, and so their fighters had no time to climb against the new menace. Altogether, these dive-bombers numbered fifty-four, and they divided their attentions between three of the Japanese carriers, the *Akagi*, the *Kaga* and the *Soryu*. Hurtling downwards and meeting practically no opposition, they loosed a cascade of bombs towards their respective targets.

All three Japanese carriers were heavily hit and burst into flames. *Akagi* was abandoned in the afternoon and sank next morning. *Kaga*, still burning, sank the same evening. *Soryu* was abandoned almost at once, but as the fires seemed to subside attempts were made to take her in tow. At about noon, however, the American submarine *Nautilus* happened to sight her. Two hours later, the submarine fired three torpedoes, all of which hit. That finished the *Soryu*, which sank before nightfall.

Almost in a flash, the Japanese carrier force had been reduced by three. Moreover, the planes of the stricken ones had gone with them. As he had hoped, Admiral Spruance had caught the Japanese refuelling and rearming. Three-quarters of the Japanese striking aircraft had been eliminated.

The one remaining Japanese carrier was the *Hiryu*, now alone against three Americans. She did her best to retrieve the situation. By 11.00 she had eighteen dive-bombers and six fighters in the air, all she had by then been able to get ready. An hour later, they were closing on the *Yorktown* just as the latter's own returned dive-bombers were waiting their turn to land on. These latter were waved away as the Japanese attack came in.

Despite the utmost endeavours of the Wildcat fighters, some of the Japanese got through and three hits were made. Fires broke out and the ship came to a stop. But the fires were got under control, and in about an hour and a half the *Yorktown* was steaming again. But not for long. The *Hiryu* had been organizing another striking force of ten torpedo planes and a few fighters, and flew it off about 1.30 p.m. An hour later, it was dashing through the *Yorktown's* fighter patrol to drop torpedoes from all round the American carrier. Two of them hit, jamming the rudder, breaching the port oil fuel tanks and causing the ship to list heavily. This time the blow was mortal. Though *Yorktown* remained afloat for more than two days, during which she received two more torpedo hits from a submarine, she finally rolled over and sank.

The *Hiryu* had got in two attacks on the *Yorktown* without being attacked herself. But her turn was now to come. Before her first attack on *Yorktown* (that is, sometime before noon), Admiral Fletcher had ordered his Flag Captain to send off a search flight to see how matters stood with the Japanese carriers. They found nothing for several hours, but at a quarter to three a report was received of one carrier, with attendant gun vessels. By this time, *Yorktown* was incapable of operating aircraft and *Hornet* was empty of both torpedo planes and dive-bombers. *Enterprise*, however, flew off twenty-four dive-bombers, of which ten were *Yorktown* survivors. They found the *Hiryu* group at 5 p.m. and, although without fighter escort, broke through the defence and scored four hits. Severe damage was inflicted on the Japanese carrier. Fires broke out which could not be controlled, and she sank early next morning.

The Japanese carrier squadron which was to have inflicted further losses on the American fleet had been wiped out. Too late, Admiral Yamamoto began to regret the dispersion of his air power between Midway and the Aleutians. He signalled for the light carriers *Ryujo* and *Junyo* in the latter area to come over to Midway at high speed; but they were a long way away and could not arrive under about two days. Had they been present from the start, they could well have turned the scale against the American carriers; for though there were two of these intact after all four of the large Japanese carriers had been knocked out, their combined surviving aircraft totalled only 3 torpedo planes and 43 dive-bombers or less than the 50-odd mixed torpedo planes and dive-bombers that represented one American carrier's complement of aircraft when the battle started. Moreover, some of the American 46 were damaged and all the aircrews were weary.

Then there were the light carriers *Zuiho* (with the transport force) and the *Hosho* (with the battleships) which together with the *Ryujo* and *Junyo* would have made four. There was also the large carrier *Zuikaku*, which was at sea two or three days later and could probably, on the example of the *Yorktown*, have been at sea two or three days earlier. Had Admiral Yamamoto kept in mind a modernized naval version of Napoleon's dictum to the effect that 'one light carrier often decides the day', the critical battle of June 4th would probably have ended with his triumph.

He made the further mistake of pursuing two conflicting objects simultaneously. The use of the Japanese carrier aircraft to bombard Midway Island clashed with the requirements of the naval battle that he was anxious to bring about. Nagumo's agitated vacillations about whether he would arm his second striking force with bombs for Midway or torpedoes for ships vividly illustrates the essential antagonism between the two duties his Commander-in-Chief had imposed upon him; just as the fact that he was eventually caught by enemy air attack with all his torpedo planes and dive-bombers on board demonstrates the danger of such dual briefing. It was an error of strategy that went a long way towards losing the Japanese the battle.

That sea-borne aircraft from somewhere might be required to soften up the Midway defences prior to the landing merely serves to underline Yamamoto's failure to concentrate his air power for the decisive operation. Such concentration would at least have allowed him to keep some carriers free to watch for the appearance of enemy ships. It may, however, be argued that the Japanese could reasonably have looked for surprise at Midway and so for long enough time to complete the bombardment of the island before having to meet American warships. If this consideration was what determined their strategy, the disastrous outcome stands as a solemn warning that comfortable assumptions of the enemy's absence, always hazardous, are particularly so in the air age.

For, as the course of the battle brought out with especial clarity, aircraft carriers are subject to awkward periods of operational paralysis, from which gun vessels are free. A battleship or cruiser which has been bombarding one target can switch its guns round to another in a matter of seconds, and can go on firing with hardly a break till its ammunition runs out. But the carrier, as at present constituted, suffers embarrassing lacunae when its aircraft are coming down, going up, or refuelling and rearming, during which it is peculiarly vulnerable to attack. Even with skilfully planned and directed operations, these 'dead' periods introduce an inevitably high degree of chance into carrier warfare, which tends to make an encounter between two carrier fleets unusually speculative. It was the successful exploitation of one of these enemy periods by the Americans at Midway that was the basic cause of the smashing victory of three carriers over four. But it required only a small turn of fortune's wheel to have swung the advantage hard over the other way. Another half-hour would have had all four Japanese striking forces in the air. Again, the *Enterprise's* dive-bombers, flying on blind calculations and without the aid of regular reconnaissance reports, very nearly missed the enemy as completely as the *Hornet's*, which would, as it happened, have left three surviving Japanese carriers instead of one.

The high degree to which luck seems to dominate carrier operations of this kind, to the detriment of skill, training, and experience, invites the query whether a carrier strategy which aims at the destruction of the enemy carriers is the correct one. There is no practicable way of disposing of the menace of the gun vessel except by sinking or capturing it. But carrier air attack can be dealt with by shooting down the aircraft, as well as by sinking the carriers from which they fly. It is to be remembered that the aircraft complements of the carriers at Midway, both Japanese and American, represented a compromise between the two above-mentioned principles of victory by destroying the enemy's carriers and by destroying his aircraft; and the same is true to-day. Some fighters were and are provided for the second purpose and some torpedo planes and dive-bombers for the first, each contingent being included at the expense of more of the other. At Midway, the fighters formed just about a third of the total complement of planes: yet their influence on the result of the battle was considerable, handicapped as those of the Japanese were by lack of radar in their carriers and those of the Americans by inferior quality to the enemy. Were the proportion of fighters to be much increased, even to 100 per cent, the chance of enemy torpedo planes and bombers penetrating the fighter screen and so reaching their ship objectives might become too small to be worth the attempt.

This 'fighter' theory was given practical test in the battle of the Philippine Sea later in the war when about 550 Japanese aircraft endeavoured to reach the American fleet. They were met by about 300 fighters who shot down 400 enemy aircraft at a cost of about 20 of their own. Only a few of the Japanese attackers got past the fighters and some of these were accounted for by the anti-aircraft artillery; and the damage to the fleet was negligible. Now that rockets and proximity fuses have increased the power of the artillery, a fleet that relies on destroying the enemy's aircraft rather than his carriers should be more secure still.

Such reliance would solve a number of problems that proved difficult at Midway. It would greatly reduce the 'paralysis' periods of refuelling and rearming, the rearming of fighters being a quick and simple matter. Since fighters would not operate so far from their carriers as the so-called striking forces, it would simplify control and would shorten the time that carriers were tied to a 'recovery' course for the benefit of returning aircraft. And it would bring the carriers back from distant and separate battles of their own to the proximity of the fleet to which they belonged. Above all, it would diminish the element of pure luck in carrier operations.

Some people might condemn such a strategy as 'defensive'. But this is a wrong term to use; and indeed there has been much confusion of thought on the subject of the offensive and defensive since air power was held by its devotees to have necessitated a new idea of strategy through its introduction of the third dimension into warfare. The basis of this claim is false, since it was the submarine and not the aircraft that ushered in the third dimension, and, being false, it would not be surprising if it gave rise to further fallacies. The terms offensive and defensive have traditionally related to the enemy's armed forces. Aircraft are therefore being at least as offensive if they reserve their attentions for the enemy's aircraft as if they devote them to his airfields, whether territorial or floating.

The fact that under a 'fighter' strategy the enemy (if he still believes in bombers and torpedo planes) comes to the fighters does not necessarily put the latter into a defensive role. What it does do is to confer on them the advantage of position. They are saved the labour of looking for the enemy over large areas of sea, with the chance that he may not be found but instead may slip in an attack on the fleet while the searching aircraft are away. The fighters remain always with the fleet and so are always on the spot where they are most wanted, and where the enemy is most likely to be encountered.

The benefit of forcing the enemy to come to you, if he wishes to do any harm, by remaining in the vicinity of what he wants to harm is well illustrated in the case of convoy protection. British naval officers have ever disliked the drudgery of convoy escort and have frequently tried to break away from it by labelling it as defensive and therefore inferior to an offensive policy, which they interpret in terms of dashing off in search of enemy vessels and chasing enemy reports, sometimes to extravagant distances. There were cases in the last war of destroyers being sent to hunt submarines reported 500 miles away; which, when the destroyers reached the spot, could have been three or four hundred miles somewhere else themselves and usually were. Despite the argument against the enemy being left with the initiative, it is nevertheless the fact that in two wars it has been in the vicinity of the convoys that the greatest number of German submarines has been destroyed, all the 'hot pursuits', the bombing of production centres and U-boat bases, the air sweeps, and Bay of Biscay offensives notwithstanding. And a system that leads to the destruction of the highest proportion of enemy warships cannot have much wrong with it, whatever it be called.

In gun warfare, since the gun is inseparable from the ship that mounts it, the sinking of the ship ends the career of that particular gun. This does not apply to carrier warfare, where the sinking of a proportion of the carriers may not immediately impair the combat air power of the carrier fleet at all, as the sunken ships' aircraft, if in the air when their parent carrier was attacked, can probably go on operating from others. There may not even be much over-crowding, as the aircraft casualties among the surviving carriers may leave plenty of vacancies. Of course, in the extreme case of all the carriers present being sunk, as at Midway, the aircraft will have no deck to land on and so may all be lost.[1]

On the other hand, if the primary aim is to destroy the enemy's aircraft rather than his carriers, his air strength automatically diminishes proportionately to the destruction. The emptying carriers may later be refilled with new machines; but they cannot be refilled with the same experienced airmen. It might not matter a great deal for the enemy carriers to remain afloat if they can only send off striking forces manned by progressively lower quality air crews, the bulk of whom are annihilated at each strike with little achievement. Regarded as objectives, there is much to be said for preferring the aircraft to the carriers. At the Philippine Sea battle, the American fighters won as important a victory as Midway, though they sank no ships. And they won it much more cheaply: for whereas at Midway the American losses in ships were 1 to 4 Japanese and in carrier aircraft over 1 to 3, their aircraft losses in the Philippine Sea fighting were under 1 to 20.

In the Philippine Sea, Admiral Spruance had known from his air searches that the Japanese fleet was coming eastward to attack him. He deliberately refrained, however, from advancing to meet it. His object was to cover the invasion of Saipan, then in progress, and he argued that if he remained where he was the

[1] Though their crews may be rescued by friendly cruisers and destroyers.

Japanese would have to come to him and fight him on his own ground if they wished to interfere. So he waited for them with his fighters ready. In due course, the Japanese bombers arrived, and the Americans shattered all their attacks, one after the other, with the slaughter previously listed.

Yet so prevalent is the feeling among fighting men that they ought to dash straight at the enemy in all circumstances that Admiral Spruance made an apologetic statement after the battle that he wished he could have steamed westward in search of the Japanese fleet instead of waiting in a covering position for them to attack him. That the victor should have felt constrained to make excuses for his victory can be thought to indicate a certain sense of guilt on his part at winning in what others might regard as an unorthodox way. Yet it is the victory that matters, not the manner of achieving it; and it is obviously possible that Admiral Spruance gained his striking success for the very reason that he acted as he did. Nevertheless, he felt it necessary to point out, as though in extenuation of his behaviour, that had he advanced towards the enemy he might have been drawn off on a false scent while the Japanese relieved Saipan behind his back. Precisely. As it was, the position he chose made this impossible and the Japanese had no option but to try to fight their way through. And in the attempt they suffered a devastating defeat.

Another and a famous example of victory gained in the same way is provided by the Battle of Britain. The enemy bombers came to the fighters which were covering Britain and were shot to pieces. The peculiar thing is that some of the highest R.A.F. dignitaries persist to this day in rather scornfully referring to the fighter as a defensive weapon but at the same time claim the highest distinction of the whole war for this victory that the fighters won.

The employment of aircraft in a similar role at sea would not necessarily imply a strategical defensive on the part of the fleet they were accompanying. On the contrary, it might increase that fleet's general offensive freedom by eliminating the worst of the uncertainties and elements of unpredictable chance seemingly inherent in inter-carrier combat; which at Midway caused a Japanese fleet superior in carriers and enjoying a monopoly in battleships to be severely worsted, even allowing for all Yamamoto's strategical and Nagumo's tactical mistakes.

Suppose that Admiral Yamamoto had filled his four large and two small carriers up with fighters. He could then have had —allowing for the smaller size of the fighter—about 400 Zero fighters against 104 Wildcat and Buffalo fighters and 240 mixed carrier-borne and land-based torpedo planes, dive-bombers, Flying Fortresses, Catalinas and Marauders. So armed, is it to be regarded as unlikely that Admiral Yamamoto could have captured Midway Island without overmuch loss to himself, even without radar? With radar, it would surely, on the analogy of the Philippines Sea, have been a certainty. And the odds would seem to be on the American carriers being left with no surviving aircraft.

As it was, Admiral Yamamoto suffered disastrous losses without capturing the island, and he retired discomfited to the westward. His retreat marked the real turning-point of the war. The issue at stake at Midway was the command of the sea in the Pacific and Indian Oceans. The Japanese defeat did not give the Americans the immediate command in all parts of the Pacific. But it did make certain that they would in time gain that command. Had the battle of Midway gone the other way, the command might have remained with the Japanese; and if that had happened the war must have taken a different course.

CHAPTER FIFTEEN

The End of an Epoch

*

I mentioned in Chapter Eight that 10th December 1941, was a turning point in British history, if not in the history of the world. That date marked, in fact, the end of an epoch; that of British pre-eminence as a sea Power. It was a pre-eminence that had been shared with the United States for the previous twenty years on equal terms; but before that Britain had been universally recognized as the world's dominant sea Power for well over a century, ever since Nelson had shattered the French Mediterranean fleet at the Nile in 1798. And this battle was only the culmination of two earlier centuries of naval prowess that had enabled Britain to hold her own against, and ultimately to prevail over, one maritime rival after another.

During these three centuries up to 1941, Britain had not been without her naval ups and downs. The English fleet had not always got the best of it in the fiercely contested Anglo-Dutch wars of the seventeenth century. In the battle of Beachy Head against the French fleet in 1690 the English were definitely defeated. Admiral Graves's failure to beat the French off the Chesapeake in 1781 was as good as a defeat in that it determined the surrender of Cornwallis at Yorktown and therefore the success of the revolting American Colonies. And in 1914 Admiral Cradock's armoured cruisers had been annihilated by the German *Scharnhorst* and *Gneisenau* at the battle of Coronel. But all these reverses were redeemed by victory before the end of the war in question, Beachy Head by Barfleur and La Hogue, the Chesapeake by the battle of the Saints, and Coronel by the Falkland Islands battle a month later.

The End of an Epoch

The sinking of the *Prince of Wales* and *Repulse* and the resultant passing of the command of the south-west Pacific to the Japanese was never redeemed, at least by the British. When redemption came, it was the achievement of the Americans in their victory off Midway Island.

What were the causes of the British naval collapse in December 1941 before the Japanese? The proximate one was the presence in London of a Minister of Defence so convinced of his own individual competence as a master of naval strategy that he was prepared to ignore the advice of his professional naval experts and force upon them measures for the naval defence of Malaya which they clearly did not like. Nor are their misgivings to be wondered at: for the Minister's proposition which he imposed upon the Admiralty that lesser strength is to be preferred to greater in dealing with an enemy who is stronger than oneself would appear to classify as an historical curiosity. All the strategical textbooks, based on the experience of the past and the precepts of the great masters of war, take exactly the opposite view. They agree in stating that you cannot be too strong at the decisive point. That Singapore was such a point will hardly need arguing in view of the consequences of its loss.

Mr. Churchill seems also not to have appreciated the part that aircraft were playing by 1941 as an essential element in sea power. Though the *Prince of Wales* and *Repulse* would probably have been sunk sooner or later anyway, since they were far too weak a force for the task assigned to them, the speed with which they were disposed of was due to their defencelessness against air attack, resulting from the lack of an aircraft-carrier and the extreme weakness of the shore-based Malayan Air Force. It is true that the aircraft-carrier *Indomitable* which had been earmarked to accompany the Eastern fleet became an unexpected casualty at a late hour. But there was the carrier *Hermes* already in the Indian Ocean which could have been picked up by Sir Tom Phillips on his way out but was left where she was. She was admittedly old, small, and not very fast. But even an old, small, and slowish carrier would have been better than none at all. In his memorandum of August 28th, the First Sea Lord had proposed to attach her to the Eastern fleet, so that the highest naval authority believed her suitable for that position.

Shore-based fighters could, however, have gone a long way to remedy the absence of carriers, had there been enough of them. For it would have been possible for the Eastern fleet to fulfil its role of defending Malaya while remaining in Malayan coastal waters, where shore-based fighters could have given it continuous overhead protection during daylight, if they had been present in sufficient numbers. But there were far too few of them, and what there were, were of inferior quality to the Japanese. There was a suitable east-coast chain of airfields, at Mersing, Kuantan and Kota Bharu, had there been the fighter aircraft to use them. It is ironical to think that the *Prince of Wales* and *Repulse* were sunk by air attack within an aerial stone's-throw of the airfield at Kuantan whence all the aircraft had been withdrawn the day before owing to a lack of fighters to keep away Japanese bombing attacks.

Whether or not a good supply of fighters would have saved the Colony, it would undoubtedly have raised in no small degree the chances of a successful defence. An amplitude of fighters could have been provided had Mr. Churchill chosen. But, as we have seen, he was busy handing out Hurricanes by the hundred for the defence of foreign countries while ignoring the needs of the British Far East.

Why did he display this seemingly obstinate unconcern for the defence of a key British position? I think some of the reasons are probably connected with the office of Minister of Defence, first brought into British politics by Mr. Churchill. There is a danger that this office, when joined with that of Prime Minister, may identify the head of the Government too intimately with the conduct of warlike operations. If the duties of Prime Minister and Minister of Defence are combined in one man, there is bound to be some tendency for his attention and energies to be absorbed by the day-to-day direction of the war as Minister of Defence, with the hope of personal glory from victories to come, to the detriment of that wide and judicious view appropriate to a Prime Minister, whose true wartime function is to act as free and independent referee of all the many competing strategic, industrial, and political pulls and pressures, while keeping one eye resolutely looking beyond the fighting to the peace to come.

One cannot read Mr. Churchill's books on the Second World War without feeling astonished at the amazing range of the author's mental activities during the war. Not only did Mr. Churchill personally plan the grand strategy of the war but much of the major and even minor strategy as well. In addition to all this planning, he took a very close and active part in the direction of operations, often deciding which ships, army divisions, and air squadrons should go here or there and how they were to get to their destinations. Not content with plans and operations, Mr. Churchill gave his attention to a mass of technical details of guns, tanks, air bombs, magnetic mines, and a host of other *minutiae*, including whether the flag flying above the Admiralty was clean enough and how much exercise Generals should take.

Had not Mr. Churchill chronicled his multitudinous labours between 1940 and 1945 for the perusal of the public, the ordinary person would not have believed that one man would be capable of such Himalayan endeavours. At the same time, the possibility cannot be avoided that their immense scope was bought at a price. It had been a convention in the Service departments for many years that the handling of current operational business did not go well with planning for the future. Thus, a Plans Division was deliberately created at the Admiralty to provide some officers who would have no responsibility for moving ships about the globe and so would be free to think and plan without the preoccupation of making the daily wheels go round. The latter activity, it was held, could not be doubled with planning without making efficient planning almost impossible. But Mr. Churchill took upon himself not only the combined planning and operating and technical supervision of one service but of three, with a tight control of politics, national and international, thrown in. It is therefore a tenable hypothesis that, in spite of his awe-inspiring capacity for work, he was taking on too much for the proper performance of the whole. And, of course, if anything was likely to suffer it was the time available for thinking about places like Malaya where no fighting was, before December, 1941, actually taking place and where it might never take place. The temptation to such a man as Mr. Churchill, under tremendous and urgent pressures from many directions, to leave Malaya to look after itself must have been very strong, and it is quite clear that he surrendered to it. We have it on his own authority that he had done so little to acquaint himself with the general strategic position on the Peninsula that even as late as the middle of January 1942, five weeks after the opening of the Japanese attack, he was harbouring a number of wholly false beliefs about the state of the Singapore defences. His bitter complaint in his book that no one had enlightened him as to the true condition of affairs gives a plain enough indication of the extent of his ignorance.[1]

Mr. Churchill's persistent neglect of Malaya in the general allocation of force does not, however, account by itself for the greatest British disaster of the war. Whatever he had done in the way of reinforcing the Malayan garrison, he would in any case have been under the almost insoluble handicap that there were not enough British warships to retain the command of the south-west Pacific.

The only really satisfactory way of ensuring that command was to have a fleet at least equal to the Japanese navy permanently stationed in those waters. The next best thing was a fleet equal to the Japanese navy that could have gone out at call; as the original Admiralty plan for the 'passage of the main fleet to the Far East' implied could be done. But when the need arose, Mr. Churchill had at his disposal neither a fleet ready on the spot nor a 'main fleet' to reach the spot.

Who was responsible for this lamentable lack of naval power available for the protection of our Far Eastern interests? A great many people were responsible in their different spheres and their differing ways. Mr. Lloyd George, Liberal Prime Minister at the

---

[1] *Daily Telegraph*, 11th October 1950: '. . . I cannot understand how it was I did not know this. None of the officers on the spot and none of my professional advisers at home . . . pointed it out to me. . . .'

time of the Washington Treaty, and Mr. (Earl) Balfour, ex-Conservative Prime Minister, who negotiated it, were two. Mr. Churchill himself was another in respect of his sponsoring, as Chancellor of the Exchequer, that movable ten-year-rule that proved so damaging to our national security.

Then there is the baleful effect of the British Treasury system. The Treasury is the most powerful organ of the public service in our national life, and there is a good deal of evidence that its general peacetime attitude is unsympathetic and even hostile towards adequate defence preparations. It is not merely that its duty requires it to work for economy. Its constant endeavour is to effect reductions in defence expenditure to an extent and in a manner that takes no account of the national security. Lord Chatfield has described[1] the unending fight that the defence services have to wage with the Treasury for money, and the dangerous methods to which that department is prepared to resort in order to make cuts in the Service Estimates. As an example of these methods there was the persistent pressure put on the Chiefs of Staff during the 1930's to make them accept a financial ration of so much money, but no more, for defence which they could apportion between themselves as best they could, whatever might be their separate calculated requirements. The irresponsible stupidity of such a plan from the larger national point of view is quite extraordinary. It corresponds to telling a man whose house needs urgent repairs that he cannot have enough to do them all, and that he must decide whether to let the walls tumble down or the window frames rot away or the roof let in the rain.

Treasury control is a hallowed phrase in all matters of British governmental procedure, and in principle there is a lot to be said for it. In practice, it is open to the danger that Treasury officials are human beings and that Treasury control for the public benefit can very easily become Treasury control for the sake of controlling, which latter may be far from the public benefit. The essence of good business finance is to know when to spend money with both hands as well as when to cut expenditure to the bone. Unfortunately, the Treasury official is prevented by the

[1] In his valuable book, *It Might Happen Again* (Heinemann).

nature of his employment from exercising judicious discrimination between wise spending and extravagance. He is inevitably bound to a routine opposition to all expenditure, and he therefore goes on contesting defence costs whenever and as long as he can.

His general attitude of opposition to the Service Estimates, backed by the decisive constitutional weapon of 'Treasury approval' without which money cannot be spent, was rendered all the more formidable by the creation of the post of 'Head of the Civil Service' in 1919 and its vesting with the Permanent Secretary of the Treasury. This administrative innovation, for which Parliamentary sanction was never sought, was bound to have a far-reaching effect on Government departments of all kinds. Civil Servants were thereafter compelled to look to the Secretary of the Treasury for personal advancement and benefit. The inevitable result was that the Civil Servants of the Admiralty, War Office, and Air Ministry, instead of giving the whole of their loyalty to the departments they were serving, tended to become automatic underground workers for the forces of economy at all costs. One cannot blame them. Self-interest is a dominating motive with all ordinary men. But the resulting sinister situation has been graphically described by Lord Chatfield:

'Overpowering everything was the immense power given to the Treasury. That power was to be found everywhere. Its proper function of avoiding waste and extravagance was extended until it ruled as an autocrat in Whitehall, a veritable tyrant. It possessed innumerable officials whose duty it was to be ready to counter the demands of the fighting departments; and in those departments themselves it had its familiars who could, if they used their power, oppose or delay all action involving the spending of money. It was a power that was greatly abused.'[1]

This is a very serious indictment from a man like Lord Chatfield, who had served a good many years at the Admiralty, including five years as First Sea Lord. What it comes to is this—

[1] *It Might Happen Again*, p. 198.

and it is a very startling conclusion to reach—that there is a large, well-paid, highly educated, officially encouraged, and extremely powerful sixth column in Whitehall which is, in complete safety, working away continuously to assist the country's potential enemies by trying to cut down the national defences. It is, as I say, a startling conclusion, which will no doubt be just as startling to the sixth column itself as to anyone else. But it is just as well to face realities. Not that one can necessarily blame the members of the column. They are the products of the system.

The primary defect of the Treasury system of controlling defence expenditure lies in the absence of responsibility on the part of the Treasury official for the consequences of the power that he wields; an absence that tends to lead him into dangerous courses that he would otherwise avoid. If a Treasury official were put on trial as a matter of course whenever a military disaster occurred, there would undoubtedly be a surprisingly better understanding by Treasury watch-dogs of the needs of the Services. Officials who labour for reductions in defence would then realize that a species of national Nuremberg trials might give a verdict that a place like Malaya was lost in Whitehall and go on to fix the blame on individual members of the Civil Service hierarchy for the loss. One of the worst features of the Treasury control of defence expenditure lies in the anonymity of the controllers. Though it is easy enough when things go wrong, as Mr. John Strachey once said, to sacrifice Generals to keep the politicians in their jobs, there is no present way of knowing who are the Treasury officials whose influence resulted in the Generals having no tanks or heavy artillery.

However, drastic treatment of the bureaucracy can be regarded as impracticable in this country; though apparently not in Russia, where it is said that the death penalty is applied for bureaucratic inefficiency. Nor would it be sensible. It is really not the Treasury official's fault that he may sink battleships through procrastination and endanger the country through the wooden application of departmental principles which, though they may be admirable for national education or town planning, are quite unsuitable for defence measures which have to be framed in relation to foreign countries who are not bound by Acts of Parliament. The officials, after all, have to obey the commands of the Chancellor of the Exchequer, who may previously have committed himself to the electorate as a 'no more war' man. But it would undoubtedly be a mistake to think that Treasury officials take their cue entirely from above. The Services have good reason to think that the officials very often regard defence as their natural prey.

The antidote to the evils of irresponsible power is not to chastise the irresponsibles but to remove their power. For this reason there is a lot to be said for the American system where the fighting services deal direct with the financially *responsible* body in the country; namely, Congress. Admirals and Generals take their requirements to, and argue their case before, Congressional Committees, the record being taken and being publicly available either at once or in due time. This arrangement has a double, indeed a treble, advantage. It places the original responsibility for framing the defence requirements openly where it belongs—that is, on the Service Chiefs—instead of leaving it with a civilian Minister who may be and often is a mere mouthpiece. It places the responsibility for the final decision squarely with Congress (or, with us, Parliament), the body to which the people have entrusted the national decisions. And it enables the people themselves to make personal inspection of how their vital defence interests have been handled, what was said in the process of investigation, and—most important of all—*who said it*.

It is of interest that an Admiralty Civil Servant, Sir John Briggs, reached much the same conclusion over fifty years ago. In his book of reminiscences, he said:

'One of the chief causes of the unsatisfactory state of naval and military affairs is not attributable to civilians being placed at the head of these great war departments, as some imagine, but in no small degree to the fact that there is no public record of the views and opinions of their professional advisers, which, for the good of the Service, ought to be brought under the consideration of the Cabinet, and afterwards come forward with the Navy estimates for the final decision of the House of Commons. The deficiencies of the Navy in regard to ships would never have required a vote of twenty-one millions had the representations of the naval members of various Boards of Admiralty received, from year to year, that attention they deserved. . . .'[1]

With our Treasury system, the views of the Service Chiefs remain for ever buried in official dockets and files. All that the public and Parliament have to go on are Ministerial speeches, which never reveal whether the professional chiefs concur in or dissent from what is being said.

The Ministers of the Crown who make these speeches have, of course, the principal executive responsibility for the state of the country's defences. Yet curiously enough, it is difficult to bring that responsibility home to them individually, on account of the long time-lag that usually occurs between unwise defence economies and their untoward aftermath. The fact, for instance, that Mr. Churchill struck a heavy blow at the national defences between 1924 and 1929 by the introduction of his receding ten-year rule was entirely forgotten by 1939, when he was hailed back to office as the man who had pressed for more defence expenditure—when out of office—after 1931. Nor did the vast majority of the people realize that the grave lack of small craft facing Mr. Alexander when he became First Lord of the Admiralty in 1940 was one which he himself had done most to create by his action at the London Naval Conference of 1930.

Because they are thus reasonably safe from subsequent criticism, politicians are very unreliable custodians of the national security. They will make the most reckless economies in the defence services in order to placate popular feeling or to find money for some more immediately promising political project. It requires an exceptionally candid politician to admit to this; but we have it on record that Mr. Baldwin, later made an earl (like Mr. Balfour), confessed to going slow on what he believed

[1] *Naval Administrations* 1837-1892, Sir John Briggs, Reader to the Lords and Chief Clerk of the Admiralty.

to be an urgently necessary defence programme for fear of losing the next election.

All the greater is the responsibility, however, that devolves upon the Service Chiefs. Though they receive little enough credit for the fact, they are nevertheless the main trustees of the national security. They tell the politicians what is wanted, they wage unceasing warfare against the Treasury for money, and they put pressure, if need be, on the Government itself to increase the defence vote. They seldom get all they desire. But if it were not for them, there would be a great deal less.

It is essential in the national interest that this position of the Service Chiefs as the country's 'safety men' should be adequately realized and properly safeguarded. There has been a very noticeable tendency, operating over a long period, to reduce their status to that of Civil Servants, directly subordinate to the political office-holders of the moment. The Service Chiefs are more than that. They have a semi-ministerial position in that, though they are undoubtedly subject to the orders of the Cabinet, they are not so entirely. In regard to the general question of the national security, they are answerable to the King and the people as well as, if not more than, to the Government. Therefore, if they deem that the Government is unnecessarily weakening the country's defences, it is not only their constitutional right but duty to refuse their concurrence and if necessary resign. Resignation is obviously a weapon to be used very sparingly and is, as a matter of fact, extremely rare; the last occasion being in 1915 when Admiral of the Fleet Lord Fisher 'walked out' of Mr. Churchill's Board of Admiralty owing to differences over strategy with his political chief. But a good deal can go on behind the scenes of which the public hears nothing. A comparatively recent First Sea Lord offered his resignation three times to the then Prime Minister, who each time conceded the Admiral's point.

Such concealed pressures are not, however, enough. Sir John Briggs clearly had something different in mind when he advocated that the views of the Service Chiefs should be publicly known and recorded. And one way towards meeting this requirement would be to restore to them their former right of Parliamentary membership. In Nelson's day, serving officers could be Members of Parliament and many were. Political partisanship among officers of the Services had certain disadvantages. But it also had advantages, and it did not prevent the winning of victories over the enemy, the basic test of a Service system.

It was not till the twentieth century that this right of officers on the active list to sit in the House of Commons was done away with. At the present time, officers must go on the retired list in order to enter that House—though, very undemocratically, they do not have to retire to sit and speak in the House of Lords.

The modern prohibition on Parliamentary activity by serving officers who are Commoners necessarily disallows such episodes as Lord Charles Beresford's resignation from the Board of Admiralty in the latter part of the last century and his gaining a seat in the Commons for the express purpose of using Parliamentary pressure to secure an essential naval reform which he had been unable, as a Sea Lord, to get past Treasury opposition. Lord Charles succeeded in his object, and Sir John Briggs did not think he would have succeeded by other means:

> 'Lord Charles Beresford resigned his seat at the Board because the Treasury refused to place the Intelligence Department of the Admiralty, to which he rightly attached so much importance, upon a more liberal, substantial, and permanent footing. . . . It is certain that, as an independent Member of the House of Commons, (he) was able to accomplish much more good for the Navy, supported as he was by the most distinguished officers of his profession and the Press, than if he had retained his seat at the Board.'

The good of the Navy being a matter of public as well as professional interest, it can be thought publicly unfortunate that Lord Charles' method of advancing it was later made impossible. Retired officers have neither the standing nor the up-to-date information and experience to carry anything approaching the same authority in debate, even on Service subjects, as those on the active list.

The gradual Parliamentary emasculation of the Fighting Service officer is naturally to the advantage of the politician, who obviously prefers to have professional members of the Board of Admiralty and the Army and Air Councils who are without personal political influence and are in no way political competitors. But it is much more questionable whether it has been to the advantage of the country. If Sir John Briggs is a reliable witness, the nation has lost more than it has gained through the elimination of the serving officer from Parliamentary life. There is much evidence that the civilian politician will take the most shocking security risks in order to avoid unpopularity by advancing armament proposals which the people do not like; or, to be accurate, which the people can be induced by interested parties to think they do not like.

But the ultimate responsibility, as also the ultimate power, in defence matters lies with the people. It was the people of Britain who, if they did not specifically cause the sinking of the *Prince of Wales* and *Repulse*, nevertheless rendered it reasonably certain that the command of the eastern seas would pass to the enemy in the event of a war with the Japanese. The people of Britain set their face against spending money on armaments between the wars. They were prepared to back any policy, expedient, or nostrum that offered reduction of such expenditure. They were delighted with the Washington Treaty of naval limitation, but not because it made the Empire safer. The Empire actually became much more exposed to attack. The popularity of the Treaty lay in its saving of money; and the clause whereby Britain was empowered to build the Singapore base was resented for its cost and not valued for its protective content. They leapt at the slogan of 'collective security', not giving a thought to whether it would be effective so long as it eased the national defence budget. If someone else could be found to defend Britain, so much the better. That such an attitude might be psychologically as well as strategically dangerous left them cold.

No reference in Parliament or in public speeches was more certain of drawing cheers than that to the 'crushing burden of armaments'. But just how crushing was this burden? For the

year 1936, the combined Navy, Army and Air Force estimates
came to less than £130 million, at which time the Civil Services
and Local Government expenditure combined came to over
£1,000 million. The Police were costing about twice as much as
the whole of the Air Force; yet there was never any talk of 'the
crushing burden of law and order'. It can, of course, be argued
that civil expenditure is returned to the people in the form of
benefits of various kinds. But so is expenditure on armaments,
in the shape of wages to those in the armament industries. And
lest it be thought that the beneficiaries are only the weapon
makers, let us list some of the firms that contribute to the building of an aircraft-carrier. There are, for instance, the manufac-
turers of furniture, rope, canvas, paint, polish, floor cloth, cur-
tains, cutlery, crockery, lockers, bunting, wireless gear, boats,
oars, engines, boilers, auxiliary machinery, propellors, wire haw-
sers, compasses, ladders, typewriters, seaboots, and many other
things in addition to the steel for the hull and guns and materials
for the aircraft. Armaments therefore stimulate industry over a
wide field.

We now look back on the year 1913 as typifying an amazing
period of prosperity, with income tax at only just over a shilling
in the pound. Yet in that year we possessed no less than thirty
first-line capital ships and many more second-line. Why, then,
were the fifteen capital ships of 1936 a crushing burden when we
took the thirty plus of 1913 in our stride? The answer is not too
obvious. For approximately sixpence on the income tax, we could
have kept a fleet permanently in the Pacific more or less equal to
the Japanese Navy and still have had enough at home. We could,
that is, had we not rashly allowed our hands to be tied at Washington by agreeing to a naval ratio that prevented an adequate
battlefleet being stationed in the East.

For roughly twopence on the income tax, we could have had
another 200 fast escort vessels, about the number we were short
on the outbreak of war in 1939: the shortage resulting in an
avoidable loss through submarine sinkings of possibly fifteen
million tons of allied shipping, with the cargoes, the combined
cost of which may possibly and not improbably have been as

much as £2,000 million.[1] We could have had them, that is, had we not, in order to lighten the 'crushing burden of armaments', agreed at the London Naval Conference of 1930 to cut down our smaller warship classes below the safety mark until too late to build them up again by 1939. Whatever the burden of maintaining adequate peace-time armaments may be called, it can be insignificant as compared to the fearful cost of not maintaining them.

It would conceivably be possible for a country to exhaust itself by over-arming in peace-time, but the margin of safety is much greater than we in this country have for some time been allowing ourselves to think. Every year for five or six years before 1939, the financial prophets declared that Germany, Italy and Japan could not possibly go on spending so large a proportion of their national incomes on defence without economic collapse. But the crash never came. The British finance wizards were wrong.

Admittedly, the shortest road to impoverishment is to over-extend oneself in war. But that is quite distinct from expenditure on readiness for war, and is as likely as not to be a direct result of insufficient peace expenditure leading to insufficient readiness. It would have been infinitely cheaper to have eschewed the spurious attractions of the Washington naval economies and so kept our hands free for maintaining a fleet in the East of a size that really would have deterred the Japanese from advancing into Malaya and Burma than to go to the enormous expense of turning them out after they had got there.

Again, had Sir Edward Grey (later a Viscount) understood naval strategy, he would not have committed this country, behind the back of the Admiralty, to the endeavour to defend the English Channel by an army of continental size on land instead of by a large enough fleet at sea. Sir Edward imagined that if the Germans won on the Continent they would be able to organize a combined European fleet to overtop the British. It was a supposition that history did not support, or Napoleon would have

---

[1] These figures are the best I can do by my own calculation. The Ministry of Transport informs me it has no record of the cost to the country of the shipping lost in the last war.

dealt with Britain this way in his time; as the Admiralty might have pointed out to Sir Edward had he consulted that department before coming to an amateur conclusion of his own. As it was, the results of his uninformed and secretive policy, based on a false assumption, were ruinously expensive.

The attitude of the British people during the inter-war years of armament limitation and peace propaganda was distinctly peculiar. They had enthusiastically supported the measures for reducing navies at Washington in 1921 and on subsequent occasions up to 1930. Yet when the Japanese invaded Manchuria in 1931, they clamoured for the Navy to 'stop Japan' without any regard for the fact that the naval disarmament agreements of the previous years left Britain with inadequate naval force for doing so.

A particularly significant symptom was the popular selection of the battleship as the arch symbol of the evils of war. 'Scholarships not battleships' was the fashionable cry among the 'intellectual' classes; and anti-war speeches seldom failed to include derogatory reference to the battleship to sharpen the argument.

Yet there was no weapon of war that had done more for the British people than the battleship. It had kept them safe against the Spaniards in the sixteenth century, against the French all through the eighteenth and in the early part of the nineteenth century, and against Kaiser William's Germans in the war of 1914–18 just concluded. Why, then, was the post-1918 population of Britain so bitter against the big warship? Possibly because the British had suffered a decline in their maritime instinct. No nation that had retained any strong sea sense could have used the battleship as a political bogey, as the bulk of the British did between the wars.

Real sea sense is a very rare characteristic and does not necessarily belong to people because they happen to be islanders and like a holiday at the seaside. There is a considerable difference in the maritime affiliations of the British people between Nelson's day and our own. In 1800, a very much larger proportion of the nation lived on or by the sea, as merchant seamen, as fishermen, and in the coastal trade. The subsequent industriali-

13. Singapore burning

14. Vice-Admiral Sir James Somerville

zation of the country has altered the ratio profoundly. By the 1930's, the seafaring fraction of the population had dwindled away to one three-hundredth.

Such a change may well revolutionize a nation's feeling for the sea and could greatly reduce any inherent understanding it might once have had of the possibilities and safeguards that command of the sea can offer. The actual seagoing British of the present day probably have much the same maritime outlook as their forerunners of previous centuries; but there is no inevitable reason why the workers in a Midland factory should possess much more natural sea sense than those in a factory in the Ruhr or in Smolensk. And if they do not, then the hostile attitude of the inter-war British electorate to the battleship and the Singapore base and its seeming inability to realize that the Japanese could not be coerced by a non-existent Eastern fleet begin to become understandable. It was significant that the 150th anniversary of Nelson's Battle of the Nile, one of the completest, most dramatic, and most important naval victories in history, which fell in 1948, was ignored by the British Press.

Any substantial decline in the sea sense of the British people must clearly be a factor of great if not decisive importance in their national fortunes. It was the lure of trans-Oceanic adventure and gain that started the sea-minded English off on voyages of discovery, trade and conquest in the sixteenth century. Gradually, they fought their way up to the position of premier sea Power of the world, and in so doing acquired a great overseas Empire spreading to the four corners of the world. The retention of that Empire and the secure maintenance of Britain's status as a great maritime trading nation depended on the satisfaction of one dominating condition, the supremacy of the British fleet on the seas of the world.

After nearly four centuries of oceanic enterprise, that essential condition has lapsed. British sea power received a knock-down blow on 10th December 1941, and when it got back on to its feet it was not from any independent recovery of strength but because it was helped off the ground by the American Navy. And by the time the war had ended it was plain to all, including the British, that the trident of sea supremacy had crossed the Atlantic.

As if some supernatural prompter had whispered the appropriate cue, the British Empire melted away almost overnight. India, Ceylon and Burma were handed their independence, not only without a murmur but with congratulatory telegrams and gifts of warships. Malaya was promised self-government at a later date. In the Mediterranean, Palestine was abandoned to the Jews, and British naval bases were thrown open to the American fleet, which already had access to the British West Indies and Bermuda. Nearer home, southern Ireland seceded, and American forces were established in England with extra-territorial rights that the British had relinquished for themselves in China only a few years before. There, it was conceded to be an infringement of Chinese sovereignty and an insult to Chinese national feeling, but was now apparently acceptable to the Imperial English. Proud Empires had disintegrated before in the world's history, but never with such lightning speed as the British. Apart from the British Dominions, which were in any case independent countries, and one or two small islands and rocky promontories, only the African colonies remained; and after the recent efforts of several of our Ministers it looks as if we may not have these much longer.

Curiously enough, neither the new nor the old holders of the Sea Power Championship appeared to realize the implications of the change of title. The Americans went on busily arming other nations for the distant defence of the United States; and when the Korean invasion broke upon the world, they proceeded to call up large numbers of young Americans to fight as soldiers in Asia and to form additional army divisions in Europe. Yet with the United States possessing the largest fleet in the world, the North American Continent was completely safe from invasion: and if there were any misgivings on this subject in America the sensible thing to do was to make still further increases in the Navy. Far more security far more cheaply was to be obtained in this way than by raising large armies. Sir Edward Grey, Foreign Secretary of the then principal Sea Power, could not realize this in the years before 1914, so it is perhaps less surprising than it should be that the American authorities do not appear to realize it now.

There is, of course, no absolute guarantee that superior sea power will prevent a bomb being dropped upon American soil by someone or other. But with the range of modern aircraft, no such guarantee is possible short of conquering the whole world, which even the Americans will find beyond their power. In any case, the United States cannot be defeated that way as long as she takes care to retain command of the sea. The most important lesson of the last war was not the immense power of the aircraft as a weapon of war but its limitations. All idea of Major Seversky's (and others') dream of 'victory through air power' was decisively disproved and the ancient importance of land and sea power emphatically reaffirmed. The chief pillars of American safety are therefore a dominant fleet and a powerful force of fighter aircraft.

If the Americans may not yet have appreciated the full meaning of their position as the now principal sea Power of the world, the British have to readjust their outlook in the reverse direction; and after many generations of taking sea supremacy for granted this may not be too easy. Among other things, our politicians and economists have now to consider whether the nineteenth-century doctrine of the multi-destinational export of manufactured goods, paid for by the import of food from all over the world, may not need revision. It was a doctrine that developed during the long peace (except for minor conflicts) that Britain enjoyed after Waterloo, and enjoyed precisely because the British Navy was supreme in the world. Yet the first two world wars of the twentieth century showed the danger there was of the policy of cheap imported food for the people being transformed into the stark emergency of no food for the people at all, even in a war against an inferior naval power like Germany. And now that Britain, for the first time for centuries, cannot count on the surface command of the sea, the risks of dependence on foreign food are enormously increased. It is true that our loss of the surface command could only be used to our detriment through the unfriendly action of the United States, a conflict with whom it is customary to label as 'unthinkable'. But if there is anything in Lord Acton's dictum that 'power corrupts', it would seem prudent to regard even the unthinkable with wariness. There is no man and no nation that is not subject to temptation, if temptation is put in the way. It may therefore be a healthier policy to work now for self-sufficiency in food; and, so far as supplementary imports are essential, to have these primary supply lines confined as far as possible to the Channel, the Irish and North Seas, and the Mediterranean, the protection of which is more promising under the new conditions than of those covering the wide oceans.

For the same reason, the advocates of a British Commonwealth economic *bloc* must ask themselves if it is any longer a practical policy. An economic union with insecure communications is not built on safe foundations.

These are some of the problems of the new epoch which opened on 10th December 1941. If they are to be tackled with anything like success, one basic condition must be faithfully observed. This is that policy, economic as well as foreign, must go hand in hand with strategy. Disregard of this key principle was endemic during the inter-war period and was the direct cause of many of the worst troubles of that period and of the war that followed it. Politicians who wanted some particular international policy to be pursued seemed seldom to give any prior thought to whether there was enough force available to put it into effect. Simultaneous demands for an aggressive foreign policy and an unlimited reduction in armaments make a highly poisonous mixture of ideas. All naval officers are required to pass an examination to show that they have the requisite knowledge before they are allowed to take charge of a ship of war. It is a sombre reflection that politicians can take charge of the ship of state with so little strategical understanding that they may blissfully steer it straight for the nearest minefield.

One further lesson of the Singapore affair may be mentioned. It is that loyalty should begin at home. We starved Malaya in order to supply Russia; and with what result? It goes without saying that the arms which might otherwise have gone to Malaya were of some use to the Russians who got them instead. But we do not know how much. It is possible that the tanks and aircraft sent were but a drop in the bucket of the vast Eastern front. In any case, we got no thanks for them, but only insults that our sailors who battled their way, often with heavy loss, along the grim Arctic route to deliver the arms were cowards.[1] And if we did save Russia at the cost of losing Malaya and at grave risk to Australia and New Zealand, we did so only that she might turn against us after the war and stir up trouble for us in that very Malaya whose sacrifice had been her salvation.

In so doing, Russia has been exploiting to our injury and distress the potent psychological consequences of the 'heavy forfeits' we voluntarily accepted on her behalf. The white man has held sway over large parts of Asia for two to three centuries. The British overlordship of India, of Malaya, and Hong Kong, the British and Dutch possession of the bulk of the East Indies, and the mixed European sovereignty over the International Settlement at Shanghai were each and all made possible by and rested upon one assumption. This was that the white man was a better fighting machine than the Asiatic.

It was mentioned in Chapter One that this assumption, so vitally important to the white man's position in the East, was given a perceptible jolt by the Japanese successes against Russia in 1904–5. But Russia, after all, was a semi-Asiatic country itself, and its performance in the 1914 war was so poor that the Asiatic may well have felt it hazardous to apply the deductions drawn from the Russo-Japanese conflict to the more specifically Western nations, such as Britain, Germany, France and the United States.

It can, however, be imagined what an inflammable train of thought must have been started in many Asiatic minds by the news of Pearl Harbour, the sinking of the *Prince of Wales* and *Repulse*, and the capture of Malaya and the Philippines. Here

[1] There were occasions when officers and men reaching North Russia with a convoy were angered to find the stores landed on the previous journey still lying about the jetties, untouched.

were the doughtiest representatives of the white race being utterly defeated by the yellow-skinned Asiatic Japanese. It is not very likely that this initial and exciting impression was effaced or even seriously affected by the subsequent Japanese defeats. What had been done once could be done again. The Asiatic could now believe that given the arms he could stand up to anybody. From this point of view, it was perhaps unfortunate that the atom bomb was used against an already defeated Japan that had made several proposals for surrender. The use of the bomb will have enabled the yellow peoples to say that the white men could not defeat the Japanese without bringing the most devilish contrivances of science to their aid.

The chronic unrest in the Far East since 1945 can hardly be unconnected with the Anglo-American disasters of 1941 and 1942. The banditry in Malaya and Indo-China, though it may be communist-inspired, was virtually unknown before the war. And that the northern Koreans should deliberately have challenged the whole huge might of the United States of America is a phenomenon that the pre-1939 white inhabitant of the Far East would have found utterly unbelievable. These are all by-products of aid to Russia in 1941. They would be bad enough if Russia out of gratitude were helping us to minimize their effects. That she has been doing exactly the opposite provides a very plain warning against 'forfeiting' too much of one's own in order to assist someone else. In regard to the Far East, we are now in a position to regret, too late, that when it was a question of choosing between the foreigner and members of the family, we favoured the foreigner.

It is a habit that has been growing on us and it is a dangerous one. Its outcome in the case of Malaya *versus* Russia we have seen in this book, and with this unhappy example in mind it may be well to recollect that there are British statesmen of the past who have taken a different and more domestic view of their duty. Thus, two hundred years before the Polish guarantee of 1939, Sir Robert Walpole could claim credit for having kept his country out of the war of the Polish succession in the following words. 'Madam,' he wrote to the Queen, 'there are fifty thousand

men slain this year in Europe, and not one Englishman.'
Seventy-five years later, Castlereagh replied as follows to the
Tyrolese request for British help against Napoleon: 'We wish
you well,' he said, 'but we cannot help you. We have ourselves
to think of.' That there may be a certain wisdom in this attitude
to foreign affairs seems worthy of consideration in these days
when powerful influences are at work trying to convert any
country's quarrel into everybody's agony.

Index

Index

Index

Index